Y0-BDR-259

Southern Justice

Southern Justice

EDITED BY LEON FRIEDMAN

With a Foreword by Mark DeW. Howe

GREENWOOD PRESS, PUBLISHERS
WESTPORT, CONNECTICUT

Library of Congress Cataloging in Publication Data

Friedman, Leon, ed.
  Southern justice.

    Reprint of the ed. published by Pantheon Books,
New York.
  Includes bibliographical references.
    1. Afro-Americans--Legal status, laws, etc.--
Addresses, essays, lectures. 2. Justice, Administration
of--Southern States--Addresses, essays, lectures.
3. Civil rights--Southern States--Addresses, essays,
lectures. I. Title.
[KF4757.A5F7 1975]   342'.73'085   75-33296
ISBN 0-8371-8489-4

© *Copyright, 1965, by Random House, Inc.*
© *Copyright, 1963, by Louis Lusky*

*All rights reserved under International and Pan-American
Copyright Conventions.*

Originally published in 1965 by Random House, New York

Reprinted with the permission of Pantheon Books, a
division of Random House, Inc.

Reprinted in 1975 by Greenwood Press,
a division of Williamhouse-Regency Inc.

Library of Congress Catalog Card Number 75-33296

ISBN 0-8371-8489-4

Printed in the United States of America

Our Splendid
Bauble

Ninety years ago a Federal judge delivered a charge to a grand jury assembled in Tennessee to consider the return of indictments against persons suspected of violating the Civil Rights statutes. He said:

> In no country but our own is the discreditable fact true that where murder and shocking outrages are perpetrated by a dominant party in a narrow region of country, there is no power of punishment save through the impractical instrument of those who have either committed or sympathized with the crime. When conspiracies and combinations against the property, well-being, and life of classes of persons . . . include large portions of the constabulary, the magistracy, and the jurors, grand and traverse, the inevitable consequence must be that the offenses they commit, or with which they sympathize, will be perpetrated with impunity. Unless our statesmen, state or national, create some jurisdiction of wider scope, and which will authorize

indictments and trial beyond the narrow limits a majority
of whose citizens abet the crime to be punished, the nation
must still submit to the disgrace of yearly additions of mean
and courage-wanting murders of the innocent and helpless,
without the slightest infliction of any legal penalty upon the
offenders. . . . In a very recent case it was proved that a
young man of wealth, education, and most estimable moral
character was shot to death at midday in his own house
by a band of ruffians, for no other reason than that he had
acted as chairman of a committee to wait upon the governor
of his state to solicit his action for the protection of the
Negroes of his county who were being driven from their
homes, their houses burned, and themselves murdered by
the lawless conspirators by whom he was killed. The mock
trial by which these infamous offenders were triumphantly
acquitted was a still greater stain upon our civilization than
the monstrous crime it affected to try. It is believed by many
of our best citizens that there should be here, as in every
other government on earth, some power to bring such
wicked men to justice, outside of, and uncontrolled by the
wills and hands which have united in their atrocities.[1]

To his disheartened conviction that under existing doctrine and prevailing law the Federal court could do nothing
to punish private atrocities against Negro citizens, Judge
Emmons added an expression of faltering hope. It was
grounded in the possibility that the Supreme Court of the
United States, encouraged by Mr. Justice Bradley, might
some day "find in the Thirteenth Amendment which abol-
ishes slavery, or the first clause of the Fourteenth which
creates citizenship, so much incidental power to protect what
they create, as will sustain a national law punishing the
crime, where life, liberty, and property are violently taken,
solely on account of the race and color of the party injured."
Judge Emmons realized, of course, that his hope could be
fulfilled only if Court and Congress together faced the ugliness of fact and took appropriate steps to transform the
nation's conscience from a refuge of shame into an arsenal
of power.

These reflections are not the prefatory flourishes in a
chapter on constitutional history. They are merely a re-

minder of the shameful fact that those lawyers who, in recent seasons and, particularly, in the summer of 1964,
endeavored to do what they could to make law an effective
barrier to racial tyranny in the South, were compelled to
make the effort in a structure of local insolence and national
disability very nearly the same as that which frustrated
Americans of good will in 1875. The task of making the rule
of law effective among a people, many of whom are eager
and willing to hold it in defiant scorn, is never easy. It becomes an almost hopeless endeavor when public authority
joins the insurgents and turns the agency of law against
those who are seeking its protection. How should the individual lawyer and the legal profession as a whole respond
to this malign enterprise—the turning of public power into
an instrument of lawlessness? Should the practitioner, perhaps, see his duty as essentially unchanged by the prevailing
distortions of law and the indecencies of power? Should
he, in other words, do what he can within the existing disorder of things to safeguard the client's immediate interest
—to secure his release from unlawful imprisonment by
entering a plea of guilty, urge his client to comply with unwarranted and lawless orders of the police lest he suffer
arbitrary and unwarranted arrest, advise the vestrymen
not to allow the church to be used for a Freedom School
lest it be burned down in reprisal? Doubtless there is something to be said for such cautious responses to such familiar
questions. Surely, however, an appropriate answer to the
question must take into account the framework of contrived
anarchy in which they are, today, being presented throughout the South. It may be that in existing circumstances the
lawyer who finds himself professionally engaged in "the
movement" must see his responsibility as different, almost
in kind, from what it has been in other times and other
settings. If he is to be true to his profession he must, perhaps, see himself as engaged not by a client but by a cause
—as one committed by every obligation of professional honor
to break the tyranny of insolence. This commitment may
lead him to use every lawful instrument by which the
progress of lawlessness may be impeded. Though he may

know that the statutes of Congress, the decisions of the Supreme Court and prevailing policies in the Department of Justice offer little assurance that the nation's powers will now be put to work in an effort to outlaw racially motivated brutalities, he may also feel an obligation to expose an outrage that is not beyond the nation's constitutional competence to endeavor to destroy.

Lawyers who read this searing collection of papers on the work that some of their brethren at the bar have done to keep hopes for a rule of law alive in the South, will, I feel sure, ask themselves some of the questions which I have hurriedly set forth. It is to be hoped that they, like other readers of these stories, will ask some larger questions as well. Is it not, for instance, high time for the Congress to attempt the drafting of statutes which will meet some of the problems by which Judge Emmons was agonized in 1875 and which still trouble the nation's conscience? It seems to me scarcely conceivable that today's Court would not follow the lead which Justice Bradley suggested in 1874 and recognize that the Congress is empowered, by many different means, to deal with those acts of communal violence by which racial hatred, public and private, manifests itself in crime. Of course there are decisions that obstruct desirable action and principles that condemn excesses of national power. The decisions are not, however, immutable barriers, and a Congress that possesses the wisdom to exercise power with restraint would surely be sustained in an effort to make national authority a reality when a state's processes of law support and sanction violence, terror, and outrage.

Justices of the Supreme Court have twice spoken of the danger that the Constitution may become "a splendid bauble." The danger that brought the warning from John Marshall in 1819 was that doubts, instead of confidence, would measure the right of Congress "to legislate on that vast mass of incidental powers which must be involved in the constitution."[2] In 1883 Mr. Justice Harlan renewed the warning in another context. "Unless the recent amendments be splendid baubles, thrown out to delude those who deserved fair and generous treatment at the hands of the nation" we must acknowledge that the most crucial privilege of citizenship is "exemption from racial discrimination in respect of any civil right belonging to citizens of the white race. . . ."³ Surely the time has come for the nation, disgraced by hatred, passion and violence, to heed the warnings of Marshall and Harlan.

MARK DeW. HOWE

Mark DeW. Howe is Professor of Law at the Harvard Law School.

Contents

Southern Justice

Introduction

"Liberty is not the mere absence of restraint, it is not a spontaneous product of majority rule, it is not achieved merely by lifting underprivileged classes to power, nor is it the inevitable by-product of technological expansion. It is achieved only by a rule of law."

J A C K S O N , The Supreme Court in the
American System of Government, p. 76 (1955).

Some years ago Edmond Cahn defined justice by analyzing the human response to its absence. " 'Justice' . . . means the *active process* of remedying or preventing what would arouse the sense of injustice."[1] This sense, Cahn wrote, derives from the sympathetic reactions of outrage, horror, shock, resentment and anger that men feel when they identify with a victim of injustice. Cahn concluded that a fair legal system must satisfy the human demand for equality, dignity, conscientious adjudication, and confinement of government to its proper functions. It must also fulfill the community's expectation of regularity and consistency while being responsive to change in the social order.[2]

The recent operation of the southern legal institutions has provided a good test of Professor Cahn's analysis. No one expected all the public officials of the southern states to embrace immediately the new national consensus on civil rights —a consensus shown not only by the long line of unanimous Supreme Court decisions against segregation but by the overwhelming majorities in Congress that passed the recent Civil Rights Acts and the complete repudiation by the electorate of Goldwater's opposition to Negro rights. But the resistance of a large number of these officials has been carried so far beyond the limits that the Constitution allows and social peace requires as to outrage the national sense of injustice more than any other issue of our time.

At an earlier time in the civil rights movement many of these southern officials openly declared their unwillingness to obey the national law. Governor Faubus insisted that he was not bound by the Supreme Court's decision in *Brown v. Board of Education* and was under no obligation to desegregate the Arkansas schools. The Supreme Court answered his contention in the following words:

> . . . [The] federal judiciary is supreme in the exposition of the law of the Constitution, and [this] principle has . . . been respected by this Court and the Country as a permanent and indispensable feature of our constitutional system. It follows that the interpretation of the Fourteenth Amendment enunciated by this Court in the *Brown* case is the supreme law of the land, and Art. VI of the Constitution makes it of binding effect on the States, "any Thing in the Constitution or Laws of any State to the Contrary notwithstanding."[3]

Justice Frankfurter qualified this statement in a concurring opinion:

> The duty to abstain from resistance to "the supreme Law of the Land" . . . as declared by the organ of our Government for ascertaining it, does not require immediate ap-

proval of it nor does it deny the right of dissent. Criticism need not be stilled. Active obstruction or defiance is barred.[4]

What the majority opinion and Justice Frankfurter were saying was that the Supreme Court's specific orders must be obeyed by those to whom they are directed and its decisions must be followed by all Federal and state court judges until they are changed. This is the keystone to the orderly and peaceful operation of the legal process. However, this does not mean that these decisions must be accepted uncritically, universally and permanently as the law. Legal scholars are seldom satisfied with the Court's work. Future litigants are always free to urge the Court to reverse itself. Congress has, numerous times, passed new laws changing Supreme Court decisions interpreting statutory language when it was dissatisfied with the Court's conclusion. And even constitutional interpretations by the Court are subject to constitutional amendment. Opposition to the Court's decisions in this form—by criticism and peaceful political activity—is part of what Professor Louis Lusky calls "the pivotal compact of the open society, the terms of which are: ungrudging acceptance of the present law in return for effective access to the processes of orderly change."

But the southern governor who disobeys a Federal court order, the state policemen who viciously attack peaceful Negro demonstrators, the sheriff who arrests civil rights workers for passing out voter registration information, the prosecutor who presses charges against them, the justice of the peace who finds them guilty of criminal sedition, the appeal court judges who affirm the convictions or the Federal judge who refuses to stop this harrassment because he does not believe in Negro voting rights are not trying to bring about an orderly change in the law. Indeed, there never has been any serious debate or even an articulate argument on the desirability of maintaining the second-class status of the Negro. The most serious fallacy in the thinking on civil rights is equating the actions of these officials with a Negro demonstrator's disobedience of a Mississippi law against integration of restaurants or against distributing leaflets without a permit. The Negro demonstrator is testing the validity of laws he feels in good faith are unconstitutional or are being unconstitutionally applied. By refusing to obey these laws he is introducing a bill for their repeal or for a fair application of these laws in the only way he can: by deliberately letting himself be prosecuted and appealing any conviction to the Supreme Court where they can be judicially repealed. Since the ordinary political processes are closed to him, he is pursuing an alternate peaceful way of bringing about an orderly change in his society's laws. But all his activities are premised on the fair operation of the legal system and an acceptance of—indeed an insistence on—the need to obey the final orders of the Supreme Court. He is always willing to pay the price of imprisonment if his "bill" is not passed. As Professor Charles Fried has written: "in showing his readiness to suffer the penalty for disobedience he is affirming the value of law in general . . ."5

The southern governors, state policemen, sheriffs and judges we have mentioned had no such purpose in mind. Their opposition takes place at the end, and not at the beginning of the process. Their protests against change were heard, considered and rejected as finally and definitively as our political system allows. These officials do not accept the procedures by which orderly change to a system they can accept is still possible. They do not engage in political activities which can alter the law even after the Supreme Court has spoken—by Federal law or constitutional amendment. Instead they violate and threaten the entire legal structure and denigrate the law in the most dangerous way possible. They refuse to follow the basic compact of our society, and in so doing, they encourage even greater defiance of the law —by lynch mobs, arsonists, bombers and murderers.

It would be absurd to claim that sheriffs, prosecutors or judges from the North are without prejudices of any kind and impartially go about their business. Every practicing lawyer knows how much attention is paid to a judge's idiosyncrasies or bias. The element of discretion in all phases of the legal process is much wider than most laymen imagine, and that discretion is very often ruled by emotion.

What is unique in the South is that the emotional component is much more ubiquitous, virulent and monolithic than elsewhere in the country. There is no cross current that creates a rough balance of conflicting interests and neutralizes the worst expressions of prejudice. Too many southern officials let their emotions and prejudice sway their decisions in only one direction: against the Negro. The result is not isolated injustice or occasional error. An entire pattern and practice is established that effectively overrules the law in the statute books or the Constitution. A new kind of law owing its allegiance only to the hates and fears of the white community governs the day-to-day existence of the southern Negro.

The articles contained in this anthology have been written by lawyers who have had first-hand experience in civil rights cases in the South. They represent a small fraction of the lawyers who have worked in the forefront of the civil rights movement from its start. During the last great social upheaval in this country—the labor drive of the 1930's—lawyers played only a minor role. In fact, jurisdiction over labor disputes was taken away from the courts. The weakness of labor's position in the 1930's was primarily the result of economic and not legal forces. While the courts were a separate and important ally of management, the power applied against the labor movement only incidentally and occasionally had its source in the law.

In the civil rights movement, however, the states' legal institutions were and are the principal enemy. No law compelled a man to work 10 hours a day for less than 50 cents an hour, but laws providing for segregated schools, public facilities and restaurants, and restricting Negro voting rights were enforced everywhere in the South until they were declared unconstitutional. This did not stop the authorities. Through their control of the legal institutions, they found more indirect ways of suppressing the Negro's drive for full equality.

The articles in this collection deal with one specific phase of the administration of justice in the South: how the legal institutions have been used to cripple the struggle for Negro rights and what has been or can be done to protect Negroes from this kind of legal abuse. They do not attempt to examine, except tangentially, how the southern legal machinery has dealt with the Negro in other than civil rights cases. Many of the same problems exist in both areas—illegal arrests, conviction on the basis of flimsy evidence, and punishment far out of proportion to the crime and far greater than whites would receive. But the cavalier treatment of a Negro defendant's civil liberties when he is accused of other types of crimes is not confined to the South. Negroes receive more severe sentences in the North than do whites, and Negroes undoubtedly are handled differently from whites in many northern police stations. But northern police do not arrest Negroes for distributing handbills or trying to vote or regularly manhandle peaceful demonstrators pressing for rights guaranteed by the Constitution. In that sense southern justice is a special geographical problem and deserves special study.

The violations of constitutional rights discussed in the various articles add up to what Peter R. Teachout calls "underlaw." It has one of the attributes of law—consistency—but it is not law that can result in justice. There is no equality, desert, conscientiousness, dignity, regularity or decency in its operation.

The process begins with the state legislatures, some of which have no hesitation in passing laws that blatantly violate the Constitution. As Paul Chevigny points out, Mississippi thinks nothing of destroying 50 years of social reform in the fight for segregation. James B. Wilson shows how mayors and municipal officials often supplement state laws by ordinances and special proclamations designed to harass civil rights workers. The police and sheriffs who abuse their power to arrest civil rights workers on any pretext are the most immediate and well-known enforcers of the segregated status quo—whether in Alabama, Louisiana, Georgia or Mississippi, as Clifford J. Durr, Peter Teachout, Michael Meltsner and Jeremiah Gutman indicate. The prosecutors often use their authority to press these baseless charges or —as Jesse Brenner describes—to protect the white hoodlums in the community from the law. Jack Oppenheim shows how the lack of legal assistance by the local bar compounds the difficulties Negroes face in their legal encounters. Local judges have no difficulty in finding Negroes and civil rights workers guilty despite the lack of any evidence of a crime, and Nils R. Douglas, Robert F. Collins and Lolis E. Elie point out that some judges do not hesitate to evade Federal court orders in their eagerness to keep the Negro from maintaining his rights. Michael Meltsner shows how the errors are seldom corrected on appeal and how Federal intervention is often the only solution. The effect of these tactics on the lives of the local Negro population is touched on by Robert P. Schulman.

Charles Morgan, Jr., analyzes one of the key reasons the state's legal machinery is used as a weapon to suppress the civil rights movement rather than as a neutral umpire maintaining the social peace and harmonizing contending interests within the ambit of law: the fact that the machinery is itself segregated and no Negro has a role in it or helps to operate it in any way. The legal process is out of his hands because he has been disenfranchised and cannot vote for sheriffs, prosecutors or judges. And his lack of control of the legal machinery has left the white community free to suppress his effort to register and vote. It remains to be seen how effective the 1965 Voting Rights Act will be in breaking this circle, in making the state officials more responsive to the Negro community and allowing the Negro to enter and participate in the legal system. Unless the Negroes claiming their rights under the new law are protected by the full force of the Federal government against the kind of harrassment and abuse described in these articles, nothing will change.

The need for intervention by the Federal courts and Federal executive power is apparent at all levels. But—as Gerald M. Stern shows—Federal judges such as Judge Cox in Mississippi often act as an extension of the state's repressive machinery. And the Federal government has just begun to use the enormous power currently at its disposal —described by Haywood Burns—to counter the abuse of state authority.

Fortunately there are some prosecutors and state judges who have begun to be troubled by what has been happening. Marvin Braiterman describes the dilemma of some fairer Mississippi officials. Some appeal court judges for a variety of reasons have reversed the more blatant overreachings by lower court judges and prosecutors. Some Federal judges such as Bryan Simpson of Jacksonville, Florida, have shown great courage in enforcing the Constitution in the face of local opposition. And the initiative of the Federal Fifth Circuit Court of Appeals, described by Shirley Fingerhood, has been responsible for some significant civil rights victories. Professor Louis Lusky in his article reproduced from the *Columbia Law Review* ties together many of these diverse strands and shows how the existing procedural traps have been exploited by the opponents of civil rights. He offers a number of suggestions for making the Federal courts more effective avenues of correction.

But the final solution must come from inside the system, from the native Southerner's own awareness of the monstrous perversion of the law he has helped to create by his indifference. As long as his sense of injustice remains dormant or buried beneath his fears, these perversions will continue. The sense of injustice has begun to emerge in the South only tentatively in recent times. No doubt it will find even greater expression in the future as the full awareness of what has happened enters the consciousness of the southern community. No native Southerner can now pretend that news stories of Negro oppression are exaggerated or political propaganda. Southerners must—and no doubt will—face up to their responsibilities, to their own instincts of outrage and sympathy. And the rest of the country must insist on the full national power being marshaled, to overcome—in President Johnson's words—"the crippling legacy of bigotry and injustice."

LEON FRIEDMAN

Acknowledgments

Grateful acknowledgment must be given the various organizations who financed and sponsored the legal encounters described in this volume and thousands of others in the past decade. The NAACP Legal Defense and Educational Fund, Inc. has borne the brunt of this legal defense from the time of the school segregation cases in 1954 and even prior to it. The Lawyers Constitutional Defense Committee, which was established in the spring of 1964, sponsored the largest invasion of legal talent into the South in recent years, and a number of the contributors to this volume were sent under the aegis of the L.C.D.C. I am particularly grateful to the founders and officers of that organization and the groups that formed and supported it and have themselves been giving legal assistance in the South for many years; Dean Robert F. Drinan of the Boston College Law School; Melvin L. Wulf and John de J. Pemberton, Jr. of the A.C.L.U.; Edwin Lukas of the American Jewish Committee; Leo Pfeffer of the American Jewish Congress; John Pratt of the National Council of Churches; Howard Moore of S.N.C.C.; Carl Rachlin of C.O.R.E.; and Henry Schwarzschild, Executive Secretary of the L.C.D.C.

PAUL G. CHEVIGNY

A Busy Spring in the
Magnolia State

The State Capitol in Jackson, where the Mississippi House and Senate sit, is a monument to the Mississippi legislative mind. A handsome building, finished in 1903 at what was then the terrific cost of a million dollars, it is a delicious combination of the humbug of the back-country politician and the pomposity of the Victorian swell. The floors and walls contain sixteen different kinds of marble, and the archways under the rotunda are set with thousands of light bulbs (which cause the temperature to go up above the point of endurability in the summer). If one goes in the doorway at ground level, one faces a bronze statue of the late Theodore Bilbo in a double-breasted suit, striking an oratorical stance. If one walks up the broad marble steps

Paul G. Chevigny was graduated from the Harvard Law School in 1960. He is a member of the New York Bar and is currently legal director of the Harlem Neighborhood Legal Assistance Project.

and through the main entrance, on the other hand, one is flanked on either side by an immense color transparency of one of the two Miss Americas who have come from Mississippi.

The legislative activities of the Mississippi House and Senate have been in keeping with their decorative instincts. They have always tried to protect southern womanhood and the southern way of life, though they have devoted increasing energy to the job since 1954. After the House and Senate were convened in January, 1964, they passed the spring in prodigies of legislation designed to terrify Negroes and civil rights workers and to give law enforcement agencies the power to prevent demonstrations. Much of this activity had been completed by the time the summer volunteers arrived late in June of that year. Newspaper reporters were unable to resist the temptation to speak of the Council of Federated Organizations and its efforts to register voters in terms of a military operation. But the fact is that, aside from the lack of firearms, the COFO campaign failed in its resemblance to a military attack in one signal respect: surprise. The COFO operation was one of the major news stories of the year, and Mississippi had heard much about each step in the invasion, beginning with the initial dispute among the civil rights groups as to whether Mississippi really was the best target for the movement and including the details of the training of the summer volunteers. Furthermore, a group of SNCC, CORE and NAACP workers had been there all year, and some of them for years before, quietly trying to organize Negroes to register. White Mississippians knew a great deal more than they cared to know about field secretaries, Freedom Houses, Freedom Schools, and Negro voter registration. Their elected representatives, most of whom obtained office by being more rabid race-baiters than any of their opponents, not to speak of their constituents, undertook to throw up a wall against the foreign invasion.

As the bills were proposed and passed, the COFO office at 1017 Lynch Street in Jackson kept a running record of them, together with newspaper clippings. Law students went around to the legislative sessions, then quietly requested or filched copies of the bills.

These were no Black Codes; they were a good deal more subtle than that. Though there are still a few segregation statutes scattered through the volumes of the Mississippi Code, the legislature has learned that raw segregation by state action will be declared unconstitutional by the Federal courts, even in Mississippi. The Mississippi legislators have shifted from trying to limit civil rights to trying to limit what are loosely denoted civil liberties, although their real purpose was never in doubt. Instead of perpetuating the system of segregation directly, the legislature passes bills of attainder and impairs contracts; it interferes with the liberties preserved in the Bill of Rights, including the rights to freedom of speech, press and assembly, as well as the prohibitions against excessive fines and bail, and cruel and unusual punishment. In short, the legislature sets out to maintain segregation indirectly by controlling the protest against it. This raises the question why, if they know that segregation laws are unconstitutional, the legislators do not know that laws which infringe civil liberties are unconstitutional as well. Part of the answer lies in the fact that the purpose of the statute is often hidden, sometimes artfully and sometimes not, under a thicket of pious verbiage intended to show that the law is a health measure or a police reform. Those cases where the unconstitutional intent of the statute is obvious must be explained by the fact that the legislators in Mississippi have not had as much practice with the rest of the Constitution as they have had with the equal protection clause. Part of the civil rights lawyers' job is to give them a little more experience with the rest of the Constitution.

In a few cases the legislators do in fact think that a statute is unconstitutional, but they pass it anyhow. For example, in June, 1964, a statute was passed penalizing persons located outside the state who foment crimes to be perpetrated inside the state and later come into the state. The chairman of the Senate Judiciary Committee, Senator

Collins, was quoted in the *Greenwood Commonwealth* of May 12, 1964, as saying, "The bill may be unconstitutional, but it can't do us any harm." Why anyone who entertains this attitude should stop at a segregation statute is a mystery. It is probably because he expects that not even Mississippi judges will any longer uphold a segregation statute. But a law infringing civil liberties may survive the Mississippi courts until it is struck down by the Supreme Court. The longer the law is on the books the longer it can be used as a tool against civil rights.

Nineteen sixty-four was not the first year the Mississippi legislature had attempted to maintain the status quo by passing legislation intended to stifle protest, nor for that matter is the state legislature the first official body in Mississippi that has tried it. There is an elegantly drafted little antileafleting ordinance which seems to have been passed by the governments of most of the small towns and is said to have originated with the Citizens' Council several years ago. It does not actually forbid leafleting; instead it states that for the purpose of keeping the street clean, anyone who wishes to distribute leaflets must obtain a license from the town and post a bond to cover the cost of cleaning the papers from the streets. (The U.S. Supreme Court has found similar ordinances unconstitutional in numerous cases.) This is a fairly typical sort of statute, and it shows that Mississippi had been practicing for the spring 1964 performance in the legislature for a long time. It had the civil rights activities that have been going on for several years, and continued into the spring, to draw upon for examples.

The effort on the part of the legislators to maintain segregation indirectly results in a kind of game. When a law is passed to strengthen the police, or to prevent demonstrations, or for some other purpose that affects civil rights indirectly, there is a rule among the leaders in the legislature that, if possible, the law will be proposed and passed without comment, so as to shield it from the wrath of the Supreme Court. (This is so well known that newspapermen refer to any bill that is passed without discussion, as having "racial overtones.") On the other hand, the legislators want their constituents to know that they are giving their all to the support of segregation. A dilemma. The result is a large number of "unofficial" leaks to the newspapers, and voluminous comment in the press on the purposes of the bills. The conspiracy of silence makes the newspapers an unusually valuable source of information.

Many of the newspapers are heavily involved with the Mississippi administration. The two Jackson papers, the *Daily News* and the *Clarion-Ledger*, both owned by the same family, militantly support white supremacy and Governor Paul Johnson, just as they supported Barnett before him. The *Commercial Appeal* of Memphis publishes a special Mississippi edition that is strongly segregationist. This bias is all the more useful because these papers willingly publish the most rabid oratory from the floor, and they obtain special leaks from state officials. Quoting them is almost like telling your story straight out of the mouth of Mississippi herself. The Greenwood and Clarksdale papers generally follow the Jackson papers and the wire services in covering the legislature. The *Delta Democrat-Times*, published by Hodding Carter of Greenville, is courageously against the administration, and it occasionally publishes an account of a legislative debate as a horrible example of how the legislature operates. The New Orleans *Times-Picayune* keeps its opinions pretty much to itself, but its correspondent, Bill Minor, publishes fairly full accounts of the debates in the legislature, wisely permitting them to speak for themselves. As far as I can, I intend to follow Mr. Minor's example in this discussion.

Much to the chagrin of the leaders of both houses, but fortunately for the historian, the conspiracy of silence about the purposes of repressive statutes does not work very well. The effort to cloak segregation in the garb of police or court reform tears at the fabric of the courts and the police as institutions, and it very often raises an outcry from men who are interested in preserving those institutions. Though these mavericks are rarely more than a handful, and though they are, as one of them put it plaintively, "as good segregationists as anyone," their objections often lead to a bitter floor fight and another good news story. (Mississippi, like most other states, does not keep a stenographic record of legislative debates.)

The most interesting and ingenious laws passed during the spring of 1964 were those which were not intended to limit constitutional rights directly but rather to provide for swifter and more effective law enforcement through greater police power. One of the most fiercely debated laws in this group was House Bill 564, a double-barreled bill to increase the state highway patrol, and to permit the governor to use it as a police force, for purposes of keeping the peace (prior to this time it had jurisdiction only over traffic violations). House Bill 564 was proposed in March, but it was not passed until May, and the long debate will serve to introduce us to the *dramatis personae* at the Capitol.

The Jackson *Clarion-Ledger* reported on March 4, 1964, that Governor Johnson addressed the House and Senate, asking them to give the state highway patrol authority to act as "peace officers in the full sense of the word." At this point his proposal apparently contained almost no restrictions as to the occasions on which the patrol could be used in this way, or for how long, or upon what notice by the governor. Despite these considerable questions, the paper reported:

> In the House of Representatives, veteran lawmakers . . . were universally in favor of giving police powers to the Highway Patrol, stating that they had in years past refused such authority, but that "times have changed."

The governor had, however, failed to reckon with the fact that Mississippi is the only remaining dry state, with a complicated contraband trade based upon the continuation of prohibition. The *Clarion-Ledger* went on to say:

> But there is a deep fear among many legislators and others that a state police force could be a potent political weapon in such matters as gambling, liquor and local problems if a governor chose to make it one.

Furthermore, it appeared that Walter Sillers, Speaker of the House and one of the most powerful men in Mississippi, was enough of a conservative to be opposed to the proposal in its original form, and wanted to limit the governor to the power to act "by proclamation in emergency situations."

These influential forces had their effect on the governor. On March 16, he offered a bill to increase the state patrol from 275 to 475 men, and to limit the use of the patrol as peace officers to situations which the *Clarion-Ledger* of the following day referred to as "major problems, including racial crisis." The bill as ultimately passed stated that the use of the patrol for peace-keeping purposes was limited to "civil disturbances," and Walter Sillers was presumably satisfied.

Nevertheless, the proposal found rough going both in the House and the Senate. In the House an amendment was passed limiting the length of time for which the governor could call the patrol to ninety days, and another amendment failed which would have prevented the governor from calling out the patrol on the advice of his own investigators, requiring instead the request of local authorities. In the Senate, one of the leading mavericks, McDonnell of Biloxi, was reported to have said, "What you are about to do here is create a traveling gestapo. It besmacks [*sic*] of Nazi Germany and Russia" (*Clarion-Ledger*, 4/15/64). It appeared that the liquor interests were still afraid of the governor's investigators, and they were castigated for attempting to preserve the state's democratic institutions for their own selfish reasons. On April 23, the *Clarion-Ledger* quoted one senator as saying:

> The governor says he is not going to bother with your whiskey business. He could use the National Guard now. The question is whether you are going to put Sen. McDonnell's whiskey business ahead of the people of Mississippi, whether you are going to stop demonstrators or let the question be clouded when Sen. McDonnell says it might affect his whiskey business.

The most explosive reaction to the governor's bill was produced when the governor admitted that he did not intend to notify the public of all his proclamations. Apparently there was no public discussion about the interesting question of what sort of proclamation could be made that was not public, but several senators did express their general opposition to such a proceeding. The governor's prerogative to make a nonpublic proclamation was finally upheld in the Senate on the perfectly reasonable argument that an investigation after a public proclamation would be "advertising to our enemies what we are going to do. We'll never know what they are going to do until it is too late" (*Clarion-Ledger*, 4/23/64).

Despite the grumbling in the legislature, the bill was finally passed by both houses after the legislative leaders raised the specter of the civil rights invasion. Thompson McClellan, chairman of the House Judiciary Committee, was quoted in the Jackson *Daily News* on April 3, 1964, "If we don't have the force to cope with en masse marches on Mississippi this summer we will be helpless." And a senator asked a rhetorical question from the floor, "Isn't it a fact that the whole nation and all people who read Mississippi newspapers know that an army of agitators is coming down in June?" (*Daily News*, 5/14/64) The bill as finally passed increased the patrol from 275 to 475, and permitted the governor to use the highway patrol in civil disturbances, for a period of ninety days, on the advice of his own investigators.

The curious thing about the law was that it did not seem to change the existing situation very much; the governor admitted that the sheriffs had always been able to get the assistance of the highway patrol in case of disorder, and the first of the new men was not expected to be trained until September (*Daily News*, 5/14/64). The real point of the law, as it finally appeared in the debates, was to create a state police force in case the National Guard was federalized. The Clarksdale *Press-Register* of March 28 quoted the governor as saying that the bill would protect him from having the President "pull the national guard out from under me and leave me out on a limb trying to keep law and order without anybody to do it." The implications of this scheme for Mississippi's relations with the Federal government were not lost on everyone in the legislature. Mack Weems, the representative from Scott County, was reported in the *Daily News* of April 3, 1964, to have said:

> If we had had 2,000 patrolmen at Ole Miss, the campus would have been drenched with the blood of our boys and girls. If you want to keep from backing down to the government, you had better withdraw from the Union and join forces with Fidel Castro, Russia and Red China, and you're still going to get the daylights beat out of you. . . . If it comes to an open clash with the federal government, we must recognize the fact that we are a part of the nation. Under such conditions, the less force we can show, the better.

But Weems's was a voice crying in the wilderness. The other legislators, still bemused by the outrage of Federal troops in Mississippi during the riots over the admission of James Meredith to Ole Miss, were unimpressed by the prospect of an open conflict between Federal troops and the state highway patrol.

The legislators were less hesitant about giving increased powers to the local town and county authorities than they were about giving them to the governor. One of the first bills passed for this purpose was Senate Bill 1526, ostensibly for the purpose of permitting the pooling of fire-fighting equipment in emergencies. In its first paragraph the bill authorizes local fire departments to go outside the limits of their own municipalities "for the purpose of aiding in the extinguishing and prevention of fires or damages or injuries caused by tornadoes or other casualties in locations outside the corporate limits of such municipalities." There is much more innocuous language in succeeding paragraphs, giving the fire departments the right of way over the roads, and freeing their parent municipalities from liability for damage done, up to the last paragraph, which suddenly permits municipalities to enter into "mutual assistance pacts" for the purpose "of combatting fires, natural and enemy disasters, and the prevention and alleviation of riots or civil disturbances of the peace and tranquillity within such municipalities."

Despite the fact that this language is buried in the last

paragraph, and no legislative debate was reported, the papers were not mystified as to the intent of the statute. On February 27, 1964 the *Clarion-Ledger* ran an article on the bill:

> The CORE plans to conduct a march on the Madison County courthouse in a mass voter registration attempt at Canton, a community of 10,000 located 20 miles north of here in a farm area with a heavy Negro population.
>
> Johnson signed into law a bill authorizing municipalities to pool personnel and equipment "for the prevention and alleviation of riots or civil disturbances."
>
> Madison County Sheriff Jack Cauthen was close-mouthed about plans to deal with the demonstrators but he said detailed plans had been drawn. "Every city, large and small, is standing by to lend assistance, if needed."
>
> Mayor Allen Thompson of Jackson said his city stands "ready and willing" to furnish aid in "handling unlawful activities and in maintaining law and order."

The Clarksdale *Press-Register* reported on the same day that a member of the governor's staff said the bill was "rushed through." That was putting it mildly. It was introduced, passed in both houses and signed, all on February 26, 1964. In the end, despite all the belligerent journalism, the local authorities at Canton were able to break up all civil rights demonstrations there without any outside assistance.

An even more amazing statute was introduced and passed in the House the same day, though it did not get through the Senate to the governor's desk for another two weeks. House Bill 64, as it was called, was ostensibly a quarantine law. The first section authorized municipalities to "make regulations to prevent the introduction and spread of contagious or infectious diseases; [and] to make quarantine laws for that purpose." The second section continued in a somewhat different vein, providing power "to make regulations to protect property, health and lives and to enhance the general welfare of the community by restricting the movements of the citizens, or any group thereof, of such municipalities when there is eminent [*sic*] danger to the public safety because of freedom of movement thereof."

Although both houses were seemingly silent on the intent of the bill, once again the *Clarion-Ledger* did not fail to pick up the story. Under the headline "Paul Signs Curfew Bill," the paper reported on March 12, 1964, that the bill "aimed at helping communities cope with racial disorders, would permit curfews and other restrictions to be established by city fathers."

This law, like the highway patrol bill, did not create an entirely new situation. The Delta town of Clarksdale, for example, has had a curfew law for some years, and it did not appear that anyone in the state was going to question the power of that city to pass such a law. Apparently the legislators wanted simply to show their solidarity with the local authorities in resisting demonstrations. The fact that the legislature conceived a quarantine bill as part of a statute shows how profound is their desire for a separation of the races.

The legislature permitted local authorities to increase penalties as well as to increase the powers of law enforcement. Senate Bill 1517 raised the maximum jail term permissible under municipal ordinances from 30 to 90 days, and the maximum fine from $100 to $300. Of this law the *Clarion-Ledger* on February 12, 1964, uttered the following exegesis:

> No example was cited to show the need for the legislation, usually a good indication that the bill has racial overtones.

Senate Bill 1517 was, I take it, chiefly passed as a measure to prevent demonstrations by threats of draconic punishment, and the legislature went still further in its campaign of deterrence with House Bills 321 and 322. The first provided that municipal prisoners could be removed to the county jail or the state penitentiary, and the second that county prisoners could be removed to another county or to the state penitentiary. The *Clarion-Ledger* reported on May 5, 1964, that one senator said, "This bill applies to those visitors who might be coming into our state this summer."

This delicate hint implied more than mere mass arrests. A stranger to Mississippi cannot understand the full impact of the laws on the mind of the Negro or the white civil rights worker there, until he knows something about the state penitentiary, a huge cotton farm at the town of Parchman, in the Delta. I could detail the shocking stories I have heard about Parchman Farm, but it is more convincing simply to tell the story of the legislature's own prison reform bill, House Bill 227, passed in June, 1964.

House Bill 227 is a very long statute, of some 71 sections on 13 long-legal pages. It establishes a modern prison board. It provides for wholesome food and a limit on work for the prisoners, together with the abolition of road camps. All very worthwhile aims, to be sure. But its most impressive paragraph is Section 48, which is better quoted than paraphrased:

> The superintendent may set up rules regarding the discipline of prisoners. No prisoner may be placed in solitary confinement except under orders of the superintendent. Any prisoner held in solitary confinement shall be fed a meal at least once every day and shall be examined by a physician at least once every two (2) days. No prisoner shall be placed in the "dark hole" of the maximum security unit for a longer period than twenty-four (24) hours. Corporal punishment of any kind is hereby discouraged and shall not be administered to any prisoner except on the written authority of the superintendent and if corporal punishment is administered to any prisoner, it shall be administered in the presence of any two (2) of the following persons: the superintendent, the chaplain or a member of the board. Whenever a sergeant or other employee of the Penitentiary considers it necessary that a prisoner be punished, he must make a written report to the superintendent regarding punishment, stating in such report the offense committed by the prisoner and in the event the superintendent, after investigation, considers it necessary that such prisoner be given corporal punishment, he shall give written authority therefor directed to the sergeant specifying the number of licks or lashes, not to exceed seven (7), which may be administered. The written request of the sergeant and the written authorization of the superintendent, signed by them, as well as a statement by the witnesses attesting that they witnessed the lashing, shall be placed in the file

of the prisoner involved and a copy of same shall be placed in a permanent register available to the Governor, the board and legislative investigating committees.

Despite this little bureaucratic horror, the statute was not a sham. It was a true reform in the prison laws, resulting from a real legislative compromise. The prior law concerning corporal punishment at Parchman Farm had provided for ten lashes, and had not mentioned the existence of the "dark hole" at all. Senator McDonnell, once again the strong dissenting voice, denounced all corporal punishment as a barbarity. His objections provoked an old-fashioned southern oration proclaiming the efficacy of the threat of the whip as a protection for wives and daughters, and the limited provision for corporal punishment remained in the bill.

Parchman Farm is, by all ordinary standards, an extraordinary prison. It is intended to be a self-sustaining cotton farm, and several writers have noticed a suspicious resemblance to the Old Plantation. Its general pattern is completely paternalistic: the work is hard and the punishments medieval, but there are exceptionally liberal visitation rights for wives and families. A white Mississippi lawyer told me that in fact it was a very humane prison and certainly much better than the average Mississippi county farm. The first statement may be true according to his standards, and the second is probably true by any standard, but the county farms just do not enjoy the special reputation that Parchman does. It was, after all, the reputation of Parchman that made the bills providing for the removal of prisoners to the state penitentiary so potent.

While the legislature was passing laws to permit more severe law-enforcement, it also approved a number of bills directly to prohibit certain types of protest. The earliest of these was Senate Bill 1545, which the Jackson *Daily News* called the "Anti-Boycott Bill." This bill provides a penalty for printing or circulating "any matter for the purpose of impairing, interfering with, or preventing another person from exercising a lawful trade or calling."

The Clarksdale *Press-Register* explained the particular

occasion for the bill to the voters in the edition of February 12, 1964:

> A boycott of certain white merchants has been underway at Canton, located just north of Jackson, for the past several weeks.

In the Jackson *Daily News* of the same day, it was reported that a certain Senator Jones, "terming himself as much a segregationist as anyone in Mississippi, labeled the measure unconstitutional and said 'it could seriously impair our freedom of speech.'" The proposal also evoked pained outcries from organized labor, and an amendment to exempt labor unions was defeated in the Senate after the expression of these noble sentiments, quoted from the senator from Tupelo in the same article:

> It should apply to everyone in Mississippi, . . . regardless of race, color or creed.

In the House, a similar objection brought the opposite reaction. There, the chairman of the Judiciary Committee was quoted as saying that if any local people were accused under the bill, they would be "tried in a Mississippi court before a Mississippi jury," and he would have no "apprehension" as to the outcome (*Press-Register* 2/28/64). The bill passed both houses by the end of February with only a handful of dissenting votes.

A month later, the legislature passed House Bill 546, the so-called "Anti-Picketing Bill." It provides a maximum penalty of $500 or six months in jail, or both, for mass demonstrations "in such a manner as to obstruct or interfere with free ingress or egress to and from any public premises, state property . . . or with the transaction of public business or the administration of justice therein . . . or so as to obstruct or interfere with the free use of public streets, sidewalks or other public ways adjacent or contiguous thereto."

On March 31, 1964 the New Orleans *Times-Picayune* reported that the chairman of the House Judiciary Committee, in lieu of an explanation of the bill on the floor, stated, "This is a type of bill, by reading it, most of you will catch the significance of it without too much discussion." The newspaper further explained:

> The measure was apparently rushed to passage as a weapon against picketing by Negro voter demonstrations at Greenwood, where 14 persons were arrested Tuesday [March 31] at the Courthouse.
>
> Mayor Charles Sampson of Greenwood Tuesday said he had urged McClellan to push for immediate passage of the bill, and expressed the hope the Senate will also quickly approve it.

The Senate obliged. The Jackson *Daily News* reported on April 2, 1964, that the bill passed unanimously after Senator Collins described it as "an emergency bill for Greenwood."

This law was one of the most dependable guns in the whole arsenal of Mississippi laws passed during the spring. Dozens of arrests at Greenwood were based on it, and many more in other towns. The law was attacked as unconstitutional in a case before the Federal court in Hattiesburg. Though the Mississippi Federal judges ultimately refused to take jurisdiction of the case, under the threat of the lawsuit the statute was amended in July to penalize only demonstrations which "unreasonably" obstruct sidewalks or entrances to public buildings.

In May, 1964, the legislators undertook to prevent nearly every type of demonstration, under a rubric that is a favorite for controlling protest not only in Mississippi but in every other state: breach of the peace. House Bill 777 penalized anyone who refused to obey the order of a law enforcement officer to "arise," if he was sitting or lying down, to move from a vehicle, to get into a police car, to untie himself, or to refrain from sitting or lying, or from obstructing any vehicle, or from tying himself to any person or object, when any of these were done "with intent to provoke a breach of the peace, or under such circumstances as may lead to a breach of the peace, or which may cause or occasion a breach of the peace." This bill scarcely needed any comment, and it received none. The *Clarion-Ledger* of May 22, 1964, described it simply as "one of several [bills] hustled through the Legislature in this session in the wave of planned civil rights demonstrations by out-of-state college students."

Having passed laws to punish civil rights agitation, the legislature made sure that all the agitators would be punished equally, whether they were minors or not, by removing the offenses from the jurisdiction of the youth court. The Mississippi youth court statute, like similar laws in other states, is a reform in criminal procedure intended to protect minors, who are not thought to be entirely responsible for their actions, or at least not to the same degree as adults. The youth court proceedings could not result in a criminal conviction, and, most important, they could not result in a criminal "record" available to the public. Whatever damage the bill might do to the youth court as an institution, the legislators were determined that civil rights workers who were arrested should be sent away with a record, and a prison record if possible. In House Bill 960 they removed the crimes of breach of the peace as defined in H.B. 777, as well as every other breach of the peace statute, and unlawful picketing under H.B. 546, from the jurisdiction of the youth court. Just to make sure that they were not omitting any other possible civil rights activities, they included a few older offenses, including trespass, obstructing the sidewalk, use of abusive language, perjury, carrying a concealed weapon, and disturbing a religious congregation. When the bill came to final passage on June 5, 1964, the *Times-Picayune* reported that the chairman of the Senate Judiciary Committee commented bitterly from the floor, "you just about ruined youth courts . . . because of the threats of what may happen this summer, whether fact or fiction."

In Senate Bill 2016, passed a few days before, the legislature had not removed any particular class of cases from the jurisdiction of the youth court but instead had weakened the protection of privacy surrounding its proceedings. The bill permitted any agency of the state of Mississippi to obtain the record of a youth court proceeding "upon the request of such agency." This bill was aimed not so much at civil rights workers in general as at one Negro civil rights worker in particular—Cleveland Donald, who was seeking enrollment at Ole Miss for the summer session. The *Times-Picayune* reported on June 3, 1964:

> The Negro student, Cleveland Donald of Jackson, had been arrested in a Negro demonstration here last year, but was released to custody of his parents as a juvenile.
>
> Donald, an honor student at Jackson High School, attended Tougaloo Southern Christian College this year as an accelerated student.

Under the provisions of the previous youth court law, the university would not have been able to obtain Donald's record to use against him. That result was entirely in keeping with the law's original purpose to protect minors from having their mature careers ruined by a criminal record, but the legislators destroyed that social reform because they wanted Donald's record to follow him. They closed the circle against him by providing in the second section of the bill that anyone charged with or convicted of a crime could not be admitted to any "institution of higher learning in the State of Mississippi." They also warned Donald not to get involved in further demonstrations by providing in the law that when any minor was found to be delinquent for the second time, his name and his parents' names were to be published in the local newspaper for two weeks.

The legislature took other actions to preserve segregation by silencing individuals or institutions that were centers of protest within the state. The drive to keep Cleveland Donald out of Ole Miss was mild in comparison with the one against Tougaloo Southern Christian College, outside of Jackson, where Donald was going to school. Tougaloo has been a center of civil rights activities for years. Folk-singing sessions and student rallies were held there during the summer of 1964, and many of the summer volunteers lived nearby. The college was always a haven of rest when the going got rough in Jackson. In August, 1964, Ed King, the minister at Tougaloo, was sent to the Democratic Convention as a delegate from the Freedom Democratic party. The legislators were not able to stop this, but they took a long step toward making sure that it would not happen again.

The campaign began in February, 1964, when Lieutenant Governor Carroll Gartin called for an investigation of the activities at Tougaloo. He called the college a "cancerous growth," and according to the Greenwood *Commonwealth* of April 14, 1964, added that it was a haven for "queers, quirks, political agitators and possibly some Communists." A bill was introduced to revoke Tougaloo's charter.

But even Mississippi legislators have heard of the *Dartmouth College* case. That case held that it was unconstitutional for a state to revoke the charter of a college; and after all, it was argued by Daniel Webster, who was dead before the War Between the States. Tougaloo is a small college, but, like Dartmouth, there are those who love her. The bill was permitted to die in the Senate Judiciary Committee.

It was replaced by Senate Bill 2043, a much more sophisticated measure. That bill gave to the Mississippi Commission on College Accreditation complete power to prepare a list of accredited colleges. Under the previous law, the commission had been obliged to include all the institutions approved by the Southern Association of Colleges and Universities, and the Southern Association approved Tougaloo. On April 21, 1964, the *Delta Democrat-Times* reported:

> The loss of recognition could affect transfer of students to other colleges in the state and stop Tougaloo graduates from getting state teachers' licenses, according to Lt. Gov. Carroll Gartin, who supported the bill.

A teacher's license has special significance to a Negro college student in Mississippi, where teaching is one of the few professions open to them when they graduate. But the legislators were determined, if they could not kill the "cancerous growth," at least to isolate it from the rest of the state.

The legislators did not spend all their time beating their breasts over outside agitators, and attempting to silence the centers of protest within. They occasionally took up the direct harassment of Negroes in Mississippi, most notoriously in House Bill 180, called variously the "Illegitimacy Bill," the "Baby Bill," or, to use the phrase coined by SNCC, the "Genocide Bill." As amended and passed, it provides a fine or a prison term, or both, for any person who becomes the parent of a second illegitimate child, and a still stiffer fine or prison term, or both, for any person who becomes the parent of a third illegitimate child. (The reader will be relieved to know that the birth of twins counts as only one child.) The law illuminates, perhaps even better than the others, some of the real economic and social problems of race relations in Mississippi. The bill is intended to cut down the population of Negroes, or to drive them out of the state. In the old days, forty years ago or more, when Negroes were sharecroppers, such a bill could never have been passed. Large families were encouraged, and it was sometimes as much as a man's life was worth to try to leave the farm. But mechanical cottonpickers have largely eliminated the need for hand labor on the farms, and thousands of Negroes are out of work. They are on the relief rolls, while their fellow Negroes are clamoring for freedom from serfdom. White Mississippians would like to see most of them leave, because it would cut down on the unemployed, and it would reduce the Negroes to a more manageable minority in such areas as the Delta, where they are now in the majority. When black people are fighting for the right to vote, this consideration becomes even more important.

The version of House Bill 180 passed by the Senate, despite the lynch-law attitude which still underlies it, seems mild when compared with the version that was originally passed in the House. That bill provided for a prison term of one to three years for the birth of a second child, or in the alternative, for voluntary sterilization. The *Clarion-Ledger* reported on March 12:

> In calling up the bill, Rep. Meek cited that there were 8647 illegitimate non-white births in the state and 444 illegitimate white births.
>
> He cited that . . . Mississippi is subsidizing illegitimacy through welfare payments, and that the moral structure had completely broken down in some segments of society.

There was a stormy session in the House, and some legislators called the measure barbarous, but it was passed amidst considerable laughter. The tone of the meeting and the real purpose of the law were summed up with bloodthirsty clarity by one representative quoted in the Greenwood *Commonwealth*:

> When they start to cutting they'll [the unwed parents] head for Chicago.

By the time the bill reached the Senate, it was famous. Most of the papers in the country had picked up the story. The Senate felt obliged to eliminate the sterilization provisions and to reduce the penalties, but it did pass the bill. No doubt it agreed with the representative who said, "this is the only way I know to stop this black tide which threatens to engulf us" (*Daily News*, 5/21/64).

The Senate had at first killed the bill on May 12, 1964, but the next day it returned to the question and passed the milder version. On May 14, 1964, the Memphis *Commercial-Appeal* reported that the reason for the reversal was an angry pamphlet called *Genocide in Mississippi*, circulated among the legislators by SNCC. The *Commercial-Appeal* explained:

> Legislators were unwilling to permit their action to be considered as being influenced by the Negro Civil Rights group.

This story, if true, indicates that the Mississippi legislature was expanding its program: instead of maintaining the oppression of Negroes by the harassment of civil rights workers, it was showing its hatred of civil rights workers by harassing Negroes.

When the summer volunteers arrived at the end of June, 1964, the initial flurry of legislative activity was over, but the legislature was not quite through with its fight against civil rights through interference with civil liberties. Relieved from the burden of having to exercise its own vivid imagination, the legislature began to learn from the summer volunteers what laws it ought to pass. By July, COFO workers were complaining that the local authorities had the power to fingerprint and photograph them only if they were arrested for a felony, not for a simple misdemeanor. The legislature thereupon passed a law to permit local police to take fingerprints and photographs in misdemeanor cases.

It was only the effort of the legislature to foresee and forestall the civil rights campaign of the summer that was over. The attempt was largely unsuccessful, though dozens of arrests were made under the new statutes. The attempt failed because the statutes were intended to prevent mass demonstrations, while COFO's work depended not so much on demonstrations as on quiet organization and educational activities which the laws did not effectively prevent. Such demonstrations as there were, were easily broken up without the assistance of the massive system of law enforcement created by the legislature.

The laws were a vindictive reaction to the drive for equal rights for Negroes, and a grandiloquent gesture to draw the acclaim of the voters. Simply to show their ardor in the defense of segregation and their immunity to all dissent, the legislators ripped holes in the democratic institutions and progressive social reforms of Mississippi. In their eagerness for fame as race-baiters, they did more grievous damage to Mississippi than to its invaders. They gave unprecedented powers to the governor as against local authorities and the Federal government, and they increased the powers of local authorities to control the activities of citizens. They injured their welfare laws and their youth court laws. They imposed serious restraints on all forms of protest, including picketing, boycotts and street demonstrations. Their willingness to injure their own institutions shows only that they cared more for publicity than they cared for democratic institutions or social reforms for any of their constituents, white or black.

JAMES B. WILSON

Municipal Ordinances,
Mississippi Style

In the summer of 1964, Ruleville, Mississippi, became the headquarters for a voter registration program for Negro citizens in the surrounding area. It was here that Mrs. Fanny Lou Hamer, one of the leaders of the Mississippi Freedom Democratic party, lived. In spite of the white community's opposition, a group of young civil rights workers was soon able to establish a Freedom School and community center in a small frame house on the edge of the town, and registration activities were under way.

Their initial success in Ruleville was followed by further success in Indianola, some twenty miles to the south. Three

---

James B. Wilson is an Assistant Attorney General for the State of Washington and is Counsel to the University of Washington. He is a graduate of the University of Washington Law School and was the Democratic nominee for Congress in 1956 from Seattle's First Congressional District.

workers from Ruleville had gone to Indianola in mid-July and, after gaining the support of the local Negro leadership, were given an old abandoned school owned by a local Negro church and were able to create an excellent classroom setting from supplies and materials donated by supporters in the North.

After these two initial successes, the Ruleville leaders turned to the town of Drew, a few miles north of Ruleville. On August 13, 1964, Joseph Smith, a white summer volunteer attached to the Ruleville center, went to Drew to attempt to establish a beachhead in the Negro community. He had stopped by the Negro high school to watch the students practice football and was arrested by the local police chief. He was charged with trespassing. Smith stated that at the time of his arrest he was talking to two Negro boys in a voice so low that the arresting officer could not have heard what he was saying. He was told that it didn't matter what he was doing; he was not allowed on the school grounds and his presence there constituted a crime. When the police realized there was no law preventing a person from going on the school grounds, the charge was changed to "conduct tending to incite a breach of the peace."

A conference was held between the police chief, the city attorney, and Al Frerichs, a volunteer attorney from Waterloo, Iowa, who had been assigned to the Ruleville area by the Lawyers Constitutional Defense Committee. Frerichs was advised by the mayor and city attorney that civil rights workers would not be permitted to remain in the town of Drew overnight, and if they tried, they would be seized and held in the city jail overnight in "protective custody." Frerichs' objections to this incredible procedure were of no avail. He was simply warned that if the workers tried to test the will of the city officials, those incarcerated might be released at four o'clock in the morning—an ominous threat to anyone familiar with the dangers that lurk in the Mississippi night for an individual identified with the civil rights movement. Drew's city jail is a one-room building, at one time used as a utility office. It is not even attended. The concept of "protective custody" under these conditions is particularly ludicrous, for it would simply assemble the civil rights workers in one accessible location where they would be at the mercy of any mob that might wish to do them harm.

In spite of these obvious dangers, the Ruleville workers would not be stayed. Three of them had made arrangements to go to Drew the next night, attend a civil rights meeting at one of the Negro churches and remain overnight at the home of a Negro family.

Meanwhile the mayor of Drew called a meeting of his board of aldermen and at three o'clock on August 14, issued the following proclamation:

PROCLAMATION

WHEREAS, the Board of Mayor and Aldermen find that it has been necessary to hire additional policemen to protect and insure the safety of the civil rights workers now in the City of Drew, and

WHEREAS, all civil rights workers have repeatedly proclaimed that they are constantly threatened, harassed and live in constant fear; and

WHEREAS, the Board of Aldermen of the City of Drew, at a special meeting duly called and held at 3:00 o'clock, P.M. on this the 14th day of August, A.D., 1964, directed that all civil rights workers be given special protection;

By virtue of the authority vested in me as Mayor of the City of Drew, Mississippi, I hereby proclaim;

That all civil rights workers in the City of Drew at the close of the normal working day of the day City Policemen be taken into protective custody and held in the City Jail until the beginning of the next normal working day of the police force, and that the night policemen attend to the needs of said persons while in protective custody.

This proclamation shall take effect and be in force from and after this date.

Given under my hand and official seal on this the 14th day of August, A.D., 1964.

W. O. WILLIFORD, MAYOR
City of Drew

In spite of this proclamation, the civil rights workers proceeded with their plans and went to Drew, and by 7:30 p.m. on August 14, had been seized by the police chief, placed in the city jail and held there until the following morning.

Frerichs had been acting as lawyer, counselor and emissary for the civil rights group in Ruleville. He had no office, no secretary, and no telephone. He was staying with a Ruleville minister and used the Freedom Center for an office. By now Frerichs was in touch with the L.C.D.C. office in Jackson, for it was obvious that if further injustices were to be prevented, he would need the resources of a law office, meager as the one in Jackson was. I arrived in Mississippi as the events just described were developing. While Frerichs prepared a petition removing Smith's case from the jurisdiction of Drew's police court to the Federal District Court, I took over the preparation of a lawsuit to enjoin the city officials of Drew from enforcing their proclamation and from interfering with the peaceful and lawful activities that the civil rights workers intended to undertake in Drew.

A lawsuit which seeks to prevent wrongs from being committed is often prepared hastily due to the urgencies of the situation calling for the suit. Under the most favorable circumstances, it takes a certain amount of co-ordination to get the affidavits signed, the suit filed, the parties served, and the judge available to hear motions for temporary restraining orders before damage is done.

In Mississippi all the problems were aggravated by the conditions under which the civil rights lawyers had to practice. Most of the lawyers were volunteers from other sections of the country and were not familiar with such vital details as the location of the courthouse, the names of the judges, or the whereabouts of a notary public. While most of these could be quickly learned, it still slowed down the preparation. The atmosphere of the Jackson law office was one of continued chaos, for all the lawyers were working on urgent matters, frequently affecting the freedom and immediate safety of their clients. Much of the secretarial help was done by volunteers, some of whom came to the L.C.D.C office after their regular jobs and worked late into the night on petitions, affidavits, complaints and the like.

Preparation of the Drew case required affidavits from all the parties who were incarcerated as well as certified copies of the proclamation and affidavits of other witnesses to the situation, such as Smith and Frerichs. Once these had been prepared, we had to meet at Greenville with all the parties and affiants, as there were no notaries whom we could expect to notarize the documents. Frerichs had found the clerk's office at the Federal courthouse in Greenville cooperative, so I brought the petitions and affidavits to Greenville from Jackson, and Frerichs brought the plantiffs and affiants to Greenville from Ruleville. The papers were then notarized by the deputy clerk at the courthouse and filed.

In addition to the complaint which sought a permanent injunction, we had asked the court for a temporary restraining order enjoining the Drew officials from enforcing the ordinance pending a hearing. Federal courts have the power, in their discretion, to issue temporary restraining orders without formal hearing so long as the order provides for a hearing at a later date.

Judge Clayton, Federal District Judge for the Northern District of Mississippi, resides in Tupelo, which is on the opposite side of the state from Greenville. The clerk in Greenville arranged an appointment for us at 3:00 p.m. that afternoon in the judge's office in the Federal Building in Tupelo. We could there present him our petition for a temporary restraining order and urge him to sign it, so long as we first served the city attorney of Drew.

Fortunately, Drew was on the route from Greenville to Tupelo, so we were able to serve the city attorney and even invite him to come to Tupelo and be heard by Judge Clayton that afternoon on our request for a temporary restraining order.

The city attorney declined our invitation, so we hurried on to Tupelo, but not before our driver was arrested by Drew's chief of police, who had been waiting as we left the attorney's office. In our haste to be on our way, our driver thoughtlessly made a U-turn in the middle of the empty street in front of the attorney's office. A siren sounded immediately and the driver was cited for reckless driving. Fortunately he was not immediately jailed, so our trip was not unduly delayed.

We drove north and east some 150 miles across the state to Tupelo, arriving at the Federal Building exactly at our appointed time of 3 p.m. Judge Clayton arrived shortly thereafter and ushered us into his chambers. He politely heard our argument urging him to issue a temporary restraining order pending a hearing on our petition. A judge's power in such a case is limited by procedural due process which entitles all persons to notice and hearing before a court will order them to do something. But when serious harm is threatened, a judge may temporarily restrain the harmful act pending notice and hearing. Generally speaking, there is a greater willingness to sign such an order if it will maintain the status quo. We argued that issuing the restraining order would only maintain the status quo as it existed before the issuance of the proclamation by the mayor. Putting the proclamation into effect was an unconstitutional deprivation of liberty without due process of law, as flagrant a flouting of basic rights by official act as one could expect to find. The court would be most justified in stopping the city officials from applying it.

Judge Clayton was reluctant, however, to interfere with the peacekeeping responsibilities of the Drew city officials without first having given them an opportunity to be heard. He told us that he had never granted an *ex parte* restraining order (an order granted without notice to the defendants) except on one occasion when a bankrupt was about to flee the jurisdiction of his court with all the assets of the bankrupt estate. He was willing, however, to sign an order which would require the defendants to appear in three days and show cause at that time why he should not restrain their enforcement of the proclamation.

By now it was after 4 p.m., and the order still had to be prepared for his signature and taken to his clerk's office in

Oxford, fifty miles away, for certification and service upon the defendants. We borrowed paper from the judge's secretary and a typewriter from the Internal Revenue Service office across the hall and quickly typed an order conforming with the judge's statement. He signed the order and called his clerk in Oxford asking her to hold the office open for us so that we could get it certified and ready for service on the Drew officials.

We were able to serve the city attorney for Drew the following morning and at the same time arrange for a reduction of our driver's charge from reckless driving to illegal turn, which called for a $15 fine instead of the possible $500 fine for the reckless charge.

At the time of the hearing Drew's attorney complained that many of his witnesses could not be present to testify, and the hearing was postponed. When it finally was heard, the city officials maintained that the drastic action taken by their proclamation was necessary to maintain law and order in their community. They claimed that it was the only way they could prevent dire harm to civil rights workers who might attempt to remain in their community overnight. Judge Clayton acknowledged that the officials of Drew had stepped outside the bounds of the Constitution in their peacekeeping efforts and persuaded them to withdraw the proclamation with the understanding that when they did so, he would dismiss the lawsuit.

The proclamation was withdrawn and the lawsuit dismissed early in September. By then the bulk of the civil rights volunteers were on their way back to their colleges and universities in the North.

That the Klan approved of the Drew officials' conduct was implicit in their cross-burning activities while the case was pending. The mayor of Ruleville was singled out for their expression of displeasure by the burning of a large cross on the front lawn of his home. The mayor had been known to the civil rights contingent as vehemently opposed to their activities, yet their success in establishing a center in his community was reason enough for the Klan to express its wrath. That, to date, the bloodshed in the civil rights movement has been limited to the acts of the oppressor is a credit to the leaders of the Mississippi revolution. That violence has been met with nonviolence gives strength to the cause of these revolutionaries. It also gives added importance to the role of the lawyer and the courts, for the unique factor in the Mississippi revolution is the presence of the Federal courts.

Because Mississippi is not a foreign republic, but one of the fifty United States, where the Constitution of the United States is the supreme law of the land, the revolution is properly channeled through the Federal courts. The chroniclers of this revolution in large part will be legal historians, and the historic battles will be the landmark civil rights cases such as the school desegration cases, the sit-in cases and now the voter registration cases.

The case against the city of Drew was a skirmish in the long war, and an indecisive one at that. But without the recourse to the Federal court and the protection of the Constitution, frustrations among the civil rights workers would have mounted. They would have tested the will of the city officials, been jailed, and the fuse of a powder keg would have been sparked. Fortunately, the Federal court spared us this explosion.

C L I F F O R D   J.   D U R R

Sociology and the Law:
A Field Trip to
Montgomery, Alabama

On the evening of March 30, 1960, ten students from
MacMurray College, led by Dr. Richard A. Nesmith, and
chaperoned by his wife, arrived in Montgomery, Alabama,
on the last leg of a sociological field trip through the Deep
South. The next day they found themselves involuntarily
involved as participants in the scene they had come merely
to observe. As a result, they had to forego a visit to a cattle
farm to study the sociological implications of the changeover from cotton growing to cattle raising and also an appointment with the mayor of Atlanta, Georgia, scheduled
for the next day. But the involuntary change in role from

Clifford J. Durr has recently retired from private practice in Montgomery, Alabama. He is a former Commissioner of the Federal Communications Commission and held numerous positions with the
Reconstruction Finance Corporation. A former Rhodes Scholar at
Oxford, he is the author of numerous articles.

observers to participants was not without educational value. As one of the students wryly put it, "I learned more sociology in my first thirty-six hours in Montgomery, Alabama, than I have learned at MacMurray in three years, and that is no reflection on MacMurray's sociology department."

MacMurray College is a co-educational liberal arts college of the Methodist Church, located at Jacksonville, Illinois. It is, and was at the time, racially integrated, but the students engaged in the southern trip were all white— six young women and four young men. Dr. Nesmith, an ordained Methodist minister, was Dean of Men and chairman of the sociology department. Field trips were a part of the curriculum for sociology majors, and previous trips had included a visit to several penal institutions, a study of race relations and cultural minorities in Chicago, and a trip to Arizona and New Mexico for study of some Indian tribes and their relations with the surrounding white communities.

While the study of racial and intergroup relations was a major purpose of the southern visit, the group's range of interests included the shift of population from rural to urban communities, the dislocations caused by the changeover in agriculture from cotton to cattle and timber, and the culture of the South generally.

In planning the southern trip, letters had been written to Methodist churches and chambers of commerce along the proposed route to arrange interviews with people representing a wide variety of points of view and interests. However, the interviews were not limited to persons with whom prior appointments had been made but were conducted with people, both white and Negro, encountered on the streets, at filling stations, in stores, and other like places. Before reaching Montgomery, the group had been, among other places, to Little Rock, Arkansas, Jackson and Vicksburg, Mississippi, and New Orleans, Louisiana.

A subject of particular interest in Montgomery was the use of nonviolence as a technique of social change, as illustrated by the Montgomery bus boycott that had taken place several years before. To this end an interview had been arranged with some Negro leaders who had been involved in the boycott. This interview was held as scheduled at the office of the Montgomery Improvement Association on the morning of March 31. But areas of interest soon opened up which had not been anticipated, so, to meet the requirements of a tight schedule, the interview was recessed to the private dining room of the Regal Café in order that it might be continued during the luncheon period. This café was Negro-owned and operated, and located in a predominantly Negro neighborhood. The interview in the café was conducted in a somewhat distracting atmosphere. Just as the luncheon was being served, a city policeman entered the room, asked if all present lived in Montgomery, and after receiving a negative answer, remained in the room for some eight minutes without other questions or remarks to anyone present. (The policeman had been sent to the café after the Police Department had received an anonymous tip that some young white girls had been seen going into the café with Negroes). Ten minutes after his departure another policeman entered the room, looked around for a few minutes, and left. Some fifteen minutes later, an investigator from the State Department of Public Safety entered the room, spent about a quarter of an hour taking pictures of the assembled group, and then left. He was followed by an investigator from the City Police Department who took more pictures and was, in turn, followed by a local TV news cameraman who took more pictures. Then came the Chief of Police with a retinue of four or five lesser officers, and then the City Police Commissioner. The Chief and his retinue remained in the room about forty-five minutes, at the end of which time he addressed the group with the laconic command, "Let's go," and, as he later recounted the event, "I pointed the people out . . . and they were put in the patrol wagon, the white men and Negro men and the white ladies and the Negro women were sent out to different cars and were sent to jail."

Just why the MacMurray group and their Negro friends were arrested remained a mystery, at least to them, for some time to come. They were certainly not trespassers in the café but invited guests. On their arrival they had been politely and even cordially welcomed by the manager. They had done nothing in the café except eat and talk, ask questions, and make note of answers. A policeman later testified on the witness stand, "There were some white females and colored people participating in the café." But in view of the fact that a former city ordinance requiring racial segregation in cafés and restaurants had already been repealed on the advice of the city attorney that it was unconstitutional, "participating"—at least in the mere form of eating and talking—was hardly a legal offense. At no time did the Chief of Police or any other police officer suggest to the group that they were violating any law or that their presence in the café might cause trouble, and that it would be advisable for them to leave. In fact, not a single remark was addressed to them by any police officer during the hour-and-three-quarter interval between the question as to whether or not all present were from Montgomery and the Chief's command, "Let's go." They could obtain no enlightenment as to the nature of their offense from any warrant served on them, for there were no warrants served.

Upon arrival at the city jail, Dr. Nesmith requested permission to make a telephone call to arrange for counsel and advise the college of what had happened in order that word might be passed on to the parents of students involved. But this request was refused. Instead, he and the group were photographed again, fingerprinted, and otherwise "processed" for about three hours, after which he was permitted to call the college. The "processing" was then resumed and continued for another hour and a half until the arrival of a local attorney, accompanied by a bondsman.

The bondsman, on learning of the nature of the "offense," refused to make bond. This left the Nesmiths faced with quite a difficult problem. They had brought with them on the trip their two-year-old daughter, who had never before been separated from them at night. At the time of their arrival at the jail, the little girl had been taken from them and turned over to an officer of the Juvenile Court. After considerable insistence on the part of the attorney, the bondsman reluctantly agreed to meet bond for the Nesmiths alone.

Upon their release from the city jail, the Nesmiths and their attorney rushed across town to the juvenile detention ward at the county jail where they had been assured that the child could be found. But upon arrival there, the matron in charge denied that she had custody of the child or knowledge of her present whereabouts. The child, she said, had been turned over to Mrs. Blank, of the County Welfare Department. A telephone call from the attorney to Mrs. Blank brought assurance that there was no cause for concern, because the child was in the competent hands of a licensed "foster mother" and would be delivered in good condition to the parents the next day. At the attorney's insistence that the parents wanted their child then and there, Mrs. Blank replied that no subordinate employee of the Welfare Department was available to make formal delivery of the child and that she herself was upset by a death in her family that had occurred a few weeks before; and she saw no reason why she should be expected to go dashing around at night to turn the child over to her parents when they could just as well wait until the next day. The attorney offered to spare her the inconvenience of venturing out into the night air if she would only provide the name and address of the "foster mother," but she responded that she did not feel at liberty to reveal confidential information of this nature.

A call from the attorney to the Juvenile Court Judge at his home brought the promise that he would immediately call Mrs. Blank and order her to deliver the child to the attorney, as an officer of the court, and also instruct her to call the attorney back promptly with advice as to where the child could be picked up. After waiting in vain for the call from Mrs. Blank, the attorney, accompanied by the Nesmiths, drove to Mrs. Blank's home. Their reception there was less than cordial. This time Mrs. Blank assigned a visit from her daughter as sufficient reason why she should not be expected to bother herself about immediate delivery of the child. She admitted that she had received a call from the judge but said he had only told her to turn the child over to the attorney and hadn't said in so many words that she should do this right away. Besides, she said, after putting the child to bed, the good "foster mother" had washed the child's clothes and they couldn't possibly dry before morning. She was assured that Mrs. Nesmith had an abundance of dry clothing for the child in the car and that if Mrs. Blank would only give the name and address of the "foster mother" they would be on their way to pick up the child. But still, for reasons never explained, the name and address of the "foster mother" remained a matter of unrevealable confidence.

Further phone calls to and between Mrs. Blank, the matron, and the Probation Office, in which suggestions of habeas corpuses and even kidnaping warrants were mixed with tearful pleading, resulted in the production of the child at the Sheriff's office at around 10:30 p.m.

The cases were set for trial before the City Recorder the next morning, April Fool's Day, at 8:30, on the basis of warrants and supporting affidavits executed a few minutes earlier. The affidavits threw only a dim light on the legal nature of the offenses. They charged as to each of the accused that he or she

> Did disturb the peace of others in violation of Ordinance 11-60 of the Montgomery City Code.

Prior to the opening of the court, the students were transported in "paddy wagons" from the jail to the city hall and confined in a small anteroom just off the courtroom pending the usual morning parade of drunks, vagrants, etc. The "evidence" presented by the prosecution consisted in great part of the introduction of photographs and a showing, over the objections of defendants' attorney, of the newsreel made by the TV cameraman. It was conceded by the prosecution that the segregation ordinance had been repealed the week before. The Chief of Police and the other officers called by the prosecution admitted on cross-examination that those present in the dining room were doing no more than eating and talking together. But, contended the Chief, a crowd was caused to gather and this might have created a dangerous situation. When asked why he did not arrest those present in the dining room immediately upon his arrival, he said it was because they were not violating the law at that time and so he waited until the crowd became large, at which time he decided that they should be arrested. The first and second policemen to arrive on the scene admitted that the number of people on the street was normal at the time of their arrival. It further developed upon cross-examination that during the course of the luncheon a total of some twenty police or police officials, state and city, had appeared on the scene and, in addition, at least one and possibly two Fire Chiefs' cars. The Chief, as an expert in such matters, also conceded that the presence of a police car was quite likely to attract people, the presence of two police cars was likely to attract even more people, and the presence of seven or eight police cars and some twenty police officials, including such dignitaries as the City Police Commissioner, the Chief of Police, the Director and the Deputy Director of the State Department of Public Safety, and a couple of Fire Chiefs in their red cars, might attract quite a large number of people.

The crowd, it was admitted, except for the police and a few newsmen, was made up entirely of Negroes. When asked if any threats or evidence of actual or potential violence or even boisterous behavior on the part of any member of the crowd was observed, the response was negative. When asked if the "crowd" was ordered to disperse, the Chief replied in the affirmative but admitted that the order to disperse was given only after the arrests had been made. When asked what the crowd did when ordered to disperse, the response was that it dispersed quietly. Two Negroes who lived in the neighborhood and had made up a part of the "crowd," when asked the reason for their presence, responded that they were attracted by so many police officers and cars and stopped out of curiosity as to what was going on.

At the conclusion of the testimony, which was around

noon, the judge announced that he was finding all of those present in the dining room, including some nine Negroes in addition to the MacMurray group, guilty of "disorderly conduct" but that he was recessing the court until three in the afternoon, at which time he would pronounce sentence. In answer to the attorney's motion for a dismissal, made at the conclusion of the testimony and based on the ground that no legal offense had been shown by the evidence, he replied that his decision was based on the clear language of the City Code reading as follows:

It shall be unlawful to disturb the peace of others by violent, profane, indecent, offensive, or boisterous conduct or language, or by conduct calculated to provoke a breach of the peace.

It was true, he conceded, that the segregation ordinance had been repealed the week before. It was also true that the defendants themselves had been behaving in an orderly manner, and it was also true that there had been no violence on the part of any member of the crowd. But, he said, for whites to eat with Negroes was so offensive to southern customs that a breach of the peace might have been committed by whites if they had learned of this behavior, and that the defendants were therefore clearly guilty of "conduct calculated to provoke a breach of the peace." The court was thereupon adjourned to 3 p.m., and the students were again placed in "paddy wagons" and transported back to jail.

During the period of recess, the recorder devoted himself to the drafting of an "Opinion and Order." When the court was called to order, the "Opinion and Order" was solemnly read. It consisted of a solemn lecture to the Nesmiths and the students on the impropriety of their behavior. The recorder told them of the possible dangers to which they had subjected, not only themselves, but the entire city of Montgomery—a danger which, according to his view, was averted only by the prompt, wise, and firm behavior of the police.

However, in concentrating upon the solemnity of his words, the recorder overlooked a rather important detail. The students were still locked up in the anteroom and the lecture had been delivered to empty benches. Upon discovery of this omission, the bailiff was ordered to bring the students into the courtroom, whereupon the lecture was reread. The recorder announced that, in view of the fact that the defendants were from the North and perhaps did not fully understand the southern way of life, he would be lenient and impose only fines rather than sentences at hard labor. Dr. and Mrs. Nesmith were then fined $100 and the students $50 each.

The Nesmiths and the students were now faced with the decision of whether to pay the fines, return to college and charge the whole matter up to a mere unpleasant personal experience, or whether to appeal and request a new trial in the Circuit Court before a jury. The easy answer would have been to pay the fines. Trials are unpleasant, time-consuming and expensive. The mere cost of returning to Montgomery for a new trial, to say nothing of the loss of time from the classroom, would be greater than the amount of the fines themselves. But does not a citizen have some responsibilities in such a situation—responsibility for the law itself, responsibility to protest against the apparatus of the law becoming an instrument of illegality? In an atmosphere where free discussion is stifled, the courtroom can serve as an important public forum. Judges and juries faced flatly with the necessity of decision might be forced to think through the consequences of their behavior. In the arena of the courtroom, principles become tested against facts and the common-sense realities of human behavior. Moreover, the conflicts of the courtroom are "news." Here, perhaps, was an opportunity of taking away from the good responsible people of Montgomery the excuse of saying that they did not know what was happening in the Police Department, an opportunity to make the police themselves think about the responsibilities that accompany their power.

The decision was made in favor of an appeal. Cash bonds were raised and the group returned to MacMurray and their classrooms.

At the trial before the recorder, the Negro defendants and the MacMurray group had been represented by separate lawyers. The two attorneys had decided to keep the issue of academic freedom and freedom of inquiry separate from the race issue. On his appeals, the lawyer for the Negroes waived the right of trial by jury and asked that all the issues be decided by a judge alone. The MacMurray lawyer asked for a trial by jury.

Both sets of cases were set for trial *de novo* in separate courtrooms on the same day, May 9, 1960.

Following the call of the MacMurray case, the parties proceeded with the qualifying and selection of the jury. In response to the question put by the defendants' attorney as to whether or not any members of the jury panel were or had ever been members of White Citizens' Councils, five responded in the affirmative. The defendants' attorney then moved that these five be disqualified for cause, but the judge responded that the mere fact that they were members of an organization dedicated to the principles of maintaining racial segregation did not mean that they could not be fair and objective, and the motion was denied. The attorney then asked if any of the jurors were or had ever been members of the Ku Klux Klan. A gray-haired gentleman arose, walked up to the bench and said very quietly that he had been a member of the Klan in the early 1920's but had had no connection with it since that time.

The attorneys for the prosecution and defense, respectively, proceeded with the business of striking the jury. The five White Citizens' Council members were the first stricken by the defense. When the panel had been reduced to the twelve who were to try the case, the former "Kluxer" still remained on the list. The attorneys for the prosecution were gleeful. The attorney for the defendants had decided to take a gamble. Having lived through the period of the idiocy of the 1920's, when perhaps 75 per cent of the adult white Protestant males of the state had been members of the Klan, he knew that in retrospect many of them looked back on their association with this organization with a deep sense of shame.

Prior to the trial the prosecution had substituted for the

"affidavit" on which the trial had been conducted before the recorder, a "Complaint" in language a little more elaborate but hardly more specific. It alleged that the defendants:

> Did disturb the peace of others by violent, profane, indecent, offensive or boisterous conduct or language, or by conduct calculated to provoke breach of peace in violation of Chapter 20 Sec. 18, Code of the City of Montgomery, Alabama, 1952, as amended.

The attorney's motion that these complaints be stricken for vagueness and also as an infringement of freedom of speech and assembly guaranteed by both the state constitution and the First Amendment to the United States Constitution were overruled in short order, and the trial proceeded.

The evidence of the prosecution was substantially the same as that presented before the Recorder's Court. The prosecutor conceded that there had been no disorder either in the dining room of the café or on the part of any members of the "crowd" on the outside, and that the "crowd" had dispersed quite peaceably when ordered to do so.

At the conclusion of the testimony the attorney for the defendants asked for a directed verdict in favor of the defendants on the ground that the testimony had not established any violation of the law, but this motion was promptly overruled. The jury retired to come back some three and one-quarter hours later with the verdict of not guilty in favor of all the defendants except Dr. Nesmith, who was found guilty with the recommendation of a $100 fine. The "Kluxer" had been made foreman of the jury and had fought to the very last for an acquittal of all defendants. He had finally compromised on the verdict against Dr. Nesmith as the best he could do with the other eleven members of the jury, who were torn between their responsibilities as jurors and their fears of community pressure.

The Negro defendants, whose only crime had been to invite the Nesmiths to lunch or to be present when their group was eating, were tried at the same time before a judge without a jury. They were all found guilty of conduct calculated to provoke a breach of the peace, although there was absolutely no evidence of disorder during or after the luncheon.

Dr. Nesmith's attorney promptly announced his intention to appeal, advised that cash was on hand for any reasonable appeal bond, and asked the court to set the amount of this bond in order that the appeal might be taken immediately. In response to this, the judge replied that Dr. Nesmith's right to bail bond had expired with the jury's verdict of guilty, and the right to an appeal bond would not arise until he had entered a judgment of sentence, which he had no intention of entering until the next day. He ordered the sheriff to take Dr. Nesmith to the county jail and confine him until the call of the court the next morning.

The next morning the judgment was duly entered, bond made, and the conviction appealed to the Court of Appeals to the State of Alabama. Both Dr. Nesmith's conviction and the conviction of the Negro defendants were reversed on the same day nearly a year later, on the narrow technical grounds that the language of the "Complaints" was too vague and indefinite to put the defendants on reasonable notice of the nature and cause of the accusations against them.

Again the MacMurray group was faced with the question of their responsibilities as citizens, for furthering the ends of justice and making good law. They were all now free and the "taint" of their conviction was erased from the record. But others were being subjected to the ordeal of trial, and more would be subjected to similar ordeals on equally irrelevant grounds. What do legal and constitutional rights mean if they cannot be enjoyed short of a final judgment of an appellate court and, in some cases, perhaps the United States Supreme Court itself? The ordeal of trial is in itself punishment, and litigation can be costly. "Disorderly conduct" and like ordinances and statutes are a most effective substitute for the old segregation laws and ordinances that had been declared unconstitutional, and people of small means facing the ordeal and costs of arrest and trial would be reluctant to exercise the rights which the Supreme Court had declared were theirs. If the police themselves could be made personally accountable for their unlawful arrests, would not this have a useful effect on their actions in the future?

After considering the matter very carefully and discussing it with their attorney, Dr. and Mrs. Nesmith and two of the students filed suits for damages in the Federal court against the Police Commissioner, the Chief of Police, and several other police officers. They knew that as a practical matter there was little chance of any Alabama jury, even in the Federal court, bringing in a verdict for more than nominal damages. The complaints were based on three counts: false arrest, malicious prosecution, and a denial of civil rights.

Again, at the trial in the Federal court, the testimony was substantially the same as that presented in the other trials before the recorder and in the Montgomery County Circuit Court. At the conclusion of the testimony, the attorney asked the court for a jury charge that under an interpretation of the testimony most favorable to the defendants, no probable cause had been shown to justify the arrests, prosecutions, and imprisonments. This charge the court refused, and the jury, after short deliberation, brought in verdicts in favor of the defendants.

Once more there was a question of what to do. Even if attorneys offer their services free of charge, appeals are costly, for records have to be prepared and printed. College students and even college professors are generally rather limited participants in our "Affluent Society." In the interests of minimizing costs, it was decided that the two Nesmiths alone would appeal. An important principle of law was at stake, so the two filed their appeals to the United States Circuit Court of Appeals for the Fifth Circuit.

Finally the opinion of the Court of Appeals came down, reversing the court below and holding that under the undisputed facts the arrests were illegal as a matter of law.* Following the denial of *certiorari* by the United States Supreme Court, the cases were settled upon agreement that

---

* Nesmith v. Alford, 318 F. 2d 110 (5th cir. 1963), *cert. den.*, 375 U.S. 975 (1963).

the defendants would pay all court costs and the Nesmiths' out-of-pocket expenses.

The reward of the Nesmiths, the students, and the local Negroes for all their trouble may be summed up in one short paragraph in the majority opinion in the Court of Appeals:

> But liberty is at an end if a police officer may without warrant arrest, not the person threatening violence, but those who are its likely victims merely because the person arrested is engaging in conduct which, though peaceful and legally and constitutionally protected, is deemed offensive and provocative to settled social customs and practices. When that day comes, freedom of the press, freedom of assembly, freedom of speech, and freedom of religion will all be imperiled.

Because of the MacMurray College group, the rights of all citizens have become a little more secure. In Montgomery, Alabama, the police have become more careful in the exercise of their responsibilities. The fruits of victory were certainly worth the price the Nesmiths had paid.

PETER R. TEACHOUT

Louisiana Underlaw

Law in rural, Protestant northern Louisiana is different from law in the relatively cosmopolitan, Catholic southern half of the state. North of Baton Rouge, Louisiana is very much like Mississippi. The communities are small and depend on a small farm economy. Local sheriffs have traditionally enjoyed a great deal of local autonomy in enforcing the law, especially in racial matters; and most of them openly acknowledge their allegiance to the precepts of white supremacy. As a result, in the smaller communities of the north, "law and order" is nothing more than local white custom, i.e., the Southern Way of Life, "underlaw," translated quite casually into law by the local sheriff who has *carte blanche* in determining his enforcement pattern.

Peter R. Teachout of Montpelier, Vermont, is a third-year law student at Harvard. He spent the summer of 1964 in Louisiana under the auspices of the Law Students Civil Rights Research Council.

As in Mississippi, cross burnings and church burnings and beating of Negroes involved in civil rights activity are not uncommon. (A publication of the local Klan, entitled *The People's Voice,* begins: "In time of war, many who are innocent must suffer, as you and I have already suffered. If you don't think this is war, you are very wrong . . .") And there has been murder; a recent incident was reported in the December 18, 1964, issue of *The New York Times:*

F.B.I. STUDIES FIRE THAT KILLED NEGRO

Ferriday, La., Dec. 16 (AP)—The Federal Bureau of Investigation confirmed Wednesday that its agents were investigating a fire here in which a Negro man active in civil rights and religious work was burned fatally. . . . Frank Morris, 51 years old, died at a hospital here Monday night. . . . A source said that two men had walked into Mr. Morris's shop and spilled gasoline. . . . Moments later there was "a burst of flames and a big pop," the source said. Mr. Morris ran out of the flaming building with his clothing on fire. . . . Local authorities declined to discuss the case.

This kind of private violence is sanctioned and often encouraged by local law enforcement officials, who, of course, are not responsible to the Negro citizens at the polls. For although Negroes outnumber whites in several of the northern parishes, nowhere are they allowed effective participation in the elective or judicial processes at any level of government, local, state, or Federal.

In the southern part of the state there is New Orleans, and radiations of this city's international mixing-bowl heritage and urban atmosphere tend to soften in the south the kind of harsh and brittle white supremacy one finds in the north and in Mississippi. But even in the relatively enlightened centers of New Orleans and Baton Rouge, the Negro citizen has no law enforcement body to which he can safely and sensibly turn for full cooperation in enforcing his civil rights. As a result, most of the daily violations go unheard and uncorrected. Local officials provide, at best, only begrudging cooperation and are often openly antagonistic. FBI and Justice Department agents are seldom of help in the immediate situation—though they are willing to take complaints, they rarely report back what they have discovered and never divulge just what action they are planning to take. Indeed, they make a poor practical substitute for an actively cooperative local police force. Moreover, because of their necessarily clandestine method of operation, these Federal agents are often considered suspect by the local Negro population, especially by those elements who are most active in civil rights activity and who want and need immediate and open official cooperation. Unfortunately, the usual response of the injured Negro citizen, who realizes he has no official body to which to turn for assistance, is to feel he has no alternative but to shrug off the whole unpleasant matter.

In spite of the differences between north and south, Louisiana, on the whole, enjoys a less extreme white supremacy than that found in Mississippi. In part this is due to the influence of New Orleans, and in part to the fact that there is a traditional sense of state law in Louisiana—much more so than in Mississippi, where militant local autonomy has been the order of the day throughout the state. The difference is one of degree; but, basically, the pull of a transcending allegiance to state authority in Louisiana (although it varies from parish to parish) tends to function as a breakwater against the kind of violent adherence to local autonomy, local custom and usage, one finds in Mississippi.

Yet for the most part, the relevant coordinates are not geographical. The southern white supremacy world pervades and permeates the forces which shape Louisiana's sense of justice.

What kind of law actually determines the daily existence of the southern Negro? Clearly it is not constitutional law, nor is it articulated state legislation. To the complex of immediate effective sanctions which actually determine the Negro's existence, we give the name "underlaw."

Basically underlaw is local white custom translated into effective law, usually without the help of articulated state legislation. Statute books are for the most part irrelevant to understanding, or enforcing, underlaw. Take for example the small yellow pamphlet containing the Louisiana Criminal Code. There is little in any of the provisions to suggest that Louisiana law enforcement is any different from that in Oregon or Vermont. The only clue is a slight tendency to "open up" legislation directed toward offenses such as breach of peace, vagrancy, or contributing to the delinquency of a minor. "Opened up" legislation is legislation which gives full play to enforcement discretion. Given certain broad legislative limits, how do officials behave? What determines the exercise of their legislatively granted discretion? What are the definable consistencies?

Seen in this light, underlaw can be defined as the systematic exploitation of areas of discretion in the legal process in order to perpetuate a system of white supremacy. The short but active history of the Louisiana breach of peace statute—a favorite of the small-town sheriff—should suffice to illustrate:

> Disturbing the peace is the doing of any of the following in such a manner as would foreseeably disturb or alarm the public:
> (1) . . . .
>
> (7) Commission of any other act in such a manner as to unreasonably disturb or alarm the public.
>
> LOUISIANA CRIMINAL CODE, Title 14,
Article 103 (7).

In March, 1960, Negro college students were arrested for peacefully "sitting in" at several restaurants in Baton Rouge. Title 14, Article 103(7) was invoked to secure convictions on the theory that the white community had been "alarmed" by this activity. A year-and-a-half later, in the case of *Garner v. Louisiana,* the Supreme Court of the United States reversed the convictions, saying that the peaceful activity of the Negro students didn't warrant application of the broad language of the statute.

Under the same statute, in the summer of 1964, Police Chief Mitchell of West Monroe arrested two white voter registration workers. This time the activity that caused "alarm" was voter registration of local Negroes (and using integrated voter registration teams). Using this statute as a potential hammer, Chief Mitchell effectively inhibited CORE's voter registration activity in West Monroe during the three days the books were open. For a period of five days it was against the law to walk down the sidewalk of that town with a person of another race. "If you go in there with integrated teams," said Chief Mitchell, "you are going to be arrested." A city attorney expressed his views of the Supreme Court disposition of Article 103(7) in the *Garner* case: "They haven't declared it unconstitutional up here yet. . . ."

These are just two of many similar applications of the statute. (The West Monroe incident will be examined in greater detail below.) Though the language of Article 103(7) is racially neutral, the application of the statute has not been. Enforcement, not legislation, has been the significant variable. It is this distance between the articulated legislative mandate and the consistent enforcement pattern, in kind and degree, that has proved one of the most significant manifestations of underlaw.

The enforcement impulse comes not from the legislation but from outside, from the southern white social and political norms. The machinery for translating these norms into law without the help of legislation has been historically established.

From the time Louisiana became a state in 1812 until the end of the Civil War in 1864, only free white males could vote or hold office. Color, and not slavery or education or poverty, was determinative: For example, in 1803, one-ninth of the population of New Orleans was free Negro; by 1830, there were 17,000 free persons of color in Louisiana; by 1860, free Negroes owned property and slaves valued at $50,000,000.[1]

Shortly after the Civil War, Confederate veterans were disenfranchised and Negroes were enfranchised. In 1867, 84,527 Negroes were registered to vote in Louisiana as compared with only 45,189 whites. A number of Negroes held high office in both state and Federal government. Someone complained: "We are completely under the rule of ignorant and filthy negroes scarcely superior to the orang outang. . . ."

Confederate veterans were not happy with "illiterate Negro" officials, and the first citizens' groups were formed "to suppress crime, to compel the authorities to perform their duties, to watch the city government." At this moment in time, the efficient officialdom of the community shifted out of the hands of the elected authorities into the hands of makeshift supervisors appointed *ad hoc* by the white community. "Law and order" began to flow from this extrademocratic authority, especially in the smaller rural communities.

After the Federal troops were pulled out of Louisiana in 1877, a radical group of whites, who pressed for total Negro disenfranchisement, gradually took over. The climax came in the Constitutional Convention which convened in New Orleans on February 8, 1898. Judge Thomas J. Semmes, a former president of the American Bar Association, set the theme:

> We [meet] here to establish the supremacy of the white race, and the white race constitutes the Democratic party of this state. . . .

The Grandfather Clause device (which required that an applicant or his ancestors had to have voted *before* the Civil War) was eventually adopted. The device was effective: 130,334 Negro voters were registered in Louisiana in 1896; eight years later, there were 1,342 (who qualified under other sections of the bill, by passing literacy and property tests not required of whites). Ninety-nine per cent of the Negro voters had been disenfranchised.

The Constitutional Convention of 1898 met for one purpose: to disenfranchise the Negro. It did not pretend to be establishing an honest or intelligent or openly realistic law. Its one transcending allegiance was to white supremacy and its one purpose was to avoid the prohibitions of the Fifteenth

Amendment. Indicative of the spirit of the convention is this statement of its president, a Mr. Kruttschnitt:

> WHAT CARE I whether the test we have put be a new one or an old one? What care I whether it be more or less ridiculous or not? Doesn't it meet the case? Doesn't it let the white man vote, doesn't it stop the Negro from voting, and isn't that what we came here for? (*Applause*)

Even more curious is that convention's *rejection* of the Interpretation Test device (which requires a Negro applicant to satisfy a white registrar with a "reasonable" interpretation of any selected clause of either the state or Federal constitution). It was rejected partly because there was a genuine feeling that it was based on fraud, but partly because it also "would place enormous power in the hands of the registrars, officers not of high rank nor probably of intellect."[2] This reluctance to leave registration totally in the hands of the local registrar has institutional significance. At this point in time, legislation was still the supreme directive as far as enforcement pattern was concerned. And while the Grandfather Clause contained its own *explicit* enforcement directive, the Interpretation Test left registration up to the discretion of the local registrar and required an *implicit* understanding of local white custom—i.e., that Negroes be disenfranchised—for effective enforcement. At this point in time, Louisiana lawmakers were not willing to go this "implicit understanding" route.

However, in 1915, the Supreme Court declared the Grandfather Clause device unconstitutional, and in 1921 another Louisiana Constitutional Convention convened to find a substitute. The Interpretation Test was adopted without hesitation. This meant depending on local registrars to disenfranchise Negro applicants, which meant, in turn, that the enforcement directive had to come from the outside. The "outside" however was *not* just the whim of the local official, nor was it disembodied "custom and usage." At this juncture in history, the "outside" was a mobilized and already efficient shadow officialdom (citizens' councils, citizens' groups, parish bosses) enforcing an already solidly established routine.

After the Supreme Court's school desegregation decision in 1954, the worried forces of white supremacy gathered in Huey Long's state house in Baton Rouge. A joint legislative committee was created to "provide ways and means whereby our existing social order shall be preserved and our institutions and ways of life maintained." Willy Rainach ("a young man with slick black hair and a long upper lip who was wearing a broad necktie emblazoned with a Confederate flag and who addressed a microphone with gestures appropriate to mass meetings"[3]) was mobilized. He became chairman of the new Segregation Committee. A front "amature" organization was simultaneously created, the Association of Citizens' Councils of Louisiana, of which Rainach was also appointed chairman. This "unofficial" group was also determined to "protect and preserve by all legal means, our historical southern social institutions in all of their aspects."

In 1956, local citizens' councils conducted extensive voter registration purges throughout the state. Registrars, sheriffs, and other local officials were required to attend meetings held in every parish. They were given a pamphlet which begins:

> The Communists and the NAACP plan to register and vote every colored person of age in the South. . . .

Rainach told the registrars: "The fight for school integration in the South has shifted to a fight for the voters of the Negro masses." Mr. Shaw, a co-chairman of the citizens' councils, told them:

> Constitutional tests are a test of native intelligence and not "book learning." Experience teaches that most of our own white people have this native intelligence while most Negroes do not.[4]

In Ouachita Parish in northern Louisiana all but 595 of the 5,682 registered Negroes were stricken from the rolls. Whites conducting the purges corrected the errors they made on their own registration applications, while removing

Negroes for making similar mistakes. One ground for challenging Negroes was that they had not interpreted a constitutional section, "even though that test had not been administered at the time of the registrant's application."[5]

In order to reregister, both Negroes and whites were asked to satisfy a white registrar that they could give a reasonable interpretation of a constitutional passage. Theoretically, the test was applied equally across the board but:

> Registrars were easily satisfied with answers from white voters. In one instance "FRDUM FOOF SPETCH" was an acceptable response to the request to interpret Article 1 § 3 of the Louisiana Constitution. On the other hand, the record shows that Negroes . . . have been turned down although they had given a reasonable interpretation of fairly technical clauses of the constitution. . . .[6]

Moreover, if one thing is clear, literacy wasn't the requirement. In November, 1962, the state carried 37,365 illiterates on the registration rolls. One registrar flunked eight Negro school teachers while passing eight illiterate white persons.

One peculiarly telling statement of these times comes from a session of the Louisiana legislature in May, 1959:

> Now, this registration you're talking about. . . . That was put through in carpetbag days, when colored people and scalawags were running rampant in our country. You got to interpret the Constitution. There ain't any people looking at me, including myself, who, if properly approached or attacked, could qualify to vote. They say this is a nigger bill—ain't no such. . . .

And the voice on the podium went on:

> And when you do, you got to recognize that niggers is human beings! . . .
> There's no longer slavery! . . .
> To keep fine, honorable grayheaded men and women off the registration rolls, some of whom have been voting as much as sixty or sixty-five years—I plead with you in all candor. I'm a candidate for Governor. If it hurts me, it will just have to hurt. . . .[7]

They led Governor Earl Long, still rambling to himself, away from the podium, out of the hall, and shipped him to an institution for the insane in Texas.

The Interpretation Test wasn't the only barrier to voting; dozens of others had evolved. There was economic reprisal: In 1960, Mr. Joseph Atlas, fifty-six-year-old Negro farmer from East Carroll Parish, testified before the Civil Rights Commission that he wanted to vote. The day after he testified, he was told by the local sheriff that the cotton gins in East Carroll would no longer process his cotton. When he took his cotton to a gin eighteen miles away, the manager told him that the pressure in the community was too great. Atlas could buy neither seed nor equipment for his farm.[8]

Arrests, and threats of arrests, were a primary deterrent. For example, on August 10, 1963, the Reverend Joseph Carter attempted to register to vote in West Feliciana, a southeastern Louisiana parish with a 60 per cent Negro population. No Negro had registered since 1902. Reverend Carter was told that he would have to be identified by two registered voters. When Reverend Carter approached Registrar Fletcher Harvey to inquire about his qualification, he was arrested by Sheriff W. C. Percy for "disturbing the peace" and jailed overnight.

And there were numerous other devices:

> Negroes could not find the registrars, though white persons had no difficulty . . . registrars would reject applications because they said there were "mistakes" in them. In one case . . . the "mistake" was that the applicant had underlined the word "Mr." on the card instead of circling it. . . . Voters must give their exact age, and this is construed to mean that the age must be given in years, months and days. Consider your own age in years, months and days, and how easy it would be to make an error in that computation.[9]

It was against this gloss of history that Judge Wisdom of the Fifth Circuit Court of Appeals was able to find, in 1963, "massive evidence that the registrars discriminated against Negroes . . . as a matter of state policy in a pattern based on the *regular, consistent predictable unequal application* of the test . . ."[10] (Emphasis added). Unfortunately in that decision, *U.S. v. Louisiana,* only two of the many barriers to Negro voter registration were removed: the Interpretation Test and its multiple-choice equivalent, the Citizenship Test. That this was only a partial step might be seen by what happened in the voter registration drive in West Monroe in June, 1964.

On June 20, 1964, Louisiana CORE sent three voter registration teams into West Monroe. Between noon and 2:30 p.m., over a hundred potential registrants had volunteered to attempt to register at the city hall in Monroe the following Monday. At 2:30 p.m., two local Negro girls, CORE volunteers, and a white male CORE worker, Dave Kramer, were sitting on the porch of a Negro woman's house, instructing the woman and a friend in the use of the application form. A police car drove into the café lot next door. A few minutes later, two other police cars arrived. One policeman approached the porch and called Kramer down. Kramer was searched then, in front of the porch, and led away to one of the squad cars. The police asked the girls on the porch which one was "working with him." The girls answered together, "We're both working with CORE." Each girl (fourteen and fifteen years old) was carried off in a separate squad car.

Five minutes after the workers arrived at the station, the police brought in the women who were being instructed. The canvass lists, indicating which Negro families would be willing to attempt to register, were taken from the workers and photostated.

At about 3:15 p.m., another voter registration team (Bill Yates, white, and Ruth Wells, Negro) was picked up while walking from one area to another and also taken to the station.

I was in the third team. We had just stopped at a café when a Negro man came bursting through the door behind us shouting that the police were arresting everyone. Five minutes later, I was smuggled out of West Monroe on the floor of a car driven by the son of a local minister.

At the station, Kramer and Yates had been called forward and questioned. When Yates replied he was a teacher in Boston, the interrogator said, "All of you who come down here are college people" and booked the two on charges of vagrancy. (The charges changed during the next twenty-four hours from vagrancy to soliciting to breach of peace.) They were then led off to the bullpen on top of city hall, and introduced to the regular white prisoners as "nigger lovers."

Underlaw bullpen punishment is unique. Because most southern jails are segregated, it usually applies only to white civil rights workers in white bullpens. Imagine the bullpen in a southern jail. Inside, lounging around on the bunks are a dozen or more of the usual lean, sneering toughs. Imagine yourself standing in the doorway, wearing a CORE T-shirt and the police officer at your right elbow is introducing you as a "nigger lover" and civil rights worker. The cell door slams shut behind you and they begin to line up around a pack leader and move in: "You goin to get it, niggerlover. You goin to get it, boy. You goddam niggerlover. You goin to get your balls cut off." Bob Zellner of SNCC tells about these grim ministers of justice "sharpening up their spoons and razorblades" in the East Baton Rouge Parish jail. Perhaps hyperbole, perhaps not. But there are the threats of castration. What do you do? Zellner says you back into a corner and turn to stone and wait. Sometimes it's a bluff. Sometimes they beat you until you are unconscious. Nothing is said about this kind of punishment in the statute books.

The Negro girl workers had been released after interrogation and had walked to a Reverend Brown's home in West Monroe. They wanted a ride back into Monroe. A local Negro girl came along with me to show the way. At 4:15 p.m., I was stopped on the bridge between Monroe and West Monroe by a West Monroe squad car. Captain Ray Wyles, alongside, proceeded through the routine of checking license and registration. He asked me to get out of the car. Then we were standing between our rented Chevy and the squad car and he was asking the usual questions: my name, my address, my destination. I gave him the address, the street and number, where I was staying in Monroe. He recognized the part of town, "Is that a nigger?" I had been taking notes until then (the name on his badge, what he had been saying); but I stopped and looked up. "You want me to spell it for you?" he said. He had already begun, "N . . I . . G . . ," like a schoolboy, "G . . E . ." He was at least fifty. He told me that "we have a law against associating with them down here," and he pointed to the Negro girl in my car. It was, according to Captain Wyles, against a city ordinance. Then he asked me why I was taking notes. Evidence, I said. He said that it wasn't actually against the law to ride around with them, but. After a routine check, we were released.

On Sunday afternoon, June 21, 1964, Mike Lesser, CORE field coordinator, and I went to negotiate with Chief Johnny Mitchell about bail and possible release. For more than an hour we sat with the Chief and his two city attorneys, bargaining over just what was going to be the constitutional law of the land in West Monroe. The Chief seemed worried about "our" prisoners being beaten. At the same time, he was obviously afraid—the Klan is very strong in northern Louisiana—to give them any protection. He lowered the amount of bail to forty dollars each and told us he was "going to be out of town for the next three days"—the only three days the registration books were open that month. Then he wanted a cooling-off period of four or five days. He was pleading with us to stop operations in West Monroe for the next week or so. But in the end, he laid down the law, "When you go in there in a mixed group, you are going to be arrested." As an afterthought, he added, "If there is a complaint."

When we left the station we were followed by a 1964 maroon Ford. At first we thought the passengers were plainclothes police, but when a black 1964 Chevy fell in behind, we knew they were not. Both cars carried spring-loaded antennas. When we parked near the CORE office in Monroe, the Ford pulled up beside us. There were two men, and the swarthy one in the window said, "You Mike Lesser?" After a while Mike said, "No." There was a long silence, and the men said, "We just wanted to see who you were." The cars raced off up the road. There was no number plate on the first one. Oftentimes harassment of civil rights workers is more informal, and community teen-agers join in.

"15F892 White Chevy Impala." "4F125 blue   ?   ." Taking down the license numbers of cars that were harassing voter registration workers became habit, and my notes from those days are full of them. When one is traveling down a highway after dark in Louisiana, and a pair of headlights falls in behind, one can never tell whether it is just a local farmer returning from town, or teen-agers out for kicks, or perhaps the Klan out for "revenge."

Late that Sunday afternoon, Captain Wyles stopped twenty-year-old James Donahue, Negro, out by the edge of town and asked him, "What would you do if you saw northern white men going around with your [Negro] women?" James said nothing. Captain Wyles told him to call the station if he did.

With the threat of potential arrest hanging over our heads, and operating on only a bootstrap budget, we had to abandon plans of extensive door-to-door canvassing and concentrate instead on evening voter registration clinics. On Monday evening, June 22, Chief Mitchell and Chief Kelly, of the Monroe police, were sitting in a parked squad car in front of the voter registration clinic at Reverend Brown's church. Conspicuously attached to the left front window was a large receiving antenna pointing toward the church door. A large tape recorder was on the back seat. Chief Kelly told us, "We're just listening to the meeting. Just want to find out what's goin on." This kind of conspicuous surveillance frightened most of West Monroe's Negro citizens away from coming in the first place.

The following night the police car was parked out in front again, this time with four regular policemen in it. CORE worker Ruth Wells started walking down the road, pretending to be a local registrant. The squad car followed her, passing her twice, shining its searchlight in her face. "I don't like the idea of your shining that light straight in my eyes; it scared me," Ruth complained. Three policemen jumped out of the car. One threatened, "I'm a policeman. You're headed for trouble." An elderly Negro woman, who had walked to the clinic, was afraid to go outside.

On Friday, June 26, 1964, at the trial of Kramer and Yates, the West Monroe prosecuting attorney took the case under advisement. No further action has been taken.

Convictions are largely tangential considerations to local law enforcement officials. Their primary effort is to use arrest and threats of arrest, the bullpen and costly bail, to hamstring voter registration activity the few days a month the books are open. Arrests are often used as a show of arbitrary police power to suggest to the Negro community what might happen if it becomes too involved in civil rights activity. The mere possibility of arrest is enough to deter many Negro citizens who can't risk losing their jobs. The story of these few days in West Monroe is typical: On Saturday, June 20, before Chief Mitchell and his forces had moved in, over a hundred potential registrants had volunteered to attempt to register. When the books closed on Wednesday, less than twenty registrants had applied. Underlaw had effectively frightened or discouraged hundreds of others. Moreover, of those less-than-twenty who applied, registration devices, discriminatorily applied by the registrar, eliminated more than half. The votes of the half dozen or more who passed would make negligible difference in any of the local or state elections.

The machinery of underlaw is self-perpetuating. Basically, there are three steps: (1) by one means or another the Negro population is effectively disenfranchised; (2) the legislature enacts broad discretion-dispensing statutes in the areas of voter registration and administration of justice; (3) local officials, no longer responsible to the Negro community at the polls, exploit these areas of discretion in order to perpetuate the white supremacy system and to enforce the southern way of life.

If the new voting bill, proposed by President Johnson on March 15, 1965, is energetically enforced, we well might witness in the immediate future a drastic dissolution of underlaw. The bill, which would provide for Federal registrars in many of Louisiana's parishes, should certainly go a long way toward making local officials—not now responsible to the Negro population at the polls—administer a more impartial justice.

If the bill isn't energetically enforced, we can probably expect more of the same. Officials will continue systematically to abuse discretion to perpetuate white control in the community, and Negroes will continue to have no effective remedy either through the polls or through the judicial process (which is notoriously expensive and time-consuming; and official abuse of discretion, though cumulatively effective, is often impossible to prove). Either way, however, a return to the "old" southern way of life is now impossible. The Negro community has been deeply transformed by the "movement," and Negro citizens are determined to get some kind of democratic protection, even if they have to manufacture it themselves.

The situation in Jonesboro, Louisiana, is indicative. There Negro citizens have "organized themselves into a mutual protection association, employing guns and shortwave radios. . . . The organization, called the Deacons for Defense and Justice, was organized quietly last summer."[11] The Deacons have already made a difference in one or two tight situations in Jonesboro and will probably be established on a more permanent basis unless and until the Negro population can get effective representation at the polls.

Underlaw barriers to the elective process are only part of the story. Equally impassable barriers prevent the individual Negro from access to the judicial process.

On August 23, 1964, shortly after noon, Mr. Dosie Sandfie, middle-aged family man, average citizen, was beaten in broad daylight on the concrete floor of a service station by two white men, the owner and his attendant. Sandfie had taken his Sunday meal at the previously segregated Alamo Plaza next door.

Mr. Sandfie's one good suit was ripped and bloodied, his tires slit, his windshield spidered and splintered into his front seat. Not half-an-hour after finishing dessert, Mr.

Sandfie was carried off in an ambulance to the emergency room at the municipal hospital.

And on that August evening when Mr. Sandfie told me he was going to press charges against the two men who had beaten him, and beaten him in front of witnesses—when Mr. Dosie Sandfie told me he wanted to sue those men—I told him to go right ahead. I wished him luck. *Fiat justitia, ruat coelum,* I told him.

"What?" he asked.

"Let justice be done, though the heavens fall!" I said. "Do you have any money?"

Mr. Sandfie, who is a dark man and thin (he looks over fifty, although he is probably younger), was lying on a huge double-bed in the front room. He raised up on one elbow to greet me. Both his elbows were covered with white gauze. The left lens of his glasses was shattered and his eye on that side was swollen and puffed black. The white was blood-shot. Pictures of Jesus hung from two of the walls in the living room (one of them was the top of an oil company calendar), and a torn and blood-spattered suit jacket hung on the wall behind my head. I took his story down on the yellow notepad I held in my lap. A light was turned on to help me see.

Mr. Sandfie had read about the Civil Rights Act of 1964 in the paper and heard about it on television. He told his wife and friends that he was going to eat out at the Alamo Plaza. No one thought he was serious. The next Sunday after church, he drove there alone. Mr. Sandfie was graciously served. He left a generous tip. The cashier asked him to come back again.

While he had been eating, he had noticed an attendant from the service station next door moving around his car in the parking lot out front. But he hadn't thought anything of it until he came outside and saw the car's peculiar tilt. Both tires on the right side had been slit. The outdoor payphone midway between the restaurant and service station was out of order.

When Mr. Sandfie reached the service station, the owner, a huge white man, was standing in the office doorway. "I would like to use your payphone," Mr. Sandfie told him. The owner didn't move. "I'd like to report to the police that my tires have been slit."

The owner asked, "Do you know who did it?"

Mr. Sandfie answered quietly, "Yes, I think I do."

"No nigger's going to use my payphone to call the police."

And Mr. Sandfie replied, "If you don't want me to use the phone, you don't have to tell me that way. You could have said it politely."

That is when the owner said, "No nigger's going to tell me what to do," and swung. And when Mr. Sandfie reached up to protect himself, the station attendant jumped on him from behind.

Before he was carried off in the ambulance, Mr. Sandfie overheard the owner tell the investigating policeman, that he, Mr. Sandfie, nigger, had cursed in front of the owner's (or the attendant's—Mr. Sandfie didn't remember whose) sister-in-law. At any rate, according to the owner, a struggle had ensued.

When Mr. Sandfie was through with his story, he told me he wanted to sue. I took inventory of his surroundings. Mr. Sandfie could neither afford to sue, nor could he afford what this beating was going to cost him. He would probably be out of work for several days, and he well might lose his job if the reason for his absence got out. But he told me he wanted to sue and asked my advice.

In the first place, Mr. Sandfie is a Negro, a lone Negro, and he lives in the South. He wouldn't have a mote of a chance in a civil suit in a court of law against those two white men who beat him. He wouldn't see justice done. But, more importantly, Mr. Sandfie not only wouldn't see justice done in his particular case, but he wouldn't see justice done *as a matter of course*, as a matter of law and order.

The first precept of underlaw is to make the regular working of the judicial process unavailable to the Negro citizen. The Civil Rights Act of 1964 is irrelevant. The remedy, under that act, is limited to injunctive relief; money damages aren't allowed. And medical bills won't be paid by an injunction preventing those men from beating Mr. Sandfie "next time."

State law seems more helpful. Section 2315 of the Louisiana Civil Code provides, "Every act whatever of man that causes damage to another, obliges him by whose fault it happened to repair it. . . ." Read this provision together with the equal protection clause of the Fourteenth Amendment and *theoretically* Mr. Sandfie has a right to recover from the two white men who beat him. But, of course, between the theoretical right and the remedy there is a century of contrary evolution. The underlaw system depends on the obverse of the old legal adage, "Where there's a right, there's a remedy." The underlaw doctrine of "where there's no remedy, there's no right" is a vital part of the masquerade that the average Negro citizen in the South has effective legal recourse for his injuries.

The late Dorothy Thompson once said at the annual meeting of the American Bar Association, "It has taken centuries of evolution to take the conduct of justice out of the hands of the multitude . . . and to take it into the quiet chambers, surround it with rules and restrictions, conduct it with dignity and decorum. . . ."[12] Those who rest their faith on "quiet chambers," "rules and restrictions," and "dignity and decorum" would be disillusioned, could they witness the behavior of Louisiana courts and judges from the Negro citizen's point of view. For over a century the courtroom in Louisiana has provided a theater for invidious discrimination and subtle deprivation of Negro rights. The cast of characters who sit behind the bench in Louisiana is varied. Many probably try to do their duty. Many actively participate in keeping the Negro "in his place."

There is Dual Jefferson McDuffie, city councilman and mayor *pro tem* of Plaquemine, Louisiana. Last summer, McDuffie presided over the municipal court in Plaquemine. This is how he is described in the complaint in Civil Action No. 3026 in the Federal District Court for the Eastern District of Louisiana: "(8) Defendant at that time held in his hand an empty bottle from a beverage known as 'Dr. Pepper,' and said to plaintiffs, 'The first black son-of-a-bitch that steps in here I'll knock his brains out.'" At the time, defendant McDuffie was "defending" the previously segregated City Café.

The rear bumper on the General Motors car in District Judge Rarick's carport, in West Feliciana Parish, sports a big black sticker on which is written in bold white letters: "RESIST."

Ex-Louisiana District Judge Leander H. Perez, Sr.'s reaction to the 1964 Civil Rights Act has been described as follows in a complaint filed in the Federal District Court for Eastern Louisiana:

> On or about July 6, 1964, at about 12:30 p.m., the plaintiffs entered the cafeteria in the state capitol building. . . . At the moment plaintiffs sat down to enjoy their meals in a dining room full of customers, defendant Leander H. Perez, Sr., in a loud voice ordered all the white customers to leave the room where plaintiffs were eating . . . incited a large group of whites to gather outside the door . . . to commit breaches of the peace . . . to use loud, insulting and derogatory language . . . to threaten, intimidate and punish plaintiffs. Caused a young white man who chose to stay in the dining room . . . to be harassed and, when he came to leave to be assaulted. Used unnecessarily loud, offensive . . . language, "You damn Kennedy lovers. Who told you to come here? Did John Kennedy come back and tell you to come here? You goddam black ———'s. You damn nigger, I ought to throw you through that wall. . . . Where's the F.B.I.? Paging the F.B.I. Paging rat-faced Bobby Kennedy!"[13]

But the problem runs deeper than the judiciary. Had Mr. Sandfie the most impartial judge in the world, he would still have the problem of obtaining open and unbiased witness testimony. Indeed, in Sandfie's situation there were witnesses. White patrons from the restaurant next door saw what happened from a distance, and a Negro "boy" employed at the service station also witnessed the beating.

White witnesses are out of the question. Consciously or unconsciously, they would slant their testimony to accord with their deep-seated belief that Mr. Sandfie had been violating southern "natural law" and that, whatever happened, he "had it coming." Nor could the Negro "boy's" testimony be counted upon. The ways of economic revenge are well established in the South where the white community has traditionally held the purse strings. The "boy" would be fired and he probably couldn't afford to be. To cite one example: After the Civil Rights Act was passed, a Negro employee of the *Morning Advocate,* a Baton Rouge newspaper, went to eat in the office building's "white" cafeteria. Five days later, after fifteen years of service, he was fired for parking his car in the wrong lot.

There is also the problem of obtaining full cooperation of other local officials. What kind of passionately disinterested cooperation can Mr. Sandfie expect from the investigating policeman? On July 8, 1959, at about 2:00 p.m., Mrs. Ida Mae Righteous of Clinton, Louisiana, watched while her five-year-old daughter, Wilma Jean, was struck and critically injured by a speeding pickup truck driven by a Mr. Merritt, who was employed by the state highway department in Baton Rouge. When the state trooper arrived at the scene of the accident, he asked Merritt if he had insurance. Mr. Merritt said yes. He asked him whether he had seen the child dart out in front of the truck. Merritt said no. What had happened? Merritt had been speeding because he was late for work. He had lost control of his truck.

Later that afternoon the state trooper came to see Mrs. Righteous, who was at the bedside of her injured daughter in the Clinton Infirmary. He told her that he hoped the child wouldn't die, because if the child died he would have to take Merritt's license. He didn't want to do anything which would cause the state to fire that man. He asked Mrs. Righteous to say the child had run out in front of the truck. Denying that that had been the case, Mrs. Righteous refused to do so.

I had occasion to look up the trooper's accident report. At the bottom was the simple, otherwise unsubstantiated conclusion that the child had darted out in front of the truck and that it would have been impossible to swerve or stop. The "estimated speed of vehicle" was circled at 50.

This kind of official, unpretentious uncooperation is a common occurrence. This is not police atrocity; and yet, cumulatively, it is more effective. Unlike the "sit-in" arrests, this kind of violation of Negro rights is never locked into the judicial process. The potential Negro litigant, like Mrs. Righteous and Mr. Sandfie, is effectively discouraged from invoking the judicial process machinery at the outset. Thus this kind of violation can never reach a genuinely impartial tribunal such as the United States Supreme Court; and, hence, there is little or no pressure for correction.

Still another barrier to getting justice is the local white jury. Pollock and Maitland, in *History of English Law,* tell us that "the essence of the jury . . . seems to be this: a body of neighbors is summoned by some public officers to give upon oath a true answer to some question. What are the customs of your district? What rights has the king in your district?"[14] The problem in the South is that there are two communities and the question is, Whose neighbors? whose customs? In an underlaw system, the answer is neatly resolved: (1) restricted Negro suffrage, (2) the umbroken hierarchical webwork of white officials, (3) white jury commissioners, and sufficiently-white jury lists, (4) through the mouth of a sufficiently-white jury, local white custom—underlaw—becomes law.

On top of all this is the problem of financing litigation. An informal investment-risk system has grown up to provide for the relatively indigent litigant. If a lawyer feels a potential client has a likely case, he helps with the original financing. Having a likely case is the prerequisite, however; and in our case at least four factors would be relevant to evaluation: the availability of impartial courts, reliable witness testimony, cooperation of local officials, and an unbiased jury. Needless to say, Mr. Sandfie's case would be a poor bet for any lawyer.

Police atrocity is not the only measure of constitutional injustice in the South, and hardly the most accurate one. The toll taken by the complex of immediate, effective sanctions—day-to-day underlaw—is much more telling. If a right is something that one should be able to expect in the daily grist of existence, and not something for which one has to go chasing off to the United States Supreme

Court, then the fair statement of the situation in Louisiana is that there is a continuous and total violation of the constitutional rights of every Negro citizen in the state.

What we need in the South is intelligent revision of the legal process. For the large part, the law has responded inadequately to the problems of underlaw. It has relied on *stare decisis*, old and irrelevant precedent, hallowed but impractical consistencies, last year's problems, last year's solutions, last year's reasons, last year's remedies. What we need are courts (and a body of law) willing to face openly the problems of prejudice and white supremacy. What we need is inventive injunction, novel procedure, bold experimental remedies molded to the special problems of the South. Yet, except for a nook here and a cranny there, this kind of legal response is not likely. The development of the law has been notoriously sluggish. Typical of this is Dean Griswold's prophecy in *Law and Lawyers in the United States:*

> We had one Civil War over this general issue, and understandably do not want another. . . . *With slow changes in outlook and in political leadership,* particularly in the South, we can *eventually* make *some progress,* and I hope we will do so. But *it is going to be a long slow road.* . . . (Emphasis supplied)[15]

The "long slow road" approach is one response to the legal problems in the South. To Mr. Sandfie, and to thousands of citizens like him throughout the South, it is an exceedingly hollow and cruel one.

In January, 1965 I called Attorney Bell in Baton Rouge. Mr. Sandfie had been referred to a local civil rights organization in the hope that it might help him sponsor his litigation. From what I can gather, Mr. Sandfie is still waiting.

J E R E M I A H   S .   G U T M A N

Oktibbeha County,
Mississippi

My client was Charley Taylor, an eighteen-year-old Negro freedom worker who had been forced off the road by a pickup truck. The driver of the truck had then proceeded to find a highway patrolman, with whom he lodged a complaint of reckless driving against Taylor, who was promptly arrested. He was out on bail posted for him by COFO. The witnesses, local workers and an out-of-state summer volunteer, passengers in his car, substantiated Taylor's story and one of them even claimed to have recognized the pickup truck driver as a local red-neck who had harassed rights workers in the past. The fact that Taylor's car was integrated at the time and the incident occurred after the pickup truck had followed Taylor for some miles made it likely that it was not an accident. By

---

Jeremiah S. Gutman is an attorney in New York. He was graduated from the NYU School of Law in 1949, where he was Editor-in-Chief of the *Law Review*.

the time we arrived at court, the witnesses, including the defendant, had a pretty fair idea of what to expect and what would be expected of them.

Crimes in Mississippi are either felonies or misdemeanors, distinguished by the severity of potential sentence. Traffic offenses, from improper parking to reckless driving, are misdemeanors. One accused of a misdemeanor is first brought to trial in the local court presided over by a justice of the peace. These men are not legally required to meet any particular educational or other standards, and I know of not one who is a lawyer. Court is held wherever their business is located —in gasoline stations, grocery markets or any other kind of store. In the crossroad towns and villages which are legally cities in Mississippi, the mayors are automatically created justices by virtue of their offices.

Two minutes before 10:00 a.m. we pulled into the parking area of the gasoline station where court was to be held. A group of some eight or ten young white men plus a uniformed sheriff, a highway patrolman and a few others were hanging around the entrance to the office. Taylor and the others waited near the cars. I made my way through the people who blocked the entrance into the courtroom. They made it as uncomfortable as possible by refusing to move in the slightest degree to make way for me and by following my tortuous progress through their phalanx with cold, hostile eyes. Once inside, I found a group of five or six men and one woman, all of whom stared at me without uttering a word of greeting and with stonily angry faces filled with contempt and hatred. I announced to the assembly in general that I was an attorney who had come to defend Charley Taylor. One of the men identified himself as the prosecutor and asked that I wait until the judge was ready. The small room was littered with windshield cleaners, fan belts, fuel additives and, as is usual in Mississippi service stations, boxes of shotgun shells and other ammunition. There were greasy rags, used spare parts, dirty tools and a few bald tires. The only furniture was two small chairs at a table from which all but a few grimy bolts had been removed to make way for a tattered desk pad, a few papers with oily thumb prints and a tin strongbox. The two glass exterior walls looked out, through petroleum product ads taped to the panes, on the pumps in front and the parking lot to the side. Everyone but the woman remained standing silently while we watched a man outside finish a sale of gasoline and wipe the windshield. Calling, "Hurry back and see us, you hear?" and wiping his oily hands on his uniform, His Honor entered his courtroom.

"You the lawyer I spoke with yesterday on the phone? I'm glad to see you're white. I done called your boy's name at ten o'clock and he weren't here so we forfeited his bail, found him guilty, fined him $200 and we was just fixing to get out a warrant for him. Ain't that Charley out there?"

I still had not even said good morning to the judge. I ostentatiously pulled out my pocket watch at the end of a gold chain hanging from my New York vest and asked the lady seated at the desk to please make a record that it was 30 seconds past 10:00 and that I had been waiting several minutes already and that, therefore, any default had been premature. There was a babel of voices as to accuracy of timepieces. I managed to silence the folks by firmly intoning over it, "Unless this matter is reopened and my client afforded a fair trial, I shall be compelled to force this court to produce for the inspection of the Federal courts all its records of defaults taken since it was created to determine whether, even if the court's clock is correct and I was one minute late, similar actions have been taken with other defendants so that the degree of equal protection of the law provided by this court can be examined." The prosecutor thereupon allowed as how the judge had acted correctly and had no need to give ground, but they wanted to show that everyone was entitled to equal justice in their court, no matter whether he was white, black or green.

The judge sat down behind his cluttered desk on the vacant chair next to his wife. He announced that trial could proceed, and the prosecutor thereupon asked the sheriff to bring in "the boys." The boys turned out to be six of the young men who had been blocking the doorway. I asked who they were and was told that my client had demanded a jury at the time of his arrest and that these were the jurors. (The trial

before a justice of the peace is ordinarily without a jury unless the defendant demands one, as Taylor had done.) I
inquired as to how many served on a jury and was informed
by the prosecutor that all six would serve.

. I replied, "I respectfully urge upon this Court that I am
entitled to an opportunity to question the jurors as to their
ability to render an impartial verdict. If we are to have a trial
by jury, I demand a selection from a larger group properly
drawn from the entire community so that I may select, in
conjunction with the prosecutor, six who are qualified in
accordance with the laws of the State of Mississippi, the
United States of America and the Constitutions of both."

The judge said, "Now, don't you trouble yourself none
about that, son; we done already took care of it so you can
just get on with the trial." I refused to permit the prosecutor
to proceed and made some of the more obvious objections to
drumhead justice and kangaroo courts. Meanwhile, the defendant had been brought in by the highway patrolman who
had made the arrest, and by now the tiny room was jammed
by participants, jurors, defendant, complainant, sheriff, patrolman and unidentified people whom I did not know but
knew not to be on my side. All but the judge and his wife
stood crowded together. I finally succeeded in convincing the
judge.and prosecutor that the complainant, the state highway patrolman, the sheriff, the jurors and the miscellaneous
people be cleared from the room while the prosecutor, judge
and I discussed the problem. They all went except the sheriff
and the highway patrolman, who said they were officers of
the state and had a right to be there. The complainant then
came back and the judge deputized him as a clerk of the
court so that he could stay, too.

My objections to this procedure were overruled and we
got down to the next important business, which was my right
to practice in the court. The prosecutor advised me that I
could not practice unless I had with me two members of the
local bar who requested the court to permit me to practice.
This, of course, is a perverse reversal of the true situation,
which is that an out-of-state attorney may practice unless his
qualifications are challenged in a rather technical way by

two members of the local bar. I most respectfully disagreed with my learned colleague and pointed out that my understanding of the law was the reverse of his. He stated that he was merely testing to see if I knew the Mississippi law but that I certainly could not practice in that court except for the fact that he would ask His Honor to waive my disqualification and permit the trial to proceed.

Trial in a justice of the peace court is in many ways an unnecessary formality. If you are convicted in that court, you have the right to appeal to the county court. In this second court, the appeal is in reality a trial *de novo*, or from scratch, as though the first trial, of which no minutes are kept, had not occurred. A defendant in the justice court charged with an offense in connection with his civil rights activity (such as trespass or picketing) or accused of an unrelated offense (such as reckless driving) may plead not guilty. He is certain to be convicted. However, there is no legal distinction upon appeal between a plea of not guilty or a plea of *nolo contendere* (or "no contest"). One advantage of a *nolo* plea is that the proceeding is over quickly and the crowd (including jurors) which may have gathered for the spectacle of a trial may be left before it grows into a mob. The chief advantage of a plea of not guilty is that it forces the prosecutor to put on his witnesses and disclose his case without compelling the defendant to do anything but listen and perhaps learn something that may be useful at the second trial upon the appeal. Attempts to keep a record of what the prosecution witnesses say in the JP court (in order to be able to impeach their veracity if they are better "prepared" for the second trial) have backfired into charges of perjury against defense witnesses for allegedly lying about what they heard at the first trial. Effective, even devastating, cross-examination of prosecution witnesses on the first trial has not been known to result in acquittals but has certainly educated prosecutors as to what their witnesses had better say or avoid on the second trial. From the point of view of an attorney defending such a case, the ideal is a plea of not guilty, so that the prosecution witnesses go on and are heard, followed by permission to change the plea to *nolo contendere* so that the defense need not disclose what it may have up its sleeve or put on any witnesses who might be exposed to possible later perjury charges and extrajudicial pressures and harassment.

In the case of Charley Taylor, I was interested above all in speed. The sooner I got him and his friends, including me, out of that tense scene, the better I would like it. As I looked out at the glowering jurors staring through the glass walls of the courtroom at the discussion inside and looked beyond them at the pickup trucks parked at the side of the station with the rifles and shotguns in the rear window-racks, my decision to get this procedure over as fast as possible was reinforced.

Since the prosecutor had withdrawn his objection to my status as attorney for defendant and the room was relatively empty, I adopted a very frank manner with the judge. Of all those present, besides the accused and myself—the prosecutor, the judge, the judge's wife, the two police officers and the deputized complaining driver—only the prosecutor had any but the remotest idea of what I was saying and, as I went on, ostensibly talking to the judge, all of them looked with more and more concern to the prosecutor for a clue of how to react.

My goal was to be permitted to withdraw defendant's jury demand and not-guilty plea and to interpose a *nolo contendere* plea, if I could be sure Taylor would get a small fine and no jail sentence. My method was to exploit what I suspected to be the legal ignorance on the part of all concerned.

"Your Honor," I said, "if we are to proceed with this trial before you and this jury today, I shall, and do now, interpose objections to the legality of the procedures by which you and the prosecuting attorney were elected; the manner in which the jury panel and jurors were selected; the exclusion from this room of the friends of the defendant; the fact that you have addressed Mr. Taylor by his first name in an insulting manner; the prejudicial atmosphere created by your action prior to my arrival; the fact that you have effectively disqualified yourself by making the complaining witness your clerk; the fact that at least some of the jurors are armed; the fact. . . ."

At this point, the prosecutor, not the judge, interrupted me by, "Well, that's alright, Mr. Gutman, you can make all those objections, but we can go right ahead anyway."

"In addition, sir, I warn you right now, that I regard this entire procedure and all participating in it, from the moment the complainant ran defendant off the road, as part of a conspiracy to deprive defendant and all the passengers in his automobile of their Federal civil rights and I intend immediately upon leaving here today to commence an action for damages against each and every one of you in the Federal court and to file a criminal complaint with the FBI and Department of Justice Civil Rights Division."

"Now, there's no need to get so worked up over a little old driving ticket. Why, we wouldn't deprive Charley here of no rights except a few dollars fine for not driving too good and that hardly seems worth all the fuss you're talking about."

I immediately asked him how much of a fine he had in mind and, since it was within reason, I agreed to let Taylor plead *nolo* and end the case right there. Within the next few minutes the arithmetic was completed, bail had been refunded, the nominal fine had been paid, an appeal bond was posted, a receipt taken and the change pocketed by defendant to be forwarded to Jackson COFO.

The formalities over, Charley Taylor and I left the courtroom together. Side by side, we threaded through the jurors and their friends who were again massed in the doorway. At the far side of the service station parking lot, near the cars, were the integrated group who had come with us, awaiting the result. The judge plucked at my sleeve to stop me as I emerged from the group of immobile, glaring jurors. I told Taylor to keep walking to the cars while I stopped to see what His Honor wanted.

The judge said, "I see you brought some of your friends to see the show. I hope they ain't disappointed."

I assured the judge that no one was disappointed and that we only wished to be on our way so that we could get back to work. The judge said, "I sure hope that you ain't going to say we don't know how to entertain guests what come to see a show." He pointed toward a gully or cut through which railroad tracks passed, behind and about thirty feet below the level on which we were standing. He continued, "These boys here (indicating the jurors) are from our football team and they sure would admire to play a game with your boy. We call it Dropkick the Nigger."

There was much hilarious laughter as I resumed my walk to the automobiles and signaled everyone to get going. The first car had pulled out and the car in which I was riding next to the driver was just about to complete its U-turn out of the parking space when the judge walked up to the side on which I was seated. The highway patrolman and several of the jurors had come forward and were blocking our path of withdrawal when His Honor put his hands upon the side of the car, which had been forced to stop. He said, "That'll be two dollars for parkin', Mister." I said, "I'll pay it, but I promise you I will get it back with interest." He laughed along with all his buddies who stepped aside as he waved us out.

Sometimes in these brushes with Mississippi justice a lawyer gets the feeling that, just perhaps, he is making the local community think and reappraise their actions and attitudes. The positive results of this case include the fact that a young man who would probably have received a jail sentence managed to get off without one, but more important, he, his friends, his neighbors, and many who will hear the tale without ever meeting the people, will have learned that not every white man is an enemy, that the law can be their friend, that they are not alone, that, having been urged to undertake action sure to arouse retaliation, they are not abandoned to face Mr. Charley alone.

MARVIN BRAITERMAN

Harold and the
Highwaymen

The young man sitting opposite my desk—a college student about nineteen or twenty years old—shifted uneasily in his chair as he spoke and I wrote.

On July 11, 1964, I was driving a truck carrying books for the COFO library in Gluckstadt. At an intersection, I backed around to avoid making a U-turn. A car came to the intersection, which turned out to be driven by the wife of Deputy Sheriff _____, of Madison County. I turned my truck and got out of the way, and proceeded about two or three miles to the place where we were to unload the books. There were three passengers in the truck, two of whom were Negro and one of whom was white, besides

Marvin Braiterman is an attorney in Baltimore. He was graduated from the University of Maryland School of Law in 1949. His published writings include articles on religion in the public schools, and he has also written for *Midstream*.

myself. [The deputy sheriff] came up to me, told me to get into a highway patrol car which was occupied by a highway patrolman in which [the deputy sheriff] had driven. While in the car, a blue and white pickup truck also drove up, and another officer got out and milled around us while [the deputy sheriff] talked to me. They alternately swore at me, discussed race relations with me, told me to get out of Mississippi, threatened me, and tried to "reason" with me. Before they were finished, [the deputy sheriff] had called me a Communist. They took me to a judge's house—I think his name was Judge _____, and we had more conversation about civil rights. In all of this, I remained silent except in answer to direct questions asked by the judge. Before the judge, both [the deputy sheriff] and the highway patrolman accused me of trying to start a revolution and called me a Communist. In the car and before the judge, I could not tell for a long time what I was going to be charged with, in view of all the political talk in the car and before the judge. Finally, they charged me with blocking traffic and being in Mississippi for more than thirty days with an out-of-state driving license. . . . I was held in Two Hundred Dollars bail and put in jail overnight in Canton. In the course of being transported to jail, I was required to listen to more talk from [the Deputy Sheriff] and the highway patrolman about race relations, politics, communism and revolutions. I tried to stay in the Negro section of the jail, but they made me stay in the white section. However, I was not mistreated in jail, and a lawyer called the judge, had my bail reduced to Fifty Dollars, and I was released in the morning.

Harold was giving this statement to me on a hot Sunday afternoon in the Jackson, Mississippi, office of the Lawyers Constitutional Defense Committee. He had just been released from jail, and I still remember how he looked. He wore a crew cut, had arms like a couple of toothpicks, and he probably weighed about 120 pounds soaking wet. He was very nervous, and so soft-spoken that I had difficulty hearing him. Hardly someone to strike terror in the heart of a tough Mississippi policeman.

Harold, a New Yorker, and a sophomore at Iowa State University, had come to Mississippi during his summer vacation as a volunteer in the Summer Project. His mission at that time was to transport books from Jackson to some of the outlying Freedom Schools. That is the real crime for which Harold and the Mississippi Summer Project should stand indicted—assault with a dangerous and deadly weapon; to wit, library books.

Early next morning I appeared before the justice of the peace who would try the case, a prosperous Madison County farmer who held court in a spacious garage alongside an old but neat and picturesque clapboard house. The place commanded an idyllic view of a lush, rural countryside, a peaceful place that appeared to be as unrelated to Mississippi violence as Harold was. We shared the courtroom with the judge's big Cadillac automobile, which seemed to be a bailiff of the court, standing in its brooding bulk as a silent witness to the proceedings in this peculiar judicial forum.

I spent a half hour or so chatting with the judge. I met his wife, and the three of us explained ourselves to each other pleasantly and civilly. I told the judge that I wanted to represent Harold, and would appreciate if he would extend me the courtesy of allowing this, in spite of the fact that I was not a member of the Mississippi Bar. I reviewed and explained my foreign credentials to him, and showed him certificates of admission to practice in the state and Federal courts in Maryland and in the United States Supreme Court. He was quite satisfied, assured me that he was a moderate and broadminded man—he had been around, his wife had close friends and relatives in New York—and he would certainly be capable of giving my young client a fair trial. Of course, he had to tell me that he hated what these outside agitators were doing in Mississippi that summer, but he understood that they had their rights and reasons. He saw the case as an opportunity to demonstrate to me that the stories I had heard about injustice in the Mississippi courts were not true.

We did not try the case that morning. I had asked for a postponement, explaining that I needed time to prepare a defense. The judge postponed the case until Wednesday,

July 15, and we both must have impressed each other as nice, decent people. We had been anxious to please each other, and we did.

Before leaving the judge, I reviewed the paper setting forth the charges, and Harold was substantially correct. He was charged with obstructing traffic (a sort of parking violation somewhat akin in this case to double parking), and with driving a motor vehicle after being in the state for more than thirty days without getting a Mississippi driving license, pursuant to the provisions of Section 8092 of the Mississippi statutes.

Thirty days seemed too short a period for this provision. Something appeared to be wrong with this case; and after leaving the judge to his fields and manse, I returned to the office in Jackson and checked the Mississippi statutes. I found that the provision requiring an out-of-state driver to obtain a Mississippi driving license takes effect after *sixty days* of Mississippi residence, not after thirty days. There is another provision requiring Mississippi registration of an out-of-state motor vehicle after thirty days (Section 9352 (20)), and the deputy sheriff must have confused the time provisions in the two sections. At my conference that morning with the judge, the deputy sheriff, who joined us briefly, had told me that Harold had "admitted" arriving in Mississippi "around June 7," which would be more than thirty days before the date of the offense on July 11 but less than sixty days.

Here, then, was clearly a case that had to result in an acquittal—if only we could obtain anything even remotely resembling a fair trial. Of course, my experience and the experience of all my colleagues before and after me was that acquittals of civil rights workers seldom happen in Mississippi, regardless of the facts or the law.

By this time, COFO's lawyers had adopted an unofficial policy of filing petitions for removal of nearly all criminal cases from state courts to Federal courts. We were doing this pretty much as a matter of routine in nearly every case—serious or petty—on the theory that any charge against a civil rights worker in a state court would either have been motivated initially by a policy of harassment of civil rights activity, or would result in a biased conviction because of prejudice against civil rights activity. As a practical matter, these removal petitions acted as an injunction against state prosecution of civil rights workers, and kept the movement operative in spite of repeated threats by official Mississippi that it would destroy the Summer Project by massive jail sentences and heavy fines imposed upon its workers. Admittedly, these removal petitions represented a broad and indiscriminate interpretation of the removal provisions of Federal law and amounted to a measure of counter-harassment of state officials by civil rights workers. But this was the only line of stop-gap defense against the wholesale removal of the entire civil rights movement to Mississippi jails.

There have been protest movements in history whose calculated objective was to fill the taskmasters' jails, but this was not the case in Mississippi. The state talked of filling the jails; the "agitators" talked of building—not jails, but voter projects and Freedom Schools and libraries. Harold was a library builder par excellence; he just wasn't a Bastille type fellow.

Nevertheless, we told ourselves that somewhere this summer we would find the right case and the right judge, so that we could actually go ahead and allow a trial to be held in a state court. We looked forward hopefully to finding that precious nugget—an acquittal that would prove that Mississippi justice was not quite as universally bad as we had been told. In a way, we wanted to prove this to white Mississippi as well—as a kind of first step to attaining juridical self-respect. Here, it seemed, might be the right case. I decided not to file the usual removal petition.

On the morning of the trial, I met Harold at the judge's farm. He appeared in the perfect habit, attitude, and demeanor for his great day as an about-to-be-acquitted civil rights worker. He was clean-shaven, his crew cut was neat and in order, his clothes were plain but clean and pressed, and when he spoke at all he was gentle of voice.

I was accompanied that morning by George Constantikes, a lawyer from Westport, Connecticut, who had arrived in Mississippi the day before Harold's trial to begin a two-week period of service for the Lawyers Constitutional Defense Committee. He and another group were arriving to replace five of us whose fortnight of volunteer law practice in Mississippi was about to end in a few days. Before he went into private practice, George had been a prosecutor, and he was to be at my right hand during the entire incredible proceeding. There was such an array of legal talent on a petty traffic case that, if a civil rights worker had not been involved, the case would have resembled shooting at a mouse with a cannon.

The other participants in the case gradually collected, and for a while we just exchanged banal pleasantries with the judge, the deputy sheriff, the two highway patrolmen, and the prosecutor—who, I was informed, was a former mayor of Canton, the county seat of Madison County. Everybody was out to prove to everybody else what a "nice fellow" he was—everybody, that is, except Harold. He stood outside during the preliminary chit-chat, looking wide-eyed and ingenuous. I felt a little embarrassed about that, and made a mental note that I would have to explain to Harold that it was necessary for lawyers to "fraternize" with the opposition in order to do their job effectively. Even though Harold and I are both white, it seemed he felt that I was being an "Uncle Tom." I could not help but notice that Harold was beginning to have that look on his face that expresses the dismay of one who fears his lawyer is "selling him down (or up) the river."

Harold had put into my hand some documentary evidence to prove that he had been at Iowa State University at least through June 4. The proof consisted of a wallet-sized card from Iowa State showing that Harold's term examinations were taking place on campus until that date. Lawyers love documentary evidence. It proves what otherwise may be disbelieved if it is presented as oral testimony. I fingered that card lovingly, the way a prosecutor might fondle the signed confession of a vicious criminal.

Finally, we got to the business at hand. At first, this consisted of a series of conferences among the various parties to the litigation. The prosecutor conferred with the deputy sheriff and highway patrolmen. Meanwhile, George and I spoke with the judge, who informed us that the prosecutor wanted to make a slight change in the charge, amending it to read "sixty days" instead of "thirty days." So, the state was curing the legal defect in the indictment, since it must charge facts which amount to a crime. And driving an automobile after thirty days in Mississippi without a local license is no crime.

Nevertheless, there still remained the matter of proof. There was no doubt that the deputy sheriff had been prepared to testify that Harold had admitted to being in Mississippi more than thirty days but less than sixty days. If the deputy sheriff stayed with that testimony, changing the charge would make no difference, since Harold would not be guilty, anyway. George and I went into conference with the prosecutor. He told us that his witnesses, the deputy sheriff and the highway patrolmen, were now prepared to testify that Harold had admitted to them that he arrived in Mississippi, not in the middle of June, but in the middle of *May*. Generally, this would be improbable, because the Mississippi Summer Project, which was the reason Harold came to the state in the first place, did not begin until the middle of June. However, in Harold's case, it was impossible, and I had proof that it was impossible. There was that card from Iowa State.

I told the prosecutor about the card. I guess lawyers sometimes have a sense of protective loyalty toward each other. I did not want the prosecutor to be embarrassed, and we were voluntarily exchanging information with each other in an effort to arrive at a "settlement." The prosecutor seemed like a fair-minded man, who did not like this case much. After I told him about Harold's examination card, he mused and rubbed his chin, and said he would have to take this up with his witnesses and see how they felt about it. He held another conference with them under a tall, stately tree outside the garage and returned with some novel legal theories.

"Does Harold have a copy of the grades on his examinations?"

"No, he is not carrying them around Mississippi with him."

"Well, then," said the prosecutor, "the card is *hearsay* evidence and does not prove that Harold *was* in Iowa taking his examinations, but only that he was *supposed* to be in Iowa taking his examinations."

We disagred with his view of the card as "hearsay." We told him that it may not be the only evidence, or the best evidence, but it is admissible, and it can be followed up in a new trial on appeal with further evidence that could make everybody responsible for Harold's conviction, including the justice of the peace and the prosecutor, look ridiculous. The prosecutor looked as if he had had his fill of incidents involving local law enforcement that made Mississippi look ridiculous. We also reminded him that, at least in theory, we did not have to prove when Harold came to Mississippi; he did.

In any place but Mississippi, I would end the talk then and there, begin the trial, and depend on the judge to acquit my client. But if this case finally came down to Harold's word plus the card against the word of the highway patrolmen, the judge would be left with some "discretion" as to whom he would believe. This would never do. For the judge to find Harold not guilty under those circumstances would be to make a mild declaration of war against those policemen, and that was asking for too big a donation of fairness and good will from a local justice of the peace who expected to continue living in Mississippi and holding political office.

The judge had assured us that anything I worked out with the prosecutor and deputy sheriff as to the disposition of this license charge—a stuffy paraphrase for "any deal you can make"—would be all right with him. But a tacit condition of this largess was that he not become involved in any controversy with those policemen.

George and I resumed our private discussion with the prosecutor. He had begun to be visibly upset by all this, and I told him, evenly and not threateningly, that I was prepared to holler all the way "from here to New York," if Harold was convicted of being an unlicensed driver in this case.

Idly, I began to think of this thing not only in terms of civil rights but in terms of comity among our sovereign states. After all, Harold had a New York driving license, and in my fantasy, I began to consider contacting Governor Rockefeller, asking him to retaliate against any Mississippi drivers found in the State of New York (for example, at the World's Fair) and jail them for using a New York highway without first obtaining a New York driving license. In spite of the deluge of New York civil rights workers in Mississippi, there was still more tourism from Mississippi to New York than vice versa.

(In the mind of many white Mississippians, such an idle speculation would have the ring of truth. Several of them had expressed to me their fear of driving around in the North, in places like New York, because they might be arrested by a Negro policeman and become the victims of "policy brutality." They told me about an arrangement that can be made for a white Mississippian to "borrow" out-of-state license plates at the Mississippi Department of Motor Vehicles for the very purpose of disguising themselves while they are driving in the North—a fantastic arrangement, if true.)

The prosecutor was becoming paler by the minute. He had the same sick look lawyers everywhere have when they feel trapped into putting on testimony that they patently disbelieve. He continued to confer with the patrolmen, attempting to console and conciliate them while explaining that he wanted to drop the case on the driving license. I could tell from bits of their conversation overheard when their voices rose that the patrolmen were furious with him and were telling him so in no uncertain terms. I had the distinct impression that these policemen were prepared to say anything to bring Harold within the statute requiring a Mississippi driving license; that if Mississippi law had not required a local driving license until six months of residence instead of sixty days, they were prepared to testify that Harold came to Mississippi for a New Year's Eve party and never left—"card or no card, and to hell with the burden of proof and Iowa State, whatever or wherever that is."

As they went on, it became clear that it was not the charge that they were so keen about, but the "principle" of the thing. What was the principle? The deputy sheriff's wife, whom I have never met but who I am sure is a flower of southern womanhood, had undergone "the sight of two niggers and two whites riding in a car together, and she damn near lost her lunch. We are men of the world and are used to seeing dirty things, but that is a terrible shock for a *woman* to see."

The issue was vital to Harold, because if the charge of driving without a Mississippi license could be made to stick, he could—and probably would—be sent to jail. Section 8117 of the statutes allowed the judge wide latitude as to the sentence: a fine of $5 to $250, or imprisonment from one to six months, or both. Even in Mississippi, however, the second charge against him, obstructing traffic, could not result in a jail sentence.

Finally, the prosecutor prevailed, saying over and over to the policemen, very apologetically and fearfully, words to the effect that he could do something "if it wasn't for that damn card from the college." He returned to me and asked how I would plead on the charge of obstructing traffic. He made me understand that if he was to drop the serious charge, Mississippi had to be given its pound of flesh. I told him that the question of how I would plead on obstructing traffic would depend on the disposition of the other charge and the amount of the fine that would be imposed on Harold if he pleaded guilty in the parking case. He told me that the general policy in the neighborhood was to impose lower fines and sentences on guilty pleas than if the state is "put to making its proof." If you have ever seen Gluckstadt, you would know that a charge of "obstructing traffic" there is a feeble pretense—there is seldom any traffic to obstruct. But this was no time for technical nice-

ties. We had to help get the prosecutor and the judge "off
the hook," and still keep the amount of the fine within
reasonable bounds. We agreed to a plea of guilty on the
obstructing charge, to be followed by a fine of ten dollars
and costs (to be imposed by the judge, of course), provided
that there was a finding of not guilty on the license charge.
I did not want the prosecutor simply to drop the other
charge, but to go to "trial" on it, agree to offer no evidence,
and let the court enter an acquittal. Otherwise, the case
could be reopened and Harold tried again, perhaps when
George and I were not around.

There was still another conference between the prosecutor and the policemen, and a lot of headshaking, and
dismay was expressed, but we disposed of the case according to this agreement.

"Gentlemen, are you ready to proceed?" the judge asked,
rather ceremoniously. I replied affirmatively, the prosecutor
nodded his head, and the judge proceeded to read the
charges. We entered our pleas. The prosecutor declined to
present the evidence on the license case. His Honor found
Harold not guilty on that charge and, sure enough, fined
him ten dollars and costs for obstructing traffic. Later, it
occurred to me that no evidence was offered on the obstructing traffic case, either, so the judge never officially
knew what it was that Harold had done. But enough is
enough. Suffice it to say that he knew that the arrangement
was that Harold be fined ten dollars and costs.

The COFO office had posted with this same judge, $50
in cash bail for Harold several days before. Harold owed
Mississippi $23, of which $10 was for the fine and $13
was court costs. (Eleven dollars was normal court costs
and two dollars was a jail fee for one night. Mississippi
levies this fee as part of its court costs to cover room and
board—on the American Plan.) So, instead of paying any
money that morning, Harold received from the judge $27
"change" from his bail deposit. Somehow, this provoked
the policemen as much as anything else. The sight of a
Mississippi justice of the peace tendering money to a New
York civil rights worker—even a refund of a portion of

his own money—was almost too much for them to bear. At least, there was no *woman* around to see that happen.

I thought that was the end of Harold's case. We said our goodbyes on the judge's front lawn. George and I strongly advised Harold not to drive while he was in the Madison County area, and not to drive at all until he had obtained a Mississippi driving license. He readily agreed. Harold thanked us profusely for our help, but he still had misgivings about the case. During the histrionics and ceremonial ritual in and around that garage, Harold had no speaking part. He had spent most of his time and directed most of his attention to watching those highway patrolmen. Apoplectic at the verdict and the refund of a portion of Harold's money, their faces showed that they did not agree that this was the end of Harold's case.

Of course, this is a hindsight observation of mine. I had stopped paying attention to the policemen as the case came to a conclusion, and by the time we were talking with Harold outside, we were full of smug assurances to him that the significant thing about the case was the acquittal, and that if he followed our advice about using another driver to deliver his library books, he would have no further trouble around Madison County. All I can plead in my own defense to this miscalculation is that it was made in good faith.

Harold's companion drove him to the Freedom House in Canton, a couple of miles away; and George and I returned to Jackson. We were anxious to report our success to our colleagues in the law office, and also to advise COFO that we had made a little crack in Mississippi's xenophobia. However, by the time we reached our destination, took care of some odds and ends in the law office and made our report to COFO headquarters, several hours had passed. In fact, we had not called COFO headquarters before they called us about the next chapter in the case of Harold's delivery of those library books. The books, along with the car Harold had been driving, had been virtually impounded from Saturday night, when he had been arrested, until Wednesday afternoon, when his case ended and he got back on the road again.

This time, COFO explained to us, Harold's companion

was driving. They had headed north out of Madison County, and just as they crossed the Holmes County line, they had been stopped for speeding. Mississippi has very high speed limits. The old two-lane road on which Harold and his companion had been driving out of Canton carried a speed limit of sixty or sixty-five miles per hour, and it was in such a condition that it was virtually impossible to exceed that speed limit on that road. Nevertheless, the same car was stopped. Harold could not be charged this time, because he was not driving. But the car was stopped, his friend was charged and taken before a Holmes County justice of the peace. No lawyer was present, and there was a very quick trial in which Harold's companion was fined and assessed with court costs. I do not know the amount of the fine, but the total of the fine and court costs came to exactly $27—the exact amount of the refund that Harold had received from the judge in Madison County at the conclusion of the other case.

Mississippi levies fines in five-dollar multiples, and no matter how the court costs are figured, a total levy of $27 is impossible without a contrivance to assess a fine in an odd amount, because the court costs without a jail fee come to eleven dollars. This had been carefully explained to us by the judge in Madison County. The only thing that we could conclude was the fine was sixteen dollars, a very odd coincidence that refunded to the court that same $27 which had so upset the policemen a few hours before. The boys paid the fine, because by this time, as long as they were sure that a fine would be the end of the case, they wanted to be out of the area, make their delivery, and call an end to the legal charades that the police in the neighborhood were playing with them.

But that was not the end of the case, either. While they were paying the fine to the justice of the peace in Holmes County, a highway patrolman had driven up to the filling station where this court had been convened. The patrolman claimed that Harold's car had been driven in such a way as to "intentionally" force him off the road a few miles back, in Madison County, and he placed Harold's companion under arrest, taking him—and Harold and the car, with its cargo of books—back to the county jail in Canton. More time behind bars, this time for Harold's friend, not for Harold. More bail to be raised. Another case to be handled.

I did not represent Harold's friend. By the time that case came to trial, I had left Mississippi, and George had taken over in my place. Again, he had to work things out with the same county prosecutor in Madison County whom we had dealt with on the other case. Again, apparently the county prosecutor had misgivings about the situation. It seemed that each time this car started out on the highway, there was an arrest, followed by some unsupportable or unbelievable version of a traffic offense, followed by George or me raising Cain. The only one of the three cases we had missed had been the fast disposal of the speeding fine in Holmes County, where this particular prosecutor was not involved.

After bail was made, the two youngsters were on their way again, and George told me later that he finally worked out a plea of *nolo contendere* and a fine of $35 on a charge of "reckless driving." George told me that the prosecutor in Madison County admitted that there were good grounds for skepticism about everything that had happened to these boys, and that was why he was willing to let Harold's friend off with a $35 fine. Later during his stay in Mississippi, George told the justice of the peace who had heard our first case about the incident as a partial explanation of why young freedom workers and their middle-aged Northern lawyers are a "bit critical" of Mississippi law enforcement. The judge shared the prosecutor's suspicions. First, there was the odd fine paid in Holmes County. Then, there was the case of a civil rights worker "intentionally" forcing a state highway patrolman off the road in a high-speed automobile. They must both have known that if there was any substance to this latter charge, the northern youngster would have been indicted for something akin to "assault with intent to kill." Since there was probably nothing to it, a charge and fine for "reckless driving" was sufficient.

This kind of harassment by traffic charges represented a serious problem for the civil rights movement, which must use the highways to transport its people and the instruments of the freedom movement, such as Harold's library books. To make that delivery, Harold spent a night in jail, his friend spent several hours in jail, their liberty was put in serious jeopardy, they spent a total of $85 to disentangle themselves, and it took five days to transport those books from one Mississippi Freedom House to another.

Harold's books were delivered and, by now, I suppose that Harold is back at Iowa State. Some youngsters, picked up as Harold was, were beaten or physically abused during their night in jail. And there is the specter of the most famous Mississippi traffic case, involving James Chaney, Michael Schwerner, and Andrew Goodman. They were also first stopped for a "traffic offense," and the last time anybody admits seeing them alive was after they paid a fine for speeding in Neshoba County, exactly three weeks before Harold was stopped by the Mississippi highwaymen.

On the day Harold was arrested, much of the civilized world was watching the civil rights "traffic" in Mississippi with numbness and horror. Perhaps this explains his relative good fortune. The Neshoba County case stirred the conscience—alas, the guilty conscience—of some relatively decent people in Mississippi, such as that prosecutor and that judge. Why? Perhaps, as H. L. Mencken said, conscience is "the inner voice which warns us that someone may be looking."

JESSE H. BRENNER

The Case of the Disappearing Docket

One Sunday morning, Mike and Don, two white COFO students, attempted to attend services at an all-white church in Madison County, Mississippi. Because of their COFO affiliation, they were refused admission. On their way back to their headquarters, they were viciously attacked by a gasoline station owner who took full advantage of their code of nonviolence. After finally managing to get away and receiving medical attention they were accompanied by several friends to police headquarters, where they not only reported the assault but signed a formal complaint against their assailant.

Routinely, a prosecuting attorney will keep a complaining witness informed about a trial date, but Mike had to inquire repeatedly before learning that the trial was scheduled for

Jesse H. Brenner is an attorney in New York. He is a graduate of the Columbia Law School.

the following Monday at 2:00 p.m. At the appointed time, both he and Don appeared in court. The trial, they were told, had been adjourned for a week. Although the defendant was nowhere in sight, the complainants had received no prior notice of the adjournment, nor were they given any reason for it.

When Mike and Don appeared on the adjourned date, they were accompanied by legal counsel. The lack of activity in the courtroom was puzzling. We discovered that the acting city attorney was handling the cases that day, so, after explaining our purpose to him, we checked the day's docket —the list of cases scheduled for trial that day—to learn when the case would be called.

The case was not there.

The acting city attorney appeared dumbfounded. We persuaded him to check the entire docket record—the list of all cases scheduled for trial regardless of date. Again, to his great surprise, the case was missing. "I just can't understand it," he said. "I can't understand how the case isn't on the docket somewhere. I'm sure the city attorney knows where it is. Why don't you stop in to see Bob when he comes back from Jackson tomorrow?"

And so the next day we called on "Bob." Using the same affable tone as did his acting city attorney, Bob told us he could not understand the absence of the case on the day's docket. He momentarily lost his aplomb when we informed him the case was nowhere on the docket and he realized we had examined the entire docket record, but he quickly recovered and with a genial smile confessed total incomprehension of the matter. To our question about the defendant's absence from the court he stated, "Hell, he knew the case wouldn't be heard without me and that I was up at Jackson. You city lawyers from New York don't realize we're very informal down here. Everyone in town knew I was up at Jackson." Could he set trial for the following day? "No!" He could not be ready to try the case before the following Monday and his reason was plainly transparent. Mike and Don had been assaulted toward the end of the summer. All Mississippians were aware that most of the students would be leaving shortly to return to school. Without complaining witnesses, the charge would be dismissed. The city attorney would continually misplace the case, be out of town or invent some other excuse until Mike and Don were gone. What impressed me, or better, what depressed me so about Mississippi's make-believe world of justice was that this conversation with a city attorney was typical of like conversations anywhere.

Before the bodies of Goodman, Chaney and Schwerner were found, a justice of the peace told me, "Come on, those boys are up in New York laughing at us." When a COFO worker and a minister who had been severely beaten were arrested for disturbing the peace, another justice of the peace assured me, "It was a minor ruckus. No one was hurt." After I told him I had seen the two personally and that they bore the marks of severe beatings, he became visibly angry. My first-hand knowledge had given the lie to his comment, and had shattered, if only momentarily, his belief in it.

In Mississippi, a man honorable and moral in all other respects automatically divorces himself from honor and morality in dealing with Negroes who are seeking their basic freedoms or with those who champion their cause. A man who would rarely lie under normal circumstances believes lying to be a virtue when civil rights are involved; regular churchgoers do not feel impious when they participate in Negro church burnings or bombings; and officials who otherwise take their oaths of office seriously do not feel they are violating their duty by actively participating in or tacitly sanctioning illegal acts.

This breakdown of true values has opened the door to the predators, the sadists and the others who take advantage of the lack of law enforcement for personal gain. And the disastrous effect of this breakdown on the ordinary life of the Mississippi Negro seems to compound itself. A Negro farmer came to our office to enlist our aid. As he started to talk I remembered reading his story in the Jackson paper. While he had been hospitalized, his farm was ravaged by a group of malicious vandals. The unidentified raiders filled the cylinder blocks of his two tractors with sugar, poured molasses into the gasoline tanks and slashed the tires. Then they slaughtered his prize bull. These facts were a repetition of the newspaper article, but missing from that account was any mention that the fences had also been cut and his cattle driven onto diverted land—land for which the Federal government pays if it remains unused.

This farmer's only connection with civil rights was as a passive NAACP member. Nonetheless, he was the victim of this wanton destruction. But this was not the reason he was in our office. He was seeking legal assistance concerning a letter he had received from the Department of Agriculture's local office. The letter notified him that he would no longer receive remuneration for the diverted land and demanded the return of payments he had already received. The basis for the action was the claim that he fraudulently used the diverted land for grazing cattle. The local Department of Agriculture inspector had "happened" by his farm on the day it was ravaged and had noticed the cattle on the diverted land.

Why should a Negro not involved in the civil rights movement be so victimized? According to Mississippi code, he "knew his place." Within this "place" he had managed to become a comparatively successful farmer. Yet, because Mississippi's Negroes must derive their rights not from the Constitution but from a patronizing white community, members of that community freely and comfortably ravaged his farm, knowing they would not be apprehended or, if apprehended, not punished. No fear of official action was at hand to stay or allay their activities.

ROBERT P. SCHULMAN

Clarksdale Customs

On or about July 13, 1964, I visited the Panola County Jail in Clarksdale, Mississippi, together with Philip Feiring, an attorney colleague of mine, also connected with the Lawyers Constitutional Defense Committee. The purpose of our trip to the jail was to obtain an interview with a certain Reverend Willie Goodloe, who had been arrested suddenly some days earlier, supposedly for selling cotton which was subject to his landlord's lien for rent. The arrest had been ordered by the county prosecutor, T. H. Pearson, on the complaint of a "lawyer Thompson," the owner of a strip of land in Bolivar County that he had rented to Reverend Goodloe at an agreed price of $200 for the cotton season.

Willie Goodloe grew a meager yield of cotton on the land that season, and just after harvest a third party, a man

Robert P. Schulman is a New York attorney. He was graduated from the NYU School of Law in 1952.

named Anderson, to whom Reverend Goodloe owed money for food and clothing, came to the place and took away a bale or two of cotton, his entire crop, in payment of the debt. Unable then to collect his rent from the destitute Reverend Goodloe, lawyer Thompson wrote a complaining letter to Pearson in May, 1964. In Mississippi it is a crime to sell cotton subject to a landlord's lien for rent. No action was taken, although Goodloe's whereabouts were constantly known, until about July 6, 1964, two days after Goodloe, together with a few other adventuresome compatriots, attempted to check into (and thus "integrate") a local motel in Clarksdale. Not being able to raise bail of $250, Goodloe was roasting in the county jail.

Of course there was a substantial question whether the cotton had been "sold" within the meaning of the law. But we had no hopes of persuading a Mississippi judge or jury of Goodloe's innocence. He was guilty of integrating the motel in Clarksdale and that was all that counted. We therefore filed a removal petition in the Federal court, had his bail reduced, posted bond and had him released. His case is now pending, along with thousands of others in the limbo between the state and Federal courts.

Another similar case was that of Reverend Rayford. Rayford, who swore vehemently that he detested liquor and that it never passed his lips, was arrested early in July, 1964, in Clarksdale for drunken driving. He was on his way home after driving two white persons, active in civil rights activities, to the Memphis airport. Acting on a tip from a quisling Negro gas station attendant, a police car was waiting for Rayford as he returned to Clarksdale. He protested he was not drunk, that he literally never touched liquor. "I will go to any doctor right now," he stated, "and make a test to show you I'm not drunk"; and he offered to pay for the examination. The police refused. Upon arrival at the station house, out of his change-purse dropped a button that he had put there for safekeeping after it had come off his jacket earlier. As the button clinked and twirled on the floor, he stooped over and picked it up to display to the police that he was in careful possession of his physical abilities. At the trial days later, his own testimony of his condition, his drive to Memphis, his offer to submit himself to a blood alcohol test and pay for the doctor, his picking up the button, all served to no avail. He was pronounced guilty of drunken driving.

Negroes who are caught in any way asserting rights which the authorities believe are beyond their deserts are not alone in feeling the impact of white-controlled law enforcement. An offense for which a white person would receive an admonishment, or which would be excused by the police, in Mississippi is cause for arrest and conviction if done by any Negro. And punishment meted out to any Negro is substantially more severe than punishment for the same crime committed by a white. These characteristics of Mississippi justice came to my attention in the Panola County Jailhouse where Reverend Goodloe was confined.

Philip Feiring was interviewing Goodloe on a wooden bench in a corridor of the jail, while I stood alongside. I noticed a good-looking Negro youth passing back and forth from time to time. He had spots of paint on his hair. I stopped him during one of his excursions out of curiosity, and learned that he was in the midst of painting some cells upstairs. He was just 17 years old.

"Why are you in here?" I asked.

"Breach of the peace and resisting arrest."

I asked him what the basis for his conviction was, and learned that he had been carousing with some friends on a Saturday night and was a passenger in a car when the police came and arrested him.

"Was it in the Negro or white section of town?" I asked.

"The Negro section."

Some white people had been passing by in another car and heard the noise and called the police. I asked if he had been drinking, and he conceded with a wry smile that he had consumed quite a few. So he was guilty of drinking and technically guilty of breach of the peace, if a law officer desired to interpret the law strictly.

The case sounded to me like one in which a 17-year-old boy was out on the town with friends, trying to grab some sheer fun out of life, and had too much to drink. This may be considered an annoyance no doubt, but probably was not an uncommon occurrence in Mississippi as elsewhere. I asked what happened after he was arrested. He replied he was not maltreated or roughly handled. "Did you get a trial? Did you have a lawyer?" I asked. He had not had a lawyer. "What was the sentence?" I asked. Six months in the county jail and $500 fine, he told me, and since he could not raise the fine he was serving an additional six months. I looked around at that barren, morbid place. This young boy was serving one full year in that jail for carousing on a Saturday night, an activity which anywhere else should have brought a minimum sentence.

Sometimes the authorities require less justification for punishment. An elderly Negro man consulted me at the COFO office in Clarksdale concerning his trial, which was due to come up within a few days. He had parked his pickup truck at a curb several car lengths behind a sedan, and someone pulled away from the curb, or passed the sedan, and scraped its side slightly. The police were called. Returning to his pickup, this quiet 55-year-old Negro was immediately arrested by the police for leaving the scene of an accident and breach of the peace. His truck had not come near the sedan (which was owned by a local white citizen) and he knew nothing of any accident. Taken into custody, he was ordered to empty his pockets. In doing so he did not put his wallet on the table at the same time as the other miscellaneous articles, fearing that the police would confiscate his money. The reaction of the law officers was immediate: this minor dilatory compliance was indicative to them of a nonobedient "nigger," and they tossed him against a wall, injuring his mouth and fracturing his thumb. During my interview he said that police had told him if he would bring $55 to court and plead guilty to leaving the scene of an accident, the breach of peace charge would be dropped. "I just hate to pay all that money for something I didn't do," he kept repeating to me again and again. He had been unlucky in being near a place where a white citizen found his car had been damaged, and he had been unlucky in being black.

A brush with the law by a Negro often means getting roughed up, if the whim of the law enforcement official so directs; it means no way out; it means taxation by fines upon those least able to pay. In the course of the arrest, while this Negro was being booked, he was telling the facts of his age and name and address to the clerk, a white woman.

"Don't look at her!" he was commanded. "You look at me when you talk," and the police officer turned the Negro's face away with the end of his club. In the South it is one of the customs that a Negro man not look into the face of a white woman when he speaks to her.

The Supreme Court decided not long ago that the Constitution requires integration of all courtrooms—state and Federal—and the conviction of a Negro in a segregated court must be reversed. Yet when a Mississippi judge, a woman, ordered her courtroom segregated and was told what the Supreme Court had decided, she smiled benignly and said: yes, she knew of that decision, "but we have our customs down here." The courtroom remained segregated.

However, lynching was an old southern custom too, as were segregated schools, buses, hotels and restaurants. Laws can change customs very quickly if they are vigorously enforced. It is not time that is important, but law and the force behind it. Until the Federal government is prepared to recognize that fact, the Negroes of the South will have their demands for justice met at best with a benign smile and the words, "we have our customs here."

R O B E R T   F .   C O L L I N S ,

N I L S   R .   D O U G L A S ,

A N D   L O L I S   E .   E L I E

Clinton, Louisiana

From its inception the state of Louisiana has been notoriously identified with segregation. Some of the most important Supreme Court cases in the field of civil rights have come through the Louisiana courts. In 1873 the *Slaughterhouse* cases[1] were decided by the Court. It refused to void a butchering monopoly created by Louisiana and in effect told the independent butchers they must look to the state courts rather than Federal courts for relief. The significance of that case was that the Court ignored an opportunity to give substance to the equal protection clause of the Fourteenth

---

Robert F. Collins, Nils R. Douglas, and Lolis E. Elie are the members of a New Orleans law firm. Mr. Collins was one of the first two Negro graduates of the Louisiana State Law School; Nils R. Douglas and Lolis E. Elie were graduated in 1959 from the Loyola University Law School in New Orleans. Mr. Douglas was an unsuccessful candidate for the Louisiana State Senate and the Louisiana House of Representatives.

Amendment and gave a restricted reading of its privileges and immunities clause. The victims of this narrow interpretation were Negroes of the state, whose only hope for justice was through broad protection of their rights as United States, instead of Louisiana, citizens.

In 1875 the Supreme Court whittled away the protection afforded Negroes under the Civil Rights Act of 1870. The case was *United States v. Cruikshank*,[2] in which the Court refused to punish private persons who had broken up a Negro meeting. The Court held that interference by private persons could only be a crime where the meeting was held for some purpose connected with national citizenship. Here the assembly had been convened to discuss Louisiana elections, and therefore no crime had been committed.

The infamous case of *Plessy v. Ferguson*[3] also arose in Louisiana. On Tuesday evening, June 7, 1892, Homer Adolph Plessy had bought a first-class ticket on the East Louisiana Railroad from New Orleans to Covington. Plessy boarded the train and sat in the compartment reserved for white persons. In 1890 the state legislature had passed a statute making it criminal for a person to sit in any car reserved for persons of the other race:

> No person or persons shall be permitted to occupy seats in coaches other than the ones assigned to them or [where] they belong.

The conductor asked Plessy if he was a Negro and was told yes. Plessy refused to leave his seat at the conductor's request. One Mr. C. C. Cain then stepped up and asked Plessy to go into the other coach. Again Plessy refused. Upon being threatened with jail, Plessy replied that he would rather go to jail than move. He was arrested and bond was set for $500.

Two of the many arguments made on Plessy's behalf in the Louisiana court were:

> Judge Sawyer, of the United States Circuit Court of California, declared unconstitutional a San Francisco ordinance compelling close cutting of hair of all prisoners ar-

rested on the ground that it was race legislation aimed at the Chinese.

> Daniel Webster was frequently mistaken for a colored man, and were he alive today travelling in this State, would perhaps be made to suffer under the Jim Crow Bill because of unequal provisions for the comfort of white and colored passengers on railroad trains.

The court took the matter under advisement and asked for briefs. In November, 1892, the court sustained the constitutionality of the Separate Car Act. Plessy applied to the supreme court of the state for writs of prohibition and certiorari, which were decided against him. The case was taken to the United States Supreme Court, which ruled in 1896 that the Louisiana statute was not unconstitutional. The Supreme Court rejected Plessy's argument that "the enforced separation of the two races stamps the colored race with a badge of inferiority." "If this be so," the Court said, "it is not by reason of anything found in the act, but solely because the colored race chooses to put that construction upon it." After the Supreme Court ruled against Plessy, the record shows that on January 11, 1897, Plessy withdrew his plea of not guilty and was sentenced to pay a fine of $25 and, in default of payment, to imprisonment in the parish prison for twenty days.

In more recent times the Supreme Court decisions dealing with civil rights problems in Louisiana have tended to expand rather than restrict the rights of its Negro citizens. In the spring of 1960 a number of students from Southern University, the nation's largest Negro state university, conducted sit-ins in Baton Rouge. They took seats at the lunch counter of Sitman's Drug Store, the restaurant section of the Greyhound bus terminal, and the lunch counter at Kress's Department Store. They made no speeches; they did not speak to anyone except to order food; they carried no placards and did nothing else to attract attention to themselves. However, they were arrested and convicted in the Louisiana courts on the ground that their mere presence at the lunch counters would cause a disturbance which it was the duty of the police to prevent.

The U.S. Supreme Court reversed the convictions. It said: "The undisputed evidence shows that the police who arrested the petitioners were left with nothing to support their actions except their own opinions that it was a breach of the peace for the petitioners to sit peacefully in a place where custom decreed they should not sit. Such activity in the circumstances of these cases is not evidence of any crime and cannot be so considered either by the police or by the courts."[4]

The Supreme Court's decision was announced on December 11, 1961. A few days before, Ronnie Moore, president of the Baton Rouge Chapter of CORE and a student at Southern University, contacted certain Baton Rouge merchants to complain about their segregated store facilities and discriminatory employment policies. When he received no satisfactory response, CORE prepared several news releases and two leaflets outlining the complaints and protesting against the discrimination shown by the merchants.

CORE then began to picket the stores. Twenty-three Negro college students were arrested on December 14, 1961, while picketing. That night Ronnie Moore addressed a mass meeting of students on the Southern University campus, where he spoke for about 40 minutes and announced there would be a protest march to the courthouse in Baton Rouge on the next day. On December 15, 1961 about 1,500 Negro college students walked downtown on a peaceful march protesting segregation, discrimination, and the previous day's arrest of the 23 students. Before the march, Ronnie Moore was arrested for violating an anti-noise ordinance by using a loudspeaker near the campus. Reverend B. Elton Cox then assumed leadership of the march and informed Chief of Police Wingate White that the group was going to sing some patriotic songs, say some prayers and express their protest against the jailing of the students the previous day. He told the Chief that the whole program would take about 25 minutes. The Chief told Cox to keep the group across the street from the courthouse and Cox agreed. White said nothing about stopping the march.

After taking about ten minutes to assemble near the courthouse, the group pledged allegiance to the flag, recited the Lord's Prayer, sang a couple of songs, and Reverend Cox made his short speech in which he told the assembled group to go to the lunch counters at twelve of the stores that refused to serve Negroes.

While the demonstration was going on, some 150 to 200 white persons gathered on the courthouse steps on the east side of the street. It was not a hostile group. There were also about 80 to 90 policemen present who could handle any situation which might have arisen.

As the demonstration continued, the prisoners in jail started to sing. The students quickly responded with a jubilant cheer or yell. At that point Sheriff Bryan Clemmons said through a loudspeaker, ". . . you have been allowed to demonstrate. Up until now your demonstration has been more or less peaceful, but what you are doing now is a direct violation of the law, a disturbance of the peace, and it has got to be broken up immediately." Two or three deputies came across the street and told the group to move. Almost immediately thereafter tear gas bombs were set off and the students were dispersed in the confusion. The police also used dogs to disperse the crowd.

Several hours after the demonstration, Cox was arrested and charged with disturbing the peace, obstructing the sidewalk, obstructing justice, and criminal conspiracy. He was tried in the district court and was found guilty of all but the last charge.*

* After he was sentenced, Cox criticized the way his case had been handled by the state. A Baton Rouge grand jury thereupon indicted him for defamation of the district attorney and the judge who sentenced him. When two other CORE workers criticized the authorities for bringing these second charges, they were also indicted for defamation. All the charges were dropped after the Supreme Court's decision in Garrison v. Louisiana, 379 U.S. 64 (1964), where the Court overturned conviction of the New Orleans district attorney for defaming the criminal court judges of that city.

However, the U.S. Supreme Court reversed these convictions on January 18, 1965. It wrote:

> . . . constitutional rights may not be denied simply because of hostility to their assertion or exercise.
>
>   *   *   *
>
> . . . it is clear that the practice in Baton Rouge allowing unfettered discretion in local officials in the regulation of the use of the streets for peaceful parades and meetings is an unwarranted abridgment of [Rev. Cox's] freedom of speech and assembly secured to him by the First Amendment.[5]

The charge of obstructing justice was also dismissed. The Supreme Court found that the Chief of Police had given the marchers permission to assemble across the street from the courthouse. The state would not be allowed to claim later that this was a breach of the law because it intimidated judges or jurors going in and out of the building.

In New Orleans in 1960, sit-in demonstrators had also been arrested and convicted for trespass. At the time the mayor of New Orleans, De Lesseps Morrison—certainly one of the most liberal politicians in the state—had made it very clear that he would tolerate no such demonstrations: "It is my determination that the community interest, the public safety, and the economic welfare of this city require that such demonstrations cease and that henceforth they be prohibited by the police department." The Supreme Court reversed these convictions on the basis of Mayor Morrison's remarks. Chief Justice Warren wrote:

> The official command here was to direct continuance of segregated service in restaurants and to prohibit any conduct directed toward its discontinuance; it was not restricted solely to preserve the public peace in a nondiscriminatory fashion in a situation where violence was present. . . . [These] convictions commanded as they were by the voice of the State directing segregated service at the restaurant, cannot stand.[6]

But the Supreme Court's decisions in civil rights cases have difficulty reaching into the backwoods of the state.

Away from the urban centers, the sheriffs, prosecutors and judges can do their damage long before the Supreme Court can act, and nothing the Court does at a later time compensates for the arrests, harassment and abuse that the Negroes undergo. Indeed, some Louisiana courts are not averse to ignoring Federal court orders in order to maintain segregation and smother Negro protests.

On August 19, 1963, in Plaquemine in the Parish of Iberville (not to be confused with Plaquemines Parish where Leander Perez has a stockade waiting for civil rights demonstrators), the state police, using horses, tear gas and electric cattle prods, broke up a Negro protest meeting near the local Baptist church. They severely injured a number of Negroes present, and arrested hundreds of others who had come to hear James Farmer, the national director of CORE. Farmer, who was to have taken part in the March on Washington a week later, could not attend because he was in jail for his part in the Plaquemine demonstration. In St. Francisville many voter registration workers have been arrested and beaten for trying to get at least one Negro registered in that city. And in Clinton, Louisiana, the national law as declared by the Supreme Court and enforced by the lower Federal courts has been almost totally ignored.

Clinton is in East Feliciana Parish, about one hour's drive from Baton Rouge. Two parishes, East and West Feliciana, make up the 20th Judicial District which is served by one judge, John R. Rarick, and one district attorney, Richard Kilbourne.

East Feliciana is mainly a farming area of gracefully sloping wooded plains far different from the bayous or other parts of the state. Its northernmost boundary is common with Mississippi's southern border.

The parish has a population of about 20,000, of which 54 per cent are Negroes. In 1956 there were 1,361 Negroes registered to vote in East Feliciana. By 1960 this number had been reduced to 82 through challenges to their qualifications as voters. In 1960 there were no Negroes registered to vote in West Feliciana. By early 1965, 89 Negroes had been allowed to register.

Clinton has a courthouse, originally built by slaves, which has just been renovated with not a stone changed. The city was once used as background for a Civil War movie. Rumor has it that at the end of the Reconstruction period a Negro deputy was hanged from one of the trees on the courthouse grounds. There is a rope hanging down at the end of the stairway in the Clinton courthouse. Presumably the other end of the rope is connected to a bell, the use of which has long since been discontinued.

On August 2, 1963, CORE task-force worker Michael Lesser, a young white graduate student from Syracuse University, accompanied two Negroes to the office of the registrar of voters in Clinton. When the registrar found out his business, he ordered Lesser downstairs. Later that afternoon, Lesser returned with other prospective registrants and waited downstairs. This time a deputy sheriff came out and arrested Lesser for disturbing the peace, although Lesser had done nothing more than wait silently for the registrar to admit him.

The maximum penalty for disturbing the peace is $1,000 and one year in the parish jail. Notwithstanding this, Judge Rarick set bond at $2,000 cash and would not accept a property bond.

Our firm drew up a writ of habeas corpus protesting Judge Rarick's action and appeared to argue it on August 15, 1963, at 1:00 p.m. Before our arrival, CORE had announced its plans to integrate the courtroom. When we arrived at the Clinton courthouse, we found a large group of Negroes standing outside. On inquiry, we learned that the courtroom was locked. When the time for court to open arrived, someone unlocked the door and we saw that the courtroom was filled with white persons. Not a single seat was vacant. This was East Feliciana's answer to CORE's announcement.

Although the charges against Lesser were finally dropped, CORE's registration activities and its defense of Lesser led

Clinton to counterattack. On August 20, 1963, the Town of Clinton and the Parish of East Feliciana tried to enjoin CORE from carrying out its activities in the parish. In their petition to Judge Rarick, the officials of East Feliciana claimed that CORE had forced breaches of the peace in Baton Rouge in 1961 and in Plaquemine in August, 1963. They claimed that CORE had blocked the streets and had violated state laws, and, further, that CORE was holding public meetings in Clinton for the purposes of violating the law—i.e., encouraging people to register.

Judge Rarick issued a temporary restraining order without notice to CORE and without a hearing because, he claimed, CORE's activities would create immediate and irreparable harm to the parish. The order prohibited CORE from:

> . . . unlawfully picketing and unlawfully taking possession of private places of business when having been requested to leave and failing to do so, and by congregating with others on public streets and highways and upon public sidewalks, and in or around any free entrance to any place of business or public buildings and in failing and refusing to disperse and move on when ordered to do so by any law enforcement officer.

The order was to last only ten days, until a hearing on a motion for a preliminary injunction could be held. In order to forestall any action by Judge Rarick on that motion, we filed a removal petition in the Federal court at Baton Rouge. Although merely filing a petition in a Federal court automatically ousts the state court of its jurisdiction without any further action by a Federal judge, he may, on petition from the state, remand the case back to the state courts if he feels that it was improperly removed.

Judge E. Gordon West of the Federal court in Baton Rouge—who has consistently ruled against the civil rights groups in Louisiana—remanded the case back to the state court. In the meantime Judge Rarick kept extending his temporary restraining order, although there had never been a hearing on the original petition. The trial on the petition was scheduled for October 24, 1963. On that day, we succeeded in securing from the Fifth Circuit Court of Appeals a stay of all proceedings while that court decided whether Judge West's remand order was appealable or not. However, Judge Rarick announced that he would not obey the order of the Fifth Circuit. The New Orleans *Times-Picayune* in its October 25, 1963, edition, reported:

> "The purported stay of that court," Judge Rarick said from the bench, "is without warrant in law and is an absolute nullity and is entitled to no more respect in this court than any other act of officious intermeddling designed to obstruct justice."

The trial went forward in Judge Rarick's court despite the direct order of the Federal court of appeals. A special counsel for the parish, Mr. Van Buskirk, made the following opening statement (opening statements are usually made only in criminal matters, although this proceeding was civil in nature):

> . . . We will show that the alleged purpose of the Congress of Racial Equality in Louisiana at this time, that is, voter education and registration, is a fraud, that it is simply a colorful disguise for the real intention of this organization, to foster and promote civil disturbances, racial tension, and lawlessness by mobs of emotionally aroused misled people. . . .
>
> . . . We will show that this conspiracy is directed at local government itself, that it is the intent and purpose of this conspiracy to subvert, supplant local authority by immobilizing police, immobilizing duly elected public officials by forcing them to give in to its insatiable demands by forcing them to cease protecting citizens whom it is their duty to protect.
>
> We will show that the advisory board of this organization, as an indication of its ultimate purpose, and as the intent and purpose of its activities in the State of Louisiana, on only 14 members of its advisory board, there are over 400 citations of communist-front connections and associations.
>
> We will show that included in the task force operating in the town of Clinton, was at least one individual who is an active member of a communist-front organization.
>
> We will show that the tactics of this organization are

exactly the same as the tactics of any other rabble-rousing communist-front organization; we will show that its ultimate objective is exactly the same in the field of race as the objectives of the communist party itself.

. . . I do not say, and I do not want anyone to understand me to say that the people who are engaged in this activity and the local citizens who have been misled by these people are communist, I do not say that. I say that this organization from top to bottom is infiltrated with people who have an association with communists, and with the communist-front over a period longer than the life of this organization itself, which is approximately 25 years. I say that these people, wittingly or unwittingly, are doing the work of the communist party and that these people have an intent and a purpose to come as close as they can to the edge of our sedition laws and to the edge of our criminal anarchy laws not to overthrow and destroy our local government, but simply to subvert it to their purposes, by paralyzing it and thus being able to impose their will on our local government and on the people of the community. . . .

Some witnesses appeared at this hearing, and at others that were held later. But eventually Judge Rarick evaded the orders of the Fifth Circuit simply by extending his temporary restraining order. When necessary the parish authorities could fall back on that order if nothing else would do.

In the meantime, twelve Negro residents of the parish wrote to the mayor urging him to try to settle the racial problems peacefully. The letter read as follows:

Clinton, Louisiana
September 19, 1963

JOSEPH S. FELPS
MAYOR
East Feliciana Parish

Dear Sir:

We, the undersigned individuals and organizations of East Feliciana Parish, representing the Negroes of East Feliciana Parish, hereby submit this resolution to you as our elected public officials and appeal to you to commence taking initial steps to establish a bi-racial **committee** on community relations in order to avoid civil domestic disturbance of racial tension.

We further request that the committee be composed of any white citizens that you desire, however, we reserve the right to submit an equal number of Negro citizens to serve on such committee. We respectfully suggest that the public officials to serve on the committee be composed of city councilmen, school-board members, police jury members and other elected leaders of both races for a careful consideration of the many problems facing our community.

Due to the pressing need of such a committee to establish meaningful, effective communications between all the citizens of our community we urgently request action on this resolution before September 26, 1963.

Respectfully submitted,

One of those who signed the letter was Mrs. Charlotte Greenup. Mrs. Greenup, who was 82 years old, had returned to Clinton after living in Chicago for 40 years and serving as political secretary to Oscar de Priest, the first Negro congressman elected after Reconstruction. The response which Mrs. Greenup and the other writers received was twofold. One was a letter from the district attorney:

DISTRICT ATTORNEY
TWENTIETH JUDICIAL DISTRICT
OF LOUISIANA

RICHARD KILBOURNE
DISTRICT ATTORNEY
CLINTON

Parishes of East and West Feliciana

September 23, 1963

CORRIE COLLINS	MATTIE MATTHEWS
HERBERT BELL	ROBERT THOMPSON
CHARLOTTE GREENUP	REV. ROGER TRANSPERS
HAZEL P. MATTHEWS	REV. ROBERT WASHINGTON
BETTY NERO	LAURA SPEARS
CHARLIE TAYLOR	WILLIE ADAMS

Dear Sirs and Madames:

I have before me your resolution of September 19, received by me on September 21, in which you state that you represent the Negroes of East Feliciana Parish. Fortunately, I am acquainted with all of you and with a great many other Negro citizens of East Feliciana Parish and I regard your statement that you represent the Negroes of East Feliciana Parish as an utter falsehood.

You request that initial steps be taken by me to establish a "Bi-racial committee on community relations in order to avoid civil domestic disturbances of racial tension."

At the outset, I point out that your request exhibits an inexcusable ignorance of the functions of my office under a republican form of government. So-called bi-racial committees, with semi-official status in some communities, represent nothing more than an effort on the part of spineless public officials to evade the plain, legal responsibilities of their offices. I regard such committees as wholly illegal and unconstitutional and the public officials who participate in them as being guilty of misconduct in office, subject to removal in appropriate proceedings.

It is abundantly clear that there exists in the United States today a conscious and calculated movement to overthrow the government of the United States and that of all its political subdivisions by violence disguised as "non-violence." One of the several organizations dedicated to this end is the Congress of Racial Equality with which each of you is apparently associated. I regard this organization, and all of those who see fit to associate with it, as a criminal conspiracy. One of the vehicles it uses to prey upon the ignorant, the unwary and the weak is the so-called "bi-racial committee." Simply stated, such a group is designed to undermine, subvert and ultimately destroy constitutional government as we know it since they are never elected by the people, but attempt to exercise their influence upon the elected representatives of the people through intimidation by threats of "civil domestic disturbances of racial tension."

My office has always been, and will continue to be, open to all persons whomsoever having business involving the District Attorney's office. Known criminals and those who associate with them will continue to be treated as such.

Your "resolution" set a deadline of September 26 for an

answer. Whether this date means anything or not is of no particular moment to me. Henceforth, each of you will be held personally responsible by me for any "civil domestic disturbances of racial tension" which occur in East Feliciana Parish.

Yours very truly,

RICHARD KILBOURNE
District Attorney
20th Judicial District of
Louisiana

Certified Mail-Return Receipt Requested to Each of the Above.

Copies to:

Mr. Burke Marshall, Assistant Attorney General, Washington, D. C.

FBI Office, Baton Rouge,

FBI Office, New Orleans.

The second response was given on December 3, 1963 when the grand jury indicted all twelve signers of the letter for public intimidation. Many special motions were filed challenging the validity of the indictment because of systematic exclusion of Negroes from the grand jury. The case has never been brought to trial.

During the month of October, 1963, CORE mounted a boycott against the Clinton merchants, because of their discriminatory hiring practices. One of the boycotted stores was owned by the local sheriff. As a result of their boycott activities, thirty persons, mostly Negroes, were arrested and variously charged with conspiracy to commit defamation, resisting an officer, disturbing the peace and contributing to the delinquency of juveniles. In each instance, two pickets carrying large signs bearing such slogans as "Don't Buy Segregation," "Vote With Your Dollars For Freedom," and "Freedom Now" were used. The position of the state was that these acts also constituted a violation of the temporary restraining order issued by Judge Rarick.

Of course the Supreme Court had said many times that peaceful picketing against segregation and discrimination cannot be enjoined, since such picketing falls under the constitutional protection of free speech. The authorities did not seem to be concerned with how the cases would eventually be disposed of. And in fact, these cases were never brought to trial.

Thus, in the course of three months the legal officials of East Feliciana had (1) arrested numerous CORE workers for helping in voter registrations or peacefully picketing, (2) enjoined CORE from encouraging Negroes to vote and assert their rights as citizens, (3) indicted the most respectable Negro citizens of the parish for requesting the creation of a bi-racial committee to reduce tensions in the community. In the process a direct order of a Federal court of appeals was ignored. It is no wonder that the Negroes of the parish put little faith in the fairness of Louisiana courts.

For a lawyer working in this atmosphere there are few compensations. The most important is the gratitude shown to him by all the Negroes. A brief conversation with them proves that not many understood what happened in court, but that is not important. The important thing to them is that you were there, you too were black and you answered back. What you said sounded like what should have been said.

J A C K O P P E N H E I M

The Abdication of the
Southern Bar

Sunflower County, Mississippi, is predominantly rural. Indianola, the county seat and largest town, has a population of 6,714. The county is in an area known as the Delta, which, to my surprise, is north of Jackson. It is not the delta of the Mississippi River, but a delta-shaped geographical area in the northwest part of the state. In the Delta, cotton is said to be king. To most Negroes it is a dictator. The pay for field hands is generally 30 cents an hour.

Local Negroes consider almost any job to be better than picking cotton, and very few Negroes over the age of ten have not spent some time in the fields. A job at which no Negro ever labors in Sunflower County is that of attorney. Altogether there were three Negro members of the Mis-

Jack Oppenheim is a New York attorney. A 1958 graduate of the Harvard Law School, he is a former Assistant Corporation Counsel of the City of New York.

sissippi bar in 1964. Carsie Hall and Jack Young shared an office in Jackson. Jess Brown practiced there also. The Lawyers Constitutional Defense Committee worked out of the offices of Young & Hall and was counsel to that firm. Although Hall, Young and Brown labored valiantly in support of the Summer Project, they could not furnish adequate legal services required by the thousands of Negroes throughout the state, to say nothing of the white civil rights workers who also needed legal representation. There was no legal obstacle preventing white members of the Mississippi bar from representing Negro clients. The unwillingness of the white Mississippi bar to furnish legal assistance to Negro citizens, for fee when possible, for free when not, explains the invasion of Mississippi by northern lawyers volunteering their services.

Out-of-state attorneys may represent clients in Mississippi courts if they are associated with local counsel (for the purpose of a particular case). This is a courtesy which one state traditionally accords another. However, if an out-of-state attorney's participation is challenged in writing by two or more members of the Mississippi bar, not of the same firm, the privilege is revoked until the Mississippi Bar Association determines the attorney's fitness to appear. This method of disqualification was often threatened during the summer but seldom invoked.

When I arrived in Mississippi, the leaders of the Mississippi bar had passed a resolution (proposed by one of the northern attorneys) suggesting that its white members represent persons involved in civil rights controversies. The resolution was limited to those rare instances where the prospective client could pay an adequate fee. Even thus limited, it was hoped that such participation would obviate the need for northern lawyers.

Mississippi attorneys had good reason to be wary about representing Negroes in such matters. Bill Higgs, a young white attorney who had zealously upheld the rights of Negroes in Mississippi courts, had been forced to flee the state three years before because of harassment.

I quickly came to test the efficacy of this resolution. A

young Negro, George Jones, from Indianola, had been of great asistance to COFO when it first arrived in Sunflower County. COFO found it difficult to overcome the local Negroes' fear of reprisal for attempting to register to vote. Jones accompanied the COFO workers from door to door, introduced them to each family, and helped persuade the more daring ones to register. Jones was no stranger to the law enforcement people in Indianola. At nineteen he had already served time for a number of offenses such as disorderly conduct. Many in the Negro community thought Jones was headed for fresh trouble. When, after a week, he still could be found in the vanguard, the community was greatly encouraged. However, a few days later Jones was arrested.

His arrest had occurred several days before my arrival in the Delta. Len Edwards,* a law student from the University of Chicago, brought me up to date. COFO believed that whatever the nature of the charges against him, Jones had in fact been arrested because of his prominence in the registration drive. They asked me to look into the matter.

In Indianola, Police Chief Bryce Alexander, after accepting my credentials, told us that Jones had been picked up for vagrancy and brought to the police station. He had run out of the station while being interrogated, had been rearrested a few days later, and had pleaded guilty to a charge of "fleeing from arrest." Mayor Pitts sentenced him to two months on the county penal farm. The Chief added that Jones had waived his privilege of remaining in the city jail and was already on the county farm. I asked if we might see him, to reassure his mother and friends that he was well, and also determine whether he should appeal his sentence. Chief Alexander said he had no objection, but the county farm was at Moorhead, which was Sheriff Bill Hollowell's jurisdiction.

---

* Len Edwards's father is a United States congressman from Palo Alto, California. Congressman Edwards, with several other congressmen, passed through Sunflower County and other parts of Mississippi earlier in the summer. The presence of Len Edwards during the entire summer undoubtedly was a restraining influence on local officials throughout the county.

We presented the same request to Sheriff Hollowell. He said he would allow me to see Jones if I were accompanied by a Mississippi attorney. I pointed out that Mississippi law did not require that. He suggested that we talk to County Attorney Bill Cook, who might agree to waive this "condition." We did; Cook did not. Since the three Negro members of the Mississippi bar were swamped with other cases in Jackson, over 100 miles away, we would have to find a white Mississippi attorney. I asked Cook to give me a list of all the members of the Sunflower County bar. There were fourteen attorneys in the county.

By this time the Negro community in Indianola thought that Jones might be in serious danger. Our difficulty in arranging to talk to him increased its apprehension. For my own part, I thought that I would have to resort to a habeas corpus petition to the Federal district court in Greenville. Since, in order to obtain the habeas writ, it might be necessary to show that I had diligently made effort to comply with local requirements, and because I welcomed the opportunity to gauge the attitude of the local bar, Edwards and I set out to seek the assistance of a local attorney.

Ten of the fourteen attorneys in Sunflower County have their offices in Indianola, within one block of the courthouse. We first went to the firm of Lyon and Crosswaite. Gordon Lyon, the senior partner, was away on vacation. Frank Crosswaite, Jr., listened patiently while I explained the need for his assistance. I told him that a local Negro boy had been arrested last week, and without legal counsel had apparently pleaded guilty, and was now at the county penal farm. I asked him if he would either accompany me, or arrange for me to see Jones, to ascertain the circumstances of his arrest and determine whether an appeal was warranted. Crosswaite said he "did not want to get involved in this thing one way or the other." Edwards pointed out that his involvement need only be minimal, but Crosswaite could not be persuaded.

Forest Cooper was "too busy." His partner, Richard Allen, was in the hospital. J. H. Price no longer practiced actively at the age of 96. George Ritchey was in the real estate business and no longer practiced law. Townsend, Clark and Davis considered themselves disqualified because they handled some business for the town. David Quinn was ill. In each instance I mentioned the resolution of the Mississippi Bar Association. Some knew of it. It was not persuasive.

We next headed for the town of Sunflower (population 662), Sunflower County, where Mrs. Zelda Labovitz, the county's one lady lawyer, resided. She told us that she had absolutely nothing against Negroes. Her specific ground for refusing was that she did not like to handle criminal matters. When we explained that it would not be necessary for her to do anything more than arrange for me to see Jones, she expressed a dislike for starting things she could not see through to the end. Edwards assured her that we would allow her to pursue the matter to its conclusion if she desired. She quickly reminded us that she did not want to handle criminal matters. She apologized for being unable to be more helpful and thus concluded the meeting. We did not contact the three remaining attorneys, who lived in scattered towns. The day was over, and diligent effort had been made.

Another possibility had to be checked before we applied to the Federal court. If Sheriff Hollowell would set bail at a reasonable amount, we would post a cash bond pending appeal. COFO was willing to contribute up to $100, although Jones was not a member and their funds were short. I told Hollowell I would petition for *habeas* unless he would release Jones on bail. After checking with County Attorney Cook, Hollowell decided that if $250 was posted and Jones wanted to take an appeal, he could be released. We raised the money, not without difficulty, and I was allowed to see George Jones alone.

In July the inmates at the county farm at Moorhead work in the prison cotton field. Jones was called in from the field to meet me, his one-piece black-and-white striped prisoner's uniform drenched in perspiration. I told him that I was a lawyer for COFO, offered my help and asked to hear his story. George's version of what had happened differed from Chief Alexander's in some important respects. He said that because his home was overcrowded, he often slept in the fields or in the homes or automobiles of his friends. One evening he had fallen asleep in an abandoned wagon in the Negro section of Indianola. Slim, the town's only Negro policeman (and considered "meaner than the white cops" by the Negroes), woke Jones and told him he would have to go to the police station: the Chief wanted to ask him some questions. Correctly assuming the questioning would be concerned with his cooperation with COFO, George followed Slim to the Chief's office. Slim slammed the door, saying, "George, we're gonna whup your ass for walking, and talking, and joining with them 'freedom riders.'" George did not want to be whupped on a dry throat, and asked Slim if he could have a drink of water before they got on with it. Slim said that he could, but that if he tried to run away, they would shoot him.

"I went to the fountain in the hall and decided that, since they already said they were going to beat me, and for all I knew, kill me, I'd better run. Maybe they wouldn't shoot, or maybe they'd shoot and miss." He ran. They shot at him but missed, and he escaped. He hid in the cotton fields for three days. Then he left the field and "went downtown to see if they were still mad at me." They were. A policeman told him that he was being arrested for "fleeing." After several days in the city jail he was brought before Mayor Pitts, who serves as presiding judge of town court. Mayor Pitts asked him, "George, you did run out of here the other day, didn't you?" George agreed. "In other words, you plead guilty, right?" George said, "I guess so." The mayor then sentenced him to two months on the county farm for fleeing from arrest.

Jones's narrative suggested a number of obvious defenses. He did not believe that he had been arrested by Slim, but rather that he was being taken in for questioning. More importantly, he did not flee from arrest but from a threatened beating. Although the police could produce the affidavit of the officer who picked up Jones the second time for "fleeing," they could not produce anything indicating that Jones had been initially arrested for vagrancy.

We appealed. A subsequent L.C.D.C. attorney removed the

case to the Federal court, where it will eventually be heard, unless it is remanded back to the state court. Hopefully, some out-of-state attorney will be available to handle the case at that time.

That we were unable to enlist the assistance of any member of the Sunflower County bar to help Jones can hardly be considered surprising. That the result was a foregone conclusion underlines the magnitude of the Mississippi Negro's predicament. If he becomes bothersome to the white community, he can be arrested and convicted without any legal representation. It is true that the *Gideon* case would require that a conviction of a serious crime be set aside if the defendant was not represented. But it is not clear whether the *Gideon* rule applies to the minor offenses which are a major weapon of the Mississippi authorities. Besides, with no attorney to pursue it, these convictions will rarely come to the attention of any higher court.

In the past when Mississippi Negroes were charged with crimes unrelated to civil rights, white Mississippi attorneys sometimes were appointed by the courts to represent the defendant. The extent of the defense often consisted of the attorney arranging for his client to get a less-than-maximum sentence if he pleaded guilty. Since the Negro defendant knew he could not hope to gain an acquittal if the case were tried, it was easy to persuade him to accept a short jail "visit," even if he were innocent.

In the area of civil rights, the white members of the Mississippi bar have forsaken their professional responsibilities to an even greater extent. The reluctance of these attorneys to appear is presumably because they consider the civil rights workers to be "agitators," "leftists," "mixers," "beatniks," or worse. But defendants accused of crimes, such as rape, murder, or espionage, are entitled to and receive legal counsel. It is difficult to understand why someone accused of distributing pamphlets without a permit, or even vagrancy, as in Jones's case, should be unable to find a native attorney to defend him.

The extent of the southern bar's opposition to civil rights was recently illustrated by Professor Marvin E. Frankel of the Columbia Law School. Frankel examined back issues of the *Alabama Lawyer,* the official organ of the Alabama state bar for the past ten years, and discovered an absolutely monolithic stand against the Supreme Court's decisions on Negro rights. He then wrote an article raising questions about this unanimity and sent it to that magazine for publication. The editors refused to publish it. After the article appeared in the *Columbia Law Review,* a Birmingham newspaper republished it and opened up its columns for comment by members of the Alabama bar. Its offer was met by total silence. Not a single lawyer was willing to go on record as approving the law laid down by a unanimous Supreme Court.

This total opposition has other ramifications. So loudly and unanimously has the white southern bar proclaimed its stand against civil rights, that should it now choose to enter the arena, its effectiveness would be seriously undermined. Hypothetically, if COFO were told that it was no longer necessary for the out-of-state attorneys to represent it, because white Mississippi attorneys had agreed to handle the cases, COFO no doubt would feel betrayed. The concepts of "due process" and "equal protection" in our Constitution are particularly fluid. If a lawyer can convince the court that his client has been treated unfairly, the Constitution may protect him. But only if an attorney can see the unfairness, is it likely that the necessary defense will be formulated. Because white Mississippi attorneys seem congenitally unable to recognize when a Negro is being mistreated, their effectiveness would be marred even when they are in good faith.

For the summer of 1965 the Mississippi bar has indicated that it intends to stand aside once again, and even has voiced its approval of plans by the Lawyers' Committee for Civil Rights Under Law (made up of many corporate lawyers who also dominate the American Bar Association) to have out-of-state attorneys appear in Mississippi. The Mississippi bar expressed the hope that the Lawyers' Committee group would be of a more conservative stripe than the groups it had to contend with in 1964. When it finds that these attorneys will earnestly defend the interests of their clients,

I imagine even that organization will be considered suspect by the Mississippi bar.

The utilization of out-of-state attorneys, unfortunately, was far from a complete solution. Most attorneys were considerably handicapped by unfamiliarity with Mississippi law. A more serious failing was the inability to see a case through to its conclusion. Many cases could not be resolved during the summer, and many trials and appeals are still pending. But for Mississippi Negroes legal assistance and justice are a round-the-clock problem. The abdication of responsibility by the southern bar compounds an already disastrous situation.

MICHAEL MELTSNER

Southern Appellate Courts: A Dead End

We are still witnessing a struggle for supremacy between state and Federal law a century after the Civil War supposedly settled the matter. Briefly, Federal Constitution and laws secure the Negro against all state-supported and some "private" racial discrimination. While ultimate authority on the meaning of the Constitution and Federal law rests with the United States Supreme Court, it is the duty of state judges, as well as Federal, to give content to Supreme Court decisions. In practice, however, Negroes cannot rely on southern state courts to uphold the supremacy of Federal law. In order to maintain the status quo, state judges have not hesitated to evade or ignore Federal law and to exploit a deeply rooted national tradition of deference to local au-

Michael Meltsner is an attorney for the NAACP Legal Defense and Educational Fund, Inc. He is a graduate of the Yale Law School.

thority. Or they have been content to see themselves as "a mere way-station on the route to the United States Supreme Court," where Negroes hope "in the light of supposed social and political advances, they may find legal endorsement of their ambitions."[1] Since they see the lawgiver's role this passively, delay and equivocation—the cardinal sins against justice—are easily come by.

State judges are nominated or appointed on the basis of party loyalty and service, a scale that weighs ability last and least. But judges in the South are no more creatures of prevailing political cliques than are judges in other sections of the country. The state judiciary in the North, however, is selected from a mixed bag, one filled from a society at least mouthing the rhetoric of equality. The political apparatus as a whole is subject to constant pressure from a constituency that includes articulate Negroes and white allies. In the South, the logic of political survival assures the white Southerner of judges who know and do their duty as far as the Negro is concerned. When a Negro asserts his right to freedom from racial discrimination in the courts of southern states, the decision goes against him and the political system tolerates few exceptions.

As the ranks of southern Negro voters swell, we can expect the attitude of state judges to shift gradually to acceptance of the Negro's legal equality, and eventually to something approximating impartiality. Whatever the ultimate prospects, however, little change has occurred. At present, civil rights decisions of the Supreme Court are robbed of practical effect, and settled rules of state law distorted to justify criminal convictions which would surely fail if race were not involved. For the unwary civil rights lawyer and his client, the courts of southern states are traps. Proper procedure is often indistinct, and the slightest misstep may result in forfeiture of valuable constitutional rights.

State judges who wish to remain in office and to retain the society of their fellows (judges, like the rest of us, need someone to lunch with) do not officially recognize the social consequences to the region and the nation of maintaining serfdom in place of slavery. They have shown a shocking eagerness to avoid even the appearance of fairness in areas such as jury selection, where progress could have been achieved without exposing them to great political risk. Although exclusion of Negroes from state juries had been a Federal crime since 1875,[2] and since 1880 sufficient to invalidate a criminal conviction,[3] the U.S. Civil Rights Commission could report in 1961 that it was still a widespread practice.[4]

It is not surprising, therefore, that the most prominent characteristic of state courts in the South is that a Negro will not voluntarily bring them a dispute involving his civil rights. The legal buttress of segregation has crumbled at the efforts of Federal courts. School boards, voting registrars, and police have been hailed before Federal judges and ordered to conform to the Federal Constitution. With Negroes refusing to submit their claims to state court systems, the primary opportunity for southern courts to deal with civil rights has occurred in criminal cases. Civil rights workers have been charged with "trespass" for refusal to leave all-white lunch counters, "breach of the peace" for sitting in the front of a bus, "parading without a license" when carrying picket signs, "criminal anarchy" for distribution of leaflets, and a whole host of other crimes, some petty, others extremely serious.

Convictions are appealed to courts of· statewide jurisdiction from local courts, in which justice is harsh, speedy, and predictable. Just about the only thing a civil rights lawyer can accomplish in many of these local courts is to preserve legal objections for appeal and avoid a contempt citation. Sometimes the latter is impossible. Negro lawyers moved recently in a Georgia court to disqualify a judge from presiding at a civil rights trial because of his reputed bias against Negroes, whereupon the judge gave substance to the claim by citing them for contempt because they sought his disqualification.[5]

One expects a degree of impartiality from the state appellate courts. Because they are elected by a statewide constituency, political pressure is less concentrated and more easily parried by these judges. They are somewhat removed from

the courthouse gang of prosecutors and police who dominate
southern politics in all but the larger cities. Unfortunately,
such expectations of impartiality are not fulfilled. State appellate courts have shown themselves to be as susceptible as
local courts to pressure and prejudice against Negro rights.
The major difference is that the local magistrate may be less
prone to legal cant and more likely to call what he is doing
by its right name than does the state appellate court.

On June 25, 1963, Miss Mary Hamilton was held in contempt of the circuit court of Etowah County, Alabama, and
sentenced to five days in jail and a fine of fifty dollars. She
had been testifying in her own behalf on a petition for a
writ of habeas corpus to free her from a Gadsden, Alabama,
jail, where she was held for participating in a civil rights
demonstration. The following exchange took place:

Cross examination by Solicitor Rayburn:

Q. What is your name, please?
A. Miss Mary Hamilton.
Q. Mary, I believe—you were arrested—who were you
   arrested by?
A. My name is Miss Hamilton. Please address me correctly.
Q. Who were you arrested by, Mary?
A. I will not answer a question—

By Attorney Amaker: The witness's name is Miss Hamilton.

A. —your question until I am addressed correctly.

THE COURT: Answer the question.
THE WITNESS: I will not answer them unless I am addressed
correctly.
THE COURT: You are in contempt of court.
ATTORNEY CONLEY: Your Honor—your Honor—
THE COURT: You are in contempt of this court, and you
are sentenced to five days in jail and a fifty dollar fine.[6]

Miss Hamilton's reaction to being called "Mary" by a
state prosecutor in a courtroom where, if white, she would
have been called "Miss Hamilton," was not thin-skinned
sensitivity. She was responding to one of the most distinct

indicia of the racial caste system, the refusal of whites to address Negroes with titles of respect such as "Miss," "Mrs." or "Mr.," instead referring to them as "boy" or "girl." The Supreme Court of Alabama upheld the contempt conviction in such a manner as to suggest the issue did not exist:

> The record conclusively shows that petitioner's name is Mary Hamilton, not Miss Mary Hamilton.
> Many witnesses are addressed by various titles, but one's own name is an acceptable appellation at law. This practice is almost universal in the written opinions of courts.[7]

Because use of the first name only in a formal court proceeding is one of the symbolic indignities of the caste system, the U.S. Supreme Court subsequently reversed Miss Hamilton's contempt conviction, finding it as offensive to the Constitution as segregation in the courtroom.[8]

Occasionally, there are shows of prudence and duty from state appellate courts, but they are not frequent enough to rely upon and usually flow from a recognition that a Federal court will ultimately reverse the conviction.[9] Generally, the higher state courts rubber-stamp the outrages of their inferiors. At the worst, state appellate courts throw up obstacles to review of their decisions by the U.S. Supreme Court. The Supreme Court, of course, cannot consider more than a few of the cases which lawyers ask it to decide. As a consequence, it declares guiding principles in significant cases and relies on lower courts—state and Federal—to give them flesh. That some state appellate courts "have openly flouted not only the spirit but also the letter of the Supreme Court's decisions on civil rights," as Jack Greenberg has put it, imposes a policing function to which a national court of last resort, without investigators or police at its disposal, is unsuited.

The nine justices are not equipped to save everyone enmeshed in the state criminal process, even when they decide the case is worthy of review. In the particular case, for example, application of majestic constitutional principles often depends on simple questions of fact. Did an NAACP youth leader in Columbia, South Carolina, refuse to comply with a police order that he picket close to the curb so that pedestrians could pass? The civil rights worker and his companions say no, but the police and two white witnesses disagree. The trial judge and jury and state appellate courts choose to believe the police version. It is evident that the Supreme Court does not have the capacity to revise their decision, although what in fact occurred may determine the defendant's freedom of speech.

The Supreme Court also has limited jurisdiction. It can only enter a state criminal case, for example, when questions of Federal law are controlling. A device employed by southern state courts to defeat claims that Federal constitutional rights bar conviction has been a failure to decide— one way or the other—questions involving these rights. If the highest state court refuses to decide a freedom of speech issue (a question of Federal law) and instead affirms conviction on the ground that the defendant did not follow state rules of procedure (a question of state law), the Supreme Court of the United States will not enter the case. And it will not take jurisdiction *even if the state court had misapplied Federal law,* because the state law ground of decision remains to uphold the conviction. The sole limitation on this doctrine is the power of the Supreme Court to examine, because jurisdiction turns on it, whether the principle of state law is substantial and has been applied fairly. To cope with the evasions of southern courts, the Supreme Court has expanded this power in recent years and entered cases only after deciding that procedural hurdles were not sufficient to defeat its jurisdiction. But even with this power of review, the Supreme Court is limited in the control it can exercise over state courts. Take the sorry story of the legal war between Alabama and the NAACP.

In June 1956, John Patterson, the attorney general of Alabama, went before a state circuit court and obtained a "temporary" order prohibiting the National Association for the Advancement of Colored People from doing "business of any description or kind" in Alabama. The order was obtained and the NAACP effectively excluded from the state, without giving the association any opportunity to dispute the state's contentions. This summary procedure was justified by the "irreparable injury to the property and civil rights of the residents and citizens of the State" caused by the NAACP doing business in Alabama without having registered under the state corporation law.[10]

Now, registration requirements are commonplace. They generally serve the useful purpose of ensuring that corporations can be sued in the courts of the state, for by registration the corporation agrees that a state official may be served papers in a lawsuit as its agent, thus affirming the jurisdiction of the state courts. True, the NAACP had not registered, but it had been doing business in Alabama since 1918, and no one had ever complained of its nonregistration. The association, therefore, assumed with justification that, as a nonprofit corporation, it was exempt from the registration requirement. But even if it should have been registered during these years, punishment by exclusion from the state was preposterous. Alabama had never ousted any other corporation for nonregistration, and the registration statute mentioned only a fine as penalty for failure to comply. Clearly, the remedy was to force the association to conform to the registration requirement, but the state knew that if such a request were made, the association would comply. The court order, therefore, was unconditional. Not only was the NAACP barred from Alabama, it was prohibited from attempting to register. The courts of Alabama had turned a simple housekeeping statute into a harsh, punitive sanction sufficient to end activities within its borders of the nation's most powerful civil rights organization.

Not content with barring the association from Alabama, the attorney general obtained another court order in July of 1956 requiring it to produce books, records, correspondence and membership lists. The association refused. To publish the names of its Alabama members, it argued, would subject them to economic reprisal and endanger their personal security. Judge Walter B. Jones of Montgomery, an avowed segregationist, found this failure to produce contempt of court; he ordered a fine of $10,000, to become $100,000 if the documents were not produced in five days.[11]

At the end of the five-day period the association came forward with all documents requested but the membership lists, and Judge Jones's contempt order became final.

The association appealed to the supreme court of Alabama, but that court refused to consider the appeal fully, because the association, it said, had not complied with Alabama rules of procedure.[12] The proper means of defending against contempt was to file a petition prior to the date the documents were due to be produced in court. Failure to file was enough to foreclose consideration on appeal of anything more than narrow "jurisdictional" questions. The supreme court of Alabama also ruled that until production of the membership lists, the association could not attack the legality of its ouster from the state.

The U.S. Supreme Court agreed to review this decision, but it was not until January of 1958 that briefs from both sides were submitted and the case argued. Another six months elapsed before the Supreme Court issued a decision which brushed aside the procedural ruling of the state court, calling it inconsistent with the supreme court of Alabama's own "past unambiguous holdings."[13] Reaching the constitutional issue, the Supreme Court decided that disclosure of membership lists was likely to expose members of the association "to economic reprisal, loss of employment, threat of physical coercion, and other manifestations of public hostility."[14]

Association members were now safe in their anonymity, but they had no business to transact. The Supreme Court had refused to consider the constitutionality of the exclusion of the association from the state because the Alabama courts had not yet ruled finally on the question.

The case, therefore, went back to the Alabama courts, but the association could not obtain the trial it needed to challenge the state's use of the registration requirement to keep it from doing business in the state. First, the supreme court of Alabama issued an extraordinary ruling.[15] It had considered the decision of the U.S. Supreme Court and found it erroneous and, therefore, reaffirmed the contempt judgment and $100,000 fine. By the time the U.S. Supreme

Court was informed and issued a new order summarily reversing the Alabama court once again, it was June of 1959.[16] Eventually, a reluctant supreme court of Alabama sent the case back to the trial court for a final determination of whether the association could be kept out of business in the state, but the trial court persisted in its failure to hold a hearing on the issue which had been so pressing in 1956 that the association had been ordered out of business without one.

In frustration, the NAACP went to a Federal district court, but that court refused to interfere on the ground that the route for resolution of the conflict was through the Alabama courts.[17] But, of course, those courts were blocking the route. Later, a U.S. court of appeals agreed with the district court. Federal judges, it found, should refrain from determining constitutional questions arising from the application of state statutes until state courts have been afforded a reasonable opportunity to interpret the statutes.[18] It was now May of 1961, and the Supreme Court acted again. It directed the Federal courts to consider the case, unless "within a reasonable time, not later than January 2, 1962," the state of Alabama gave the association an opportunity to dissolve the exclusion order.[19]

In December of 1961, the circuit court of Montgomery County gave the association a hearing, rejected its arguments, and, on the 29th of the month, four days before the deadline, made the "temporary" injunction permanent. The supreme court of Alabama affirmed this decision,[20] but, once again, in a manner which placed the jurisdiction of the U.S. Supreme Court in doubt. According to the Alabama court, the association had failed again to follow an important rule of state procedure by combining arguments of merit and others without merit in the same section of its legal brief:

> . . . we have a rule of long standing and frequent application that where unrelated assignments of error are argued together and one is without merit, the others will not be considered.[21]

For this reason, the supreme court of Alabama would not consider whether ouster of the association denied it and its members due process of law and equal protection of the laws as guaranteed by the Fourteenth Amendment to the Constitution.

On appeal, Justice John Marshall Harlan, speaking for a unanimous Supreme Court, again found Alabama procedure insufficient to keep the case from the Supreme Court:

> The consideration of asserted constitutional rights may not be thwarted by simple recitation that there has not been observance of a procedural rule with which there has been compliance in both substance and form, in every real sense.[23]

Eight years after the deed and four trips to the Supreme Court later, it was decided that exclusion from the state because of nonregistration violated rights of the association and its members "to associate for the collective advocacy of ideas."[24] On October 9, 1964, the NAACP resumed its activities in the state of Alabama.

Because the Supreme Court cannot substitute itself for state court systems, increasing attention has focused on attempts to transfer decision of civil rights cases to lower Federal courts. This is not to suggest that for his constitutional rights to prevail, the Negro need only find the door of the local Federal courthouse. As a group, southern Federal judges have been characterized as moderates who favor segregation and feel that the Supreme Court's desegregation decisions have been unwise. This attitude is conducive to a bland judicial statesmanship which compromises civil rights and accommodates southern resistance to desegregation. Litigation in the lower Federal courts, moreover, is costly, slow and often impractical. Only certain persons can wait for legal relief and withstand, economically and emotionally, the notoriety, pressures and demands of litigation. The shocking amount of noncompliance with the Supreme Court's school desegregation decisions, even in places where suits have been brought, hardly inspires the

confidence of Negroes who, by participating in a desegregation suit, may be risking their jobs or personal security.

The lower Federal courts, however, have been of enormous importance to the civil rights movement. They have,
of course, ordered desegregation of thousands of state-
owned, operated or supported facilities since 1954 and are
primarily responsible for enforcement of the Civil Rights
Act of 1964. They have also served what may be called a
neutralizing function, intervening, in time of crisis, in what
under normal circumstances would be the state judicial
domain. In Birmingham, for example, in May, 1963, action
by a Federal judge may be credited with saving the lives and
property of untold numbers of the city's residents. On May
20 the superintendent of schools of the riot-torn city attempted to thwart further demonstrations by suspending
over a thousand Negro school children, many within a
month of graduation, on the ground that they had been
arrested "for parading without a permit." The use of dogs
and hoses to break up these marches of school children had
already shocked the nation and was to lead to proposal of
the Civil Rights Act of 1964. In the face of evidence that
the suspensions, which were of dubious legality, would
end the uneasy peace that had settled over the city, a plea
was taken to a local Federal judge who refused to interfere.
With pressure mounting, the case was taken to the chief
judge of the U.S. Court of Appeals for the Fifth Circuit,
Elbert Parr Tuttle, who stayed the suspension order until
appeal, eventually won by the students, could be considered.[25] This willingness by some Federal judges to halt
provocative and unconstitutional administrative action by
local officials, a function that state courts should perform,
accounts for a good deal of the restraint of the Negro revolution. As violent as was that May in Birmingham, it would
have been far worse if Judge Tuttle had not acted.

When lower Federal courts have refused to intervene
and relied on the state judiciary to enforce Federal law,
consequences have been disastrous. As the Freedom Riders
arrived in Mississippi, in May of 1961, they were arrested
by state police as a matter of course and prosecuted by the

hundreds in the state courts. Attempts to stop these prosecutions by resort to the Federal courts were unsuccessful. Mississippi was permitted to try each rider and force him to vindicate in the Mississippi courts his acknowledged right to travel without meeting racial segregation, subject only to eventual review by the U.S. Supreme Court. After conviction in the police court of Jackson, Mississippi law required a new trial in a county court and two appeals before the riders could petition the U.S. Supreme Court to review their convictions. Ultimately, the supreme court of Mississippi, in the case of *Thomas v. Mississippi,* rejected their right to desegregated travel facilities by finding the arrests required to maintain order:

> In the case at bar the defendant not only knew the situation but he came to the South for the deliberate purpose of inciting violence, or, as he put it, "for the purpose of testing the Supreme Court decision in regard to interstate travel facilities." He left a trail of violence behind him in Alabama. The jury was, therefore, warranted in finding that he intended to create disorder and violence in Jackson, and that, in fact, disorder and violence were imminent at the time when Thomas refused to obey the police officer's order to move on.[26]

The over 300 riders arrested had to post $1,500 bond each to remain free pending this tortuous appellate process. Such bonds are usually purchased for a premium, but in Mississippi no surety company will write a policy in a civil rights case, and the riders were compelled to deposit over $372,000, the face value of the bonds. In addition to the cost of bond, travel expenses, printing of records and briefs and court fees, the riders were forced to maintain lawyers in almost constant attendance in Jackson, Mississippi, courts for over a year, because the state decided to try the cases one at a time although the charges concerned almost identical circumstances. By January, 1965, the Supreme Court had not yet acted on the first applications for review brought by the riders. When it does consider these cases, it is likely that the Supreme Court will reverse the convictions rendered by the Mississippi courts, but nothing the Court does will compensate for the injury to the integrity of constitutional rights and the loss of human and financial resources occasioned by deference to Mississippi justice for over three years.

The lower Federal courts are obviously reluctant to interfere with the control local officials exercise over state criminal law, even though many prosecutions are merely pretexts to harass civil rights workers. (Judging from the number of traffic tickets, for example, one would expect a high correlation between civil rights work and reckless driving.) Federal judges are ill equipped to oversee state police, prosecutors and judges and will remain so until Congress acts to recast the manner in which Federal rights are preserved and enforced; for, at present, authority to intervene is often obscure and, when acknowledged, hedged about by cumbersome procedural restrictions. These limitations on the power of the Federal courts reflect a historical preference for local authority and administration, that has been largely superseded in the economic sphere and must be modified further for the security of Negro civil rights. The absence of a tradition of Federal court intervention, however, makes each new step toward Federal regulation of southern justice a cautious groundbreaking.

Unless state courts begin to honor the Negro's Federal rights, we can expect increasing pressure on lower Federal courts to develop techniques of intervention. A good deal depends on the prudence of southern state courts. If they abdicate responsibility in cases of extreme lawlessness and brutality, they can expect Federal judges to act. If the more flagrant excesses are curbed, the state courts will probably be able to continue as they have been doing all along. A series of events in Americus, Georgia, in 1963 demonstrates the ease with which state officials maintain segregation until barbarity provokes Federal intervention.

During the spring, Donald Harris, a field secretary for the Student Nonviolent Coordinating Committee (SNCC), helped register Negro voters in Americus, Georgia, an area where officially condoned violence against Negroes is legendary. Few Americus Negroes were registered, although they constituted 50 per cent of the population. Harris, a New Yorker and graduate of Rutgers College, explained registration procedures and publicized the importance of obtaining the right to vote. After he arrived in Americus, the number of registered Negroes steadily increased.

His efforts, however, were continuously harassed by local whites. On one occasion, he was arrested for vagrancy while waiting for applicants in the corridor of the county courthouse. Shortly thereafter, signs warning against loitering appeared near the registration office. When Negroes applied in numbers, the registrar, a sister of the county sheriff, became ill and closed the office. It reopened only on a part-time basis. Ralph Allen, another SNCC worker, was beaten on the streets after he had taken a woman to the courthouse to register.

By July, when Americus experienced its first civil rights demonstration, tempers ran high. Eleven Negro teen-agers sought to enter the front door of the Martin Theatre, the city's only movie, where Negroes always had been forced to enter through a rear alley and to sit in the balcony. The youths were arrested quickly and charged with disorderly conduct. Over 200 persons met a similar fate during July and early August as a result of other attempts to protest segregation in Americus, a community with staggering Negro unemployment, where segregation was so pervasive that a Negro could not borrow a library book.*

On the night of August 8, Negroes were singing freedom songs as they left a voter registration pep rally held in a church. Police called Harris out of the group and ordered him to disperse the crowd. When he told them he was not the leader and could not order anyone to leave, he was beaten in the street. After the attack on Harris, police scattered the crowd with clubs and pistol fire. In the melee,

---

* In October, 1963, with a Federal court breathing down the neck of the city's establishment, an NAACP Legal Defense Fund lawyer arranged the "desegregation" of the public library, by betting a young Negro, Bobby Lee Jones, a dollar he could obtain a library card. Jones was greeted cordially by the librarian, who permitted him to check out a book, and was so shaken that he failed to notice that all chairs and tables had been removed from the reading room.

bricks were thrown at the police from behind a nearby café. Within the week, Harris, Allen and John Perdew, another SNCC worker, were held on charges of "attempt to incite insurrection," a crime punishable by death, as well as "riot," "unlawful assembly," "attempted escape," and "assault with intent to murder." Local merchants immediately requested peace bonds of $40,000 for each of the workers. The bonds were assurance of their "good behavior" should the workers be freed pending indictment or trial, for the police could forfeit the bonds and recommit the workers to jail if they participated in any further demonstrations. The peace bonds were of dubious legality, and they were also unnecessary. Because held on capital charges, Harris, Perdew and Allen could be kept in jail without release on bail. On August 17, they were joined by Zev Aelony, a field worker for the Congress of Racial Equality, who was also charged with "attempt to incite insurrection." Aelony's crime was supposed instigation of a march to city hall to pray for the release of Harris, Perdew and Allen. Ironically, he was not connected with civil rights activity in Americus, having come only to help establish a cooperative for impoverished Negro pecan farmers.

To add to the Alice-in-Wonderland character of the insurrection charge, in 1937 the U.S. Supreme Court had declared the statute under which they were charged unconstitutional when Georgia had applied it to a Communist party organizer.[27] But Americus authorities were not interested in applying decisions of the Supreme Court. There were no doubts that, if permitted, they would hold the workers in jail until the case reached that Court some two or three years later. The workers might, however, gain their freedom if they agreed to leave Georgia for good. The prosecutor, Stephen Pace, Jr., an ambitious son of an ex-congressman, desirous, it was said, of following in his father's footsteps, freely granted interviews with newsmen and an Atlanta reporter quoted him as saying:

> I frankly have serious doubts whether I will ever call the insurrection cases for trial. I hope something can be worked out prior to that.

The basic reason for bringing these charges was to deny the defendants or ask the court to deny them bonds. . . . We were in hopes that by holding these men we would be able to talk to their lawyers and talk to their people and convince them that this type of activity . . . is not the right way to go about it.[28]

Pace acknowledged that Harris, Perdew and Allen had not thrown bricks, but he reasoned that they had "stirred up" local Negroes and so were responsible for all lawbreaking which occurred. As they counseled protest of the city's segregation laws and customs, they were advocating resistance to the sovereign authority of the state. This was an "attempt to incite insurrection," punishable by death.

After a local court ordered the workers held for action by a grand jury in December, their attorney, C. B. King of Albany, the only Negro practicing law in southwestern Georgia at the time, moved in a county court to admit them to bail. If the judge had quickly denied the motion, a rapid appeal would have been possible; but he refused to rule one way or the other, a classic instance of justice delayed being justice denied, for each day they were held without bail was irretrievable. King then attempted to obtain a writ of habeas corpus and managed at least to obtain an order denying the writ on October 1. According to the state judge, there was sufficient evidence to believe the workers had committed the crime of "attempt to incite insurrection." He found the statute punishing insurrection to be constitutional and ignored the 1937 Supreme Court decision. King, now joined by a force of attorneys from New York, appealed to the supreme court of Georgia. He asked that court to hear the appeal immediately, declare the statute unconstitutional, and, in any event, to set bail pending a final decision. But the supreme court of Georgia refused to set bail and only agreed to hear oral argument on the appeal a few weeks earlier than it would have ordinarily. This meant consideration of the case by the supreme court of Georgia in December, or about the time the grand jury was to convene. If the grand jury indicted, the appeal could have been considered moot, forcing another time-consuming round of legal arguments before a local judge and a fresh appeal.

Fortunately, however, a special three-judge Federal court had been obtained to consider the constitutionality of the workers' detention and their claim that the arrests were part of a conspiracy of city and county officials to interfere with voter registration and peaceful protests of segregation. The court convened October 31, by which time Harris and the others had spent 83 days in the Sumter County jail.

Two days of testimony before the court revealed a sordid story of harassment and violence by city and county authorities: The Chief of Police had warned a small group to stop picketing the Martin Theatre. When the pickets refused, he went to city hall, where a council meeting was in session; an ordinance banning picketing was quickly adopted, whereupon the Chief returned to arrest the pickets for violating it.

Clubs and cattle prods, or "hot sticks" as they were called, had been used freely by the police when making routine arrests. They took special pleasure in using them on the backsides of young girls. Stitches were often required to close the wounds of demonstrators. One youth, James Williams, was set upon by police and clubbed until his leg was broken. Shirts taken from teen-agers shortly after arrest, and exhibited to the court, were hard-crusted with blood.

Rural camps for arrested youths were barely habitable. As toilet facilities were in disrepair, a shower was used as a latrine. Food consisted of four hamburgers a day, often served at the same time. There were no blankets or mattresses. The juvenile court judge, who sent Negroes under seventeen there, had never seen these camps, but he would release the children on probation if someone would pay the costs of confinement and if parents promised that their children would not demonstrate again.

For being "sassy," a sixteen-year-old girl had been kept overnight in a 4 x 5-foot windowless room, where an air-conditioner poured cold air directly down on her.

Lifelong residents of Americus were effectively denied bail on minor charges for weeks at a time when the city stopped accepting security proffered by undertaker John

Barnum, the only Negro wealthy enough to write a meaningful number of bonds. Barnum, an official of the local civil rights organization, suddenly found his embalming methods under health department investigation.

This story of perversion of the legal system into an instrument of repression was revealed by the brilliant interrogation of Pace by attorney Morris Abram. A leader of the Georgia bar before moving his practice to New York City, Abram caught Pace in a net of the prosecutor's own loose talk. Pace confirmed that the workers had been charged with crime punishable by death in order to hold them in jail without bail. They were in custody, he admitted, awaiting action by an illegally constituted grand jury, for a Negro had never served on a Sumter County, Georgia, jury, in plain violation of the Fourteenth Amendment to the Constitution and numerous Supreme Court decisions. The workers, therefore, could not have been constitutionally convicted for "attempt to incite insurrection," even if they had committed the crime. They were being held for ransom. "Agree to leave the state," they were being told, "or we will hold you in jail indefinitely."

By order of the Federal court, the "attempt to incite insurrection" and "unlawful assembly" statutes were declared unconstitutional and the workers freed to await trial on the other charges.[29] While the court found evidence of a broad conspiracy to deprive persons of constitutional rights, it refused to grant a general injunction against police and local officials until they had additional time to prepare a defense. One of the three judges, J. Robert Elliott, dissented. He made no attempt to defend the conduct of local officials but relied on what he considered essential principles of federalism: Criminal law is primarily a matter of local concern. The Federal courts cannot police every state criminal proceeding. They should, therefore, abstain from any interference until after trial and appeal in the state courts have been exhausted.

Certainly, Judge Elliott had history on his side. There have been few instances of lower Federal courts stopping state criminal proceedings, once they had begun. Although the lower Federal courts were established "for dealing with local opposition to, or disregard of, the federal law,"[30] states have been permitted to prosecute what they considered violations of local law without Federal interference, subject only to limited review by the Federal courts in special cases. But the failure of state appellate courts to enforce Negro civil rights has demonstrated the need to challenge the traditional allocation of authority between the two court systems. In the Americus case, state courts were an obstacle course to rights guaranteed by the Constitution and threatened to impose an enormous penalty on innocent persons without trial. The process of determining criminal responsibility became, at the hands of the state police, prosecutors and judges, a tool for punishment of those whose views they detest. To speak of federalism, of deference to local authority, in such a context is in reality to reject the legal equality of the Negro, for the state's legal process has become a sham, used not to grapple with tenacious questions of fact and law, guilt or innocence, but solely to maintain class and race power.

Race relations in America are characterized by an immense gap between principle and practice. Most people disapprove of racial discrimination but continue to support social policies which ensure it. As Professor Anthony Amsterdam of the University of Pennsylvania has written, "The American citizen has had a right to a desegregated school since 1954 and to a desegregated jury since 1879, but schools and juries throughout vast areas of the country remain segregated."[31] Because they are situated in a position to insulate many of the acts of state police, prosecutors and other officials from the scrutiny of Federal courts, southern judges have played an important role in maintaining this tokenism. Negro rights will continue to remain abstract and unrealized until the Federal courts develop workable techniques for prompt and effective control of southern state courts.

C H A R L E S   M O R G A N ,   J R .

Segregated Justice

Manacles removed from his arms, he glances—too quickly, some think—at the immobile faces of the twelve white men seated at his right. On the wall above the jury rests an off-time Coca Cola clock. There is a clatter as someone kicks a spittoon. Spectators fill two thirds of the wooden benches, Negroes to the left, whites to the right. Several grizzled courthouse hangers-on who have left their regular seats on the front lawn enter the courtroom. The judge, wearing his Sunday best, looks up expectantly. The foreman, a merchant in shirtsleeves, rises and stares briefly at the defendant. In flat, dry tones, he pronounces the guilty verdict. The all-male jury had been out for thirty-eight minutes. The bailiff always notes the time.

The Negro defendant, struggling in the web of white justice—its rituals and forms, trappings and entrapments—is

Charles Morgan, Jr., is Director of the Southern Regional Office of the American Civil Liberties Union. His speech before the Birmingham Young Men's Business Club following the killing of four Negro girls in a Birmingham church bombing in 1963 drew national attention. He is the author of *A Time to Speak*.

a stranger in the courthouse. Rural county courthouses, sporting their memorials to the Confederate dead, are a part of the white man's world. Ensnared by the beefy white sheriff who was elected because he "knows how to handle niggers," the defendant is convicted of the charge—rape, of a white woman. The trial, little more than a formality; the verdict puts the stamp of approval on the coming execution.

An interracial crime is reported—"NEGRO RAPES WHITE WOMAN" is the newspaper headline—and the machine begins to grind. Arrested by a member of an all-white police force, or sheriff's department or highway patrol, the Negro defendant is brought, perhaps for the first time, into the lonely world of the white South. The warrant for his arrest, if there is a warrant, was sworn out by a white man and issued by a white magistrate or commissioner. Then, transported to jail in a racially segregated patrol wagon, he is fingerprinted, photographed and assigned a number by a white clerk, and detained in a racially segregated cell in a jail run by white men. Later he is indicted by a white grand jury and pressured to confess or plead guilty. If he refuses, he is brought to a courtroom presided over by a white judge, provided a white defense lawyer, tried before a segregated audience, referred to with first-name condescension, and convicted by a white trial jury in a courthouse with segregated restrooms and drinking fountains.

The all-white state supreme court, some of whose justices are as well known for their bawdy Negro stories as for their attacks upon the Supreme Court of the United States, then views the appeal. The white lawyers write their briefs, the law is studied by white law clerks, and the jury's verdict is approved.

If an appeal to the Supreme Court of the United States fails, the Negro defendant, condemned from the beginning, now confined to a racially segregated cell on death row, will be visited by white guards, a white chaplain and a white barber, each of whom expresses regrets. He is then strapped into an electric chair (the state's desegregated instrumentality of justice) by white men and before white witnesses. A white man pushes a button or pulls a switch.

From birth in a racially segregated hospital, or no hospital at all, the Negro man, whose name was never important, has moved to burial in the Negro section of a racially segregated potter's field.

From identification by a white woman—who often says, "I can't tell one of them from the others"—to the filing of the death certificate, every decision involving the life and death of the Negro criminal defendant rested in racially antiseptic white hands.

In any society, democratic or totalitarian, unbalanced instrumentalities of justice are weapons of repression. The racially exclusionary system of southern justice, its white juries and white lawyers, judges, sheriffs and deputies, police and clerks, stenographers and segregated facilities, is the sophisticated and effective guarantor of the southern way of life.

I T E M : A Negro pedestrian is struck by a speeding automobile driven by a white college student and taken in a Negro ambulance to the Negro ward of a local hospital; he struggles for life and survives. He is paralyzed from his waist down. His background and the education provided him in racially segregated, inferior schools have limited his work capacity to waiting on tables, carrying hod, picking cotton, or the loading and unloading of trucks and ships and railroad cars. Now, unable to walk, the opportunity to earn a living has been denied him. He is visited by a white insurance adjuster who knows that the value of a Negro man's legs and working life is, in a segregated system of justice, less than a third that of a white laborer.

I T E M : A young Negro man finds his way through the ghetto, attends an all-Negro high school and college, struggles to enter a previously all-white law school, works nights and graduates. He passes a bar examination administered and graded by white bar examiners. He is required to join a state bar association governed by white men. He opens his office in a rundown building which will accept Negro tenants, struggles to find a properly trained secretary, who must, of course, be a Negro. He attempts to maintain an adequate law library on an inadequate income. He hopes to build a law practice by skill and ability, and he grasps for the dignity that attaches to lawyers. But, his name is "Sam" not "Mr. Jones" to the judges, the clerks, the bailiffs, the police. He learns to hold his hat in his hand as he laughs and acts the role of the always happy, always humble Negro. Or, he may rebel, become a leader in the community of The Movement and handle civil rights cases. He then falls heir to sleepless nights and the fears of bombs and bullets that may take the lives of his wife and children. He feels hatred at the courthouse, sees it in a judge's eyes, hears it in a lawyer's voice. Constantly he remembers the threat of disbarment and the all-white grievance committee of "his" bar association.

Professorships, judgeships, political appointments and electoral opportunities are closed to him. So are the large corporate firms and the lists of wealthy clients. So he spends most of his professional life in small claims, domestic relations, probate and police courts.

The field of personal injury law is closed to him. Even injured Negroes, of necessity, seek counsel from white men on the other side of town. White lawyers get more money from white juries.

I T E M : A Negro lawyer files a motion to quash an indictment in a murder case. Negroes have been systematically excluded from the jury, he says. Motion overruled. The case is tried, the Negro defendant convicted and sentenced to death in the electric chair. Five years later the Supreme Court of the United States reverses the conviction. The prosecution then settles the case for a term in prison. Four years later the Negro lawyer files a motion to quash another indictment on the ground that Negroes are systematically excluded from juries. The facts haven't changed. Neither have the results.

I T E M : The publisher and editor of a large, moderate daily newspaper consider editorial and news policy. High-priced libel verdicts have made them cautious. They know that the jurors and judges they alienate today may rule on their case tomorrow. They decide to "tone down" their editorials about segregation. The range of free expression, where free expression is needed most, is narrowed.

ITEM: It's a cool, moonlit night in a small southern town. Little Billy "who really hates niggers," as the townspeople say, leaves the all-night diner where he works. He drives to the nearby cut-price service station. There, he and his buddy, a kid of seventeen, have a deep, quick drink of corn, and begin their journey. They drive down a dusty, rutted road in the Negro section and park. An hour later a single shot tears through the night, followed by the sound of shattered glass. There are no white policemen patrolling the unlit, unpaved streets of "nigger town South, U.S.A." When the police do arrive, little Billy and his friend are miles away. They both take a deep drink of liquor, chase it with a warm coke, and laugh. They "didn't hurt nobody." Besides, they know they'll never be caught and, if they are, "no white jury'll ever convict us."

In 1880, the Supreme Court of the United States struck down a West Virginia statute providing that only "white male persons" were eligible for jury duty. Southern whites, unable to exclude Negroes from jury duty by law, turned to indirection. States that refused to educate Negroes required that jurors be educated. States that denied Negroes the right to vote required that jurors be registered voters. Or they required jurors to own real property. Or they required "good character," "experience" or "moral character" or "intelligence" or "uprightness." Determinations of character, experience, intelligence and uprightness, necessarily subjective, were made by white jury commissioners. Thus, for decades, most jury lists in most Deep South counties included the names of no Negroes.

A jury commissioner may include on the jury rolls the names of the few Negroes he knows—Sam, who shines shoes at the barber shop; George, the maid's husband; the Negro undertaker, and perhaps a few other "good" Negroes. Some southern jury commissioners do seek the names of other Negroes from Negroes they know. Now, the names of a token number of Negroes are often included on jury rolls. The system of selection provides for a subjective determination of juror qualifications. Thus, the important decisions are made in the mind of the white jury commissioner.

Jury commissioners make most of their selections from lists of names. Favorites are lists of registered voters, the telephone directory, real or personal property or poll tax rolls, membership lists of local junior chambers of commerce, Rotary Clubs, and similar organizations. Almost all such lists inherently exclude large numbers of poor people, and most Negroes are poor people.

Often the lists themselves bear racial designations— voter rolls may designate "C" for colored, and tax rolls are often compiled separately by race. And, where there is no racial designation, common knowledge is sufficient. Jury commissioners know where Negroes live and which addresses are in Negro neighborhoods. They know that civic clubs are racially exclusive.

Once names are selected, juror cards may be printed on different colored paper, yellow for Negroes, white for whites (now ruled unconstitutional), or Negro name cards may contain pinprick holes which can be felt, if not seen, when the cards are handled.

For many years, the qualifications of Federal jurors rested on those of the states. Many Federal jury commissioners used state jury lists to obtain names for Federal jury duty. But the 1957 Civil Rights Act formally, if not in practice, ended this.

The names of Federal jurors are selected by clerks of the United States district courts and Federal jury commissioners. Since they are assisted by the United States district judge, it is not unfair to assume that his views are considered in name selection.

Most United States courts rely on the "key man system" of name selection. "Key men" are "good citizens," who suggest the names of other "good citizens" for jury service. Key men are almost invariably middle-class white men, wedded to and dependent upon the local white community, its mores and prejudices. Their recommendations often include "good Negroes." Occasionally, a few Negroes are selected as "key men." But the number of names of Negroes included in Federal jury lists is small, and they are, in almost every instance, subject to peremptory challenge. Often, opposing lawyers simply agree to excuse all Negro jurors called for service. In this way they need not "waste" their peremptory challenges, which are limited in number. But either way, the existence of all-white trial juries is assured.

The effects of jury exclusion are evident. Most white lawyers defending a Negro charged with the commission of a crime against another Negro peremptorily challenge all Negro jurors. They believe that Negro jurors are likely to convict and severely punish Negroes for crimes against Negroes. All-white juries trying Negroes for crimes against other Negroes are more paternalistic and punish less severely. If punishment is a deterrent to crime, then its lack is a breeder of crime. Indeed, certain crimes are beyond the comprehension of many conscientious but prejudiced white Southerners. Often they simply do not believe that Negro women ever withhold consent in sexual encounter. Thus, Negro women are not protected from the crime of rape. Still other white men "know" of the dark ghetto "where everybody goes out and does some cuttin' on Saturday night." They view Negro defendants by the standard of that imagined jungle on the other side of town. Invariably, white juries demand a higher standard of conduct by white citizens in their community than by Negroes in theirs.

But when Negroes attack the white world, the system of justice moves from paternalism to patriotism. It becomes a weapon of white supremacy. For alleged crimes against white women, Negro men are easily indicted, convicted and severely punished. Juries in states that forbid racial intermarriage protect their white southern women. White women are to be believed, but Negro men lie. Even countless petty offenses are sternly punished, as are all crimes of theft or violence. For the system demands that the Negro be kept in his place. There is no corresponding harshness when white men commit crimes against Negroes. And juries are much less than anxious to indict whites for crimes with civil rights implications. When indictments are obtained, acquittals and hung juries are the rule, not the exception.

Steps are being taken to protect Negro criminal defendants. For example, prior to 1959 the Negro criminal defendant in a state court was required to claim all constitutional defenses at the time required by state law. If his lawyer failed to raise a constitutional defense at the right time, it was deemed waived. This rule was altered in *United States ex rel. Goldsby v. Harpole*.[1] Judge Rives stated:

> Conscientious southern lawyers often reason that the prejudicial effects on their client of raising the issue [the systematic exclusion of Negroes from juries] far outweigh any practical protection in the particular case. . . . Such courageous and unselfish lawyers as find it essential for their clients' protection to fight against the systematic exclusion of Negroes from juries sometimes do so at the risk of personal sacrifice which may extend to loss of practice and social ostracism.
>
> As Judges of a Circuit comprising six states of the deep South, we think it our duty to take judicial notice that lawyers residing in many southern jurisdictions rarely, almost to the point of never, raise the issue of systematic exclusion of Negroes from juries.

Thus, the Fifth Circuit recognized a fact known to every southern lawyer. A Negro defendant after conviction in the state court may now raise the jury question in later proceedings in Federal court.

In a more recent case the Fifth Circuit restated this rule. It noted that a Negro criminal defendant who had to choose between the prejudice engendered by an attack on the jury system and the prejudice inherent in an all-white jury was confronted by a "grisly 'Hobson's Choice,'" a choice he cannot constitutionally be forced to make.[2]

In *United States ex rel. Seals v. Wiman*[3] long-standing disproportionate percentages of Negroes and whites on jury rolls, which were unexplained by the state, were held to be sufficient proof of systematic exclusion of Negroes from juries. But this case clearly demonstrates both the difficulty and the expense of proving jury discrimination. The defendant with no community or organizational and financial support is hard-pressed to meet the standard of proof.

Unless new techniques of attack on the jury system are devised and an affirmative effort to select qualified Negroes for jury duty is made, the all-white jury system of the South will continue. Traditional techniques of challenging the jury venire in a particular case have not worked. But affirmative suits by Negroes to have their names included on jury lists are being filed. In a recent decision Judge Rives said, but did not rule:

> Thus it may be that the "general venire list" of three hundred persons is required to reflect a suitable cross-section of the population, and that the jury commissioners have an affirmative duty to include qualified Negroes in that list.[4]

Some state supreme courts are moving to correct state court jury practices. From North Carolina to Mississippi, criminal convictions have been reversed where jury discrimination has been proved. In Georgia, the state court of appeals ruled that a white civil rights worker is entitled to a jury from which Negroes have not been systematically excluded.

The Kraft-Rosenbluth system of jury selection offers the best hope for selection of impartial juries. John F. Kraft, a specialist in public opinion surveys, and Leon Rosenbluth, a consulting statistician, would abolish all subjective standards of juror selection. Obtaining a cross section of the population does not require the use of judgment by a jury commissioner or key man, nor the use of lists with their inherent bias. Federal jurors merely need be twenty-one years of age, able to read, write and understand the English language, and have no convictions for crimes involving penitentiary punishment for more than one year. By the use of racial, population density, sex, economic and other census data, Kraft and Rosenbluth have devised a system for the random selection of jurors' names. Thus, a true cross section of the community can be easily obtained. In a systematized canvass of a county or district, jury commissioners may acquire the names of qualified persons. The expenditure of only 500 man-days is required to select 10,000 names. By the use of sample selection techniques proved adequate in countless surveys and polls, the jury question can be put to rest.

But the utilization of new techniques in the acquisition of jurors' names is not enough. Neither the Civil Rights Act of 1964 nor Federal Civil Service rules apply to state or Federal court employment practices. The inclusion of Negroes in the system of justice will result in changes, obvious and subtle. Just as racial jokes are told more softly—or not at all—when the Negro waiter appears, the words of prejudice implicit in an all-white administration of justice can be contained. More obvious changes will occur as white attorneys associate with Negro attorneys in the practice of law. White lawyers may learn to say "Mr." and "Mrs." to Negroes. "Bloody flag" jury arguments will disappear. White lawyers may speak less as racists, more as lawyers. Newspapers, freed from the threat of libel suits in an all-white system of justice, may write for peaceful racial change. Insurance companies may hire Negro adjusters, and damages may be determined on fact rather than by skin color. Negro crime rates may begin to fall as Negroes move to mete out punishment for crimes committed in the Negro community. Negro criminal defendants in cases with racial overtones may receive fair trials—trials where guilt or innocence is not a secondary consideration.

In many areas the mere possibility of large numbers of Negroes on jury lists may deter the rough and ready soldiers of the new Confederacy. For sooner or later, the law of probabilities says, a random drawing of names from a jury box containing the names of many Negroes will result in an all-Negro jury. "No white jury will ever convict us" may become a dead phrase from a cruel past. And, white and Negro Southerners, no longer afraid, may begin to participate in the changing American society. Perhaps then the Oxfords and Birminghams, the Little Rocks, the Selmas, and all the other nightmares of contemporary America's racial struggle may become mere memories.

G E R A L D   M .   S T E R N

Judge William Harold Cox and the Right to Vote in Clarke County, Mississippi

"They've had us scared so long it's hard to get anybody to register now, but your coming made us see somebody was looking after us a little bit and we appreciate that. As soon as you came I felt better, because I knew you wouldn't have come if you didn't mean business." These are the words of an elderly Negro leader of Clarke County, Mississippi, to an attorney from the Department of Justice. Clarke County is typical of many counties in Mississippi, Alabama, Louisiana and parts of Georgia, where for years Negroes have been refused the right to register to vote on the same basis as white persons. The facts of discrimination seldom vary from county to county. In some, Negroes are denied the right to register outright; in others, more subtle means are used,

Gerald M. Stern is a former attorney with the Civil Rights Division of the Justice Department. He is a 1961 graduate of the Harvard Law School and is currently in private practice in Washington, D.C.

such as tricky questionnaires or selective economic coercion. But the relief they receive in the Federal courts can vary greatly from judge to judge.

One of the first voting discrimination suits brought by the United States involved Clarke County and was filed in the Federal court in the Southern District of Mississippi —the judicial district of Judge William Harold Cox. This is the story of Clarke County and Judge Cox.

Judge Cox was one of President Kennedy's first judicial appointments. He had been highly recommended by the American Bar Association, receiving its highest endorsement of "exceptionally well qualified." However, there are those who say Judge Cox's friendship with Senator James O. Eastland, his law school roommate at Ole Miss, may have influenced President Kennedy.[1] When Cox was appointed in 1961, there were at least 73 new judicial appointments to be cleared by the Senate Judiciary Committee, whose chairman was Senator Eastland.

Judge Cox has earned a reputation as a diligent, methodical lawyer, much like the tortoise in the story of the tortoise and the hare. The *Yale Law Journal* puts it a bit less delicately, referring to him as "leaden footed" in his disposition of civil rights cases. He has been described as "a tall heavy-set stern-faced and humorless man who rules his courtroom with a strong hand and a stronger whim. He doesn't drink or smoke himself, and has seen to it that the walls of his courtroom are plastered with 'No Smoking' signs."[2] At times he can become so furious at the smell of smoke in his library chambers that he will openly chastise anyone who is responsible for it. He rarely smiles.

Clarke County is a small rural county, south of Meridian, Mississippi, next to the Alabama border. There are about 9000 persons in the county of voting age—6000 white persons and 3000 Negroes. Most of the people farm, some haul pulpwood, and a few work at the blue-jean factory in Stonewall. Some raise cattle. Cotton is not much of a crop in this hilly country. High-school graduation day—for those who finish high school—is often their last day in Clarke County. It's the kind of place people leave when they head for the city, for Meridian or Jackson, or maybe even Birmingham or Memphis.

The white political structure of Clarke County did not admit any Negroes to register to vote for at least thirty years. This was the custom of the county—applied without question by the whites, acquiesced to grudgingly by the Negroes. Mississippians have been taught for too long that the Reconstruction days after the Civil War (called the "War for Independence" in Mississippi history books) were the bleakest days in Mississippi history because Negroes had the vote and ran the state. In Clarke County, white people outnumber Negroes two to one. But still the old fears die hard. For many years the few complaints which filtered up from rural Mississippi to the Federal government in Washington, D.C., were followed by a visit and an interview by FBI agents, and no further action from the Department of Justice.

But Congress became aware of what was happening. In 1957 and again in 1960, Civil Rights Bills were passed, authorizing the Department of Justice to initiate suits to secure Negroes the right to vote. The Civil Rights Division was set up primarily to enforce this right. In 1961, President Kennedy appointed Burke Marshall as the head of the division. John Doar, a Republican appointed during the waning days of the Eisenhower administration, stayed on as Mr. Marshall's first assistant, and late in 1964 was named by President Johnson to head the division. Under their direction, attorneys from Washington went South to interview the Negroes who had complained in vain over so many years or had suffered in silence. I was one of these attorneys.

One of the first witnesses interviewed in Clarke County was Sylvester McRee, a 71-year-old plumber, who was a member of the NAACP for 25 years. He told me that the Negro leaders of the county had been trying to register to vote under every registrar for the past thirty years. He said they would try again each time a new registrar would come into office, but they were always turned away. They waited, and prayed that the next registrar would be fair, or that someone would come to lend a hand. He told me, "I'd been reading the '57 and '60 Civil Rights Bills, and I thought you'd soon be coming to find out about us."

On July 6, 1961, the Federal government filed a lawsuit against the registrar of Clarke County, alleging that none of the 3000 Negroes but a substantial majority of the white persons of voting age were registered to vote, that Negroes had been arbitrarily denied the right to register to vote, and that they were not afforded the same opportunities to register as were white persons. On the same day it filed the action, the government filed a motion for discovery asking the court to order the registrar to let us see the public voting records of Clarke County.

Many procedural motions and arguments were immediately made by the attorneys representing the registrar and the state of Mississippi, also a defendant in the case. There were two attorneys from Clarke County and more from the state of Mississippi's Department of Justice. When we saw that we had a long fight on our hands, I returned to see the people who had talked with us and trusted us, and tried to explain that they would have to wait a while longer until we could get a hearing in the Court. I went to strengthen their resolve but soon found it was they who bolstered my spirits. They knew Mississippi better than I did and knew what they were getting into. The months of delay we fought against hardly matched the years of delay they had lived with. One of them told me, "We take your promises with grains of salt gathered from many years of tears." But they never lost faith. And our mere physical presence did lend them courage.

Under the specific provisions of the 1960 Civil Rights Act, the government has the right to inspect public voting records. But Judge Cox refused to let us see them, and it took many months and many appeals before we were permitted to inspect the voting records in Clarke County.

Even without the voting records it would seem that the statistics of Clarke County demonstrate discrimination—almost all the white persons but none of the Negroes were registered to vote, and none of the Negroes in Clarke County had ever heard of a Negro's being permitted to register to vote. Judge Brown of the United States Court of Appeals for the Fifth Circuit has said, "In the problem of racial discrimination, statistics often tell much, and Courts listen."[3] It is true that the Fifth Circuit listens. However, Judge Cox hears such statistics a bit differently. Later in his opinion in the Clarke County case he said, "There are 6000 adult white citizens and 3000 adult non-white citizens in the county as of April 1, 1960, but those statistics have no probative value in this case for the reasons indicated."[4] Of course, the important statistics are not the numbers of whites and Negroes in Clarke County, but the numbers of those whites and Negroes registered to vote.

In another one of the voting suits in Judge Cox's District (in Walthall County, Mississippi), almost all the white persons and none of the Negroes were registered to vote when the suit was filed. Judge Cox's explanation for this fact was that Mississippi Negroes really don't care much about voting, which explains the statistics:

> Such imbalance in registration is occasioned solely by reason of the fact that negroes have not been interested in registering to vote and very few have bothered to apply to register prior to 1957; whereas white people have been intensely interested in voting in elections in that county. No probative value can be ascribed to such statistics because such imbalance in registration is not due in any part to any discrimination between the races.[5]

Our motion to see the voting records was set for a hearing, but first the lawyers for the registrar filed a motion with the court to postpone our hearing and to allow them more time to answer our complaint. With their motion they filed affidavits stating they were heavily burdened with other civil rights cases and did not have time to work on this case—other than to draw up affidavits to state how busy they were.

The hearing was held as scheduled, and five frightened Negroes made the long trip from their rural country homes in Clarke County to the big Federal courtroom in the Post Office Building at Jackson, Mississippi. The trip was about 100 miles, and in the last few years many Negroes have made similar journeys, to trade their stories of the past for a better tomorrow. They come to the Federal courthouse seeking someone or something to end the discrimination they have known.

To some, the Federal courthouse itself is thought of as a sacred spot where they can be free from "the high sheriff, the lawmen, and the boss men." Negroes in Jackson, Mississippi once formed a picket line against discrimination and marched around on the steps of the Federal Post Office, thinking this an oasis of Federal land within the vast Mississippi desert. They were arrested, probably for breach of the peace.

Nor are Negroes who answer Federal subpoenas and testify in the Federal court immune from the vengeance of their white employers. Negro teachers are the most vulnerable, since they are hired and fired by the same white political establishment that refuses to let Negroes register. Negro teachers who try to teach good citizenship to their students have even been threatened or fired for giving testimony to a Federal court about violations of the Constitution of the United States. But Negroes who work for the Post Office or some other Federal agency can speak without fear of losing their jobs. This probably explains why many of the early southern Negro leaders were postmen, as for example, Reverend Robert L. T. Smith in Jackson, Mississippi.

Five Negroes from Clarke County were there in court to tell the judge they had not been allowed to vote because they were black. But they were not allowed to testify. All day, legal arguments were made in Judge Cox's courtroom in front of a beautiful mural depicting white people dispensing justice and running industry and Negro people picking cotton and singing happily along the banks of the Mississippi River.

Judge Cox finally ended this long first day by refusing to have the case proceed until the government amended its complaint to allege the names of all the Negroes ever denied the right to register and the dates on which this happened, and the names of all white applicants treated better than Negro applicants, and the dates on which they were registered. He ordered the government to give Mississippi this information without letting us first see the county voting records that told the complete story and were already in the hands of the registrar.

The first day was over, and we were where we had been when we started. But the five Negroes were out in the open, the troublemakers of the county. I went to see them after they returned home. All had been talked to by at least one white man from the county. One of our potential witnesses had not even come to the hearing. We had been told he was in the hospital, but many months later he felt free to tell me the truth. A white man had been to see him before the hearing to warn him his loan might be called in if he testified. He was also told "them young fellows don't know what they are doing. There ain't no court in the world can make you talk." Torn between his conscience and his home, he apparently decided to fall off his tractor and spend the day of the hearing in the hospital.

The defense, perhaps taking its cue from Judge Cox, immediately filed a motion for a more definite statement of the government's complaint. In October, 1961, we filed an amended complaint listing as many names and dates as we knew, and the defendants replied with a motion to strike parts of our amended complaint as prejudicial to the defendant registrar. They asked again for a more definite statement of our claims.

Time drifted on without a hearing on our motion to see the voting records. In February, 1962, we asked Judge Cox for a ruling on our motion. In March, 1962, we filed a motion for a preliminary injunction. Finally the judge set a hearing for April 2, 1962, on both of these motions. But he postponed the date, after hearing the defendants' motions to strike part of the amended complaint and to make the complaint more definite. The judge listened patiently to the defendants' motions, took them under advisement, and cancelled our April 2 hearing date.

In May we filed another motion with the court, asking for a hearing date for our discovery motion. Judge Cox then overruled the defendants' motions, and on June 30, 1962—

exactly 365 days after we had filed our complaint and asked to see the voting records—the judge gave us a hearing date for our discovery motion.

We had to find white witnesses for this hearing in order to show Judge Cox that white people in Clarke County were treated better than Negroes. So we went to the newspaper office in Clarke County and read through old newspapers to find the names of white people. We checked the county road crews—Negroes never got these patronage jobs—or took names from high-school graduating classes. At least they would be young enough to have registered recently and might remember what they had to do to register. The FBI then interviewed these people and found a few recently registered whites, some of whom were illiterate, and all of whom had registered with no trouble at all. Before the hearing, however, the defendants agreed to let us photograph the voting records in exchange for all our FBI interview statements from the Negro witnesses and white witnesses subpoenaed to testify at the hearing.

We then photographed the records, analyzed them, had the FBI interview other people picked more logically from the registration books of the county, and prepared for trial set for December 17, 1962, in Meridian. All our witnesses appeared to testify, but Judge Cox ruled the government had not fully answered interrogatories served upon it by the defendants and reset the trial for December 26.

The trial lasted three days. The defendant registrar, A. L. Ramsey, is a thin, frail, 82-year-old man. He is friendly and kind, called "Judge" because he had once been a local judge. He was not mean or vicious as are some of the registrars, but was merely trying to do his duty as he saw it and to continue a way of life he had always known.

"Judge" Ramsey had been circuit court clerk, and registrar of voters, since 1953 and registered "practically all" of the white persons now on the registration rolls. He testified it had been the practice from "time immemorial" for white people to register for each other—husbands for wives, parents for children, brothers for sisters, politicians for voters, etc. White people could register by proxy and did not have to take any test. Indeed, they did not even have to go to town to sign the registration book. An FBI handwriting expert testified there were 1500 instances where groups of two or more signatures on the registration book were written by one person—in one case one person had registered for fourteen different people. Since there were only about 5000 white persons registered in the county, the testimony of the FBI expert alone proved that at least 30 per cent of the white people had registered by proxy, without taking any kind of test.

Ramsey testified about the treatment given Negroes during this period:

Q. What did you tell Negroes when they came in to apply to you for registration?
A. What do you mean, when they would come in two or three at the time, or three or four, or one or two?
Q. Yes.
A. Well, during that time, that was when we were having a lot of trouble over the country, especially in Little Rock, and at that time Mississippi wasn't having any trouble, and whenever they would come in, when they walked in I would ask them what I could do for them and they would tell me they wanted to vote—I mean, they wanted to register—so I would always just tell them that I wasn't going to refuse them the opportunity to register but then I would just like for us to consider this matter, that due to the fact that they were having trouble in other parts of the country and that we folks here in Mississippi, white and colored, were getting along together and they were our friends and we were their friends and we weren't going to have any trouble either way, and then I just suggested to them that they go back home and consider this matter and think it over and come back later.

* * *

Q. And when they would come back what did you tell them?
A. Well, most of the time that trouble was still brewing and I would still have a little talk with them about it, and ask them to still consider.

* * *

Q. When did you decide that you were finally going to let Negroes register without telling them that they should go home and think about it?

A. Well, after all of this litigation come up and these cases were being filed in different parts of the country.

Q. This case was filed in July, 1961. Was it after that date?

A. Well, it was around that date, yes.[6]

These Negroes Ramsey was sending home were the leaders of the county. They were old and respected, not young outside agitators stirring up trouble. But that made no difference. Six of these witnesses tell the story of Clarke County.

Samuel Owens is 79 years old. He has been the principal of the Negro school in Clarke County for the past 55 years. When the county decided to comply with the Supreme Court decision declaring separate but equal schools unconstitutional by building a separate and equal school for the Negroes, they named the school after Samuel Owens. Once, more than 40 years ago, he had been registered to vote, but when he went to vote he was told that Clarke County's primary was for white Democrats only. Soon thereafter the county had a reregistration and his name was scratched from the rolls.

The last reregistration in Clarke County was begun in 1953, about the time Ramsey became registrar. Owens tried to register twice in 1958, but both times Ramsey refused to permit him to apply. He tried again around April 18, 1961, at about the time the FBI was in Clarke County checking on complaints about voting discrimination. Ramsey told him he was out of application forms and could not register him. Later the registrar testified he did have some forms that day but did not find them until after Owens left. Whether or not Ramsey actually had forms that day is not important. The point is that almost all white persons in the county registered without forms, even white persons who applied after Owens. But Ramsey refused to let Owens, whom he knew to be qualified, register without a form. Owens tried again. He was told by the deputy clerk that he would have to see Ramsey in order to apply, though for eight years the woman deputy clerk had registered white people pursuant to Ramsey's permission.

Owens tried again, and on June 1, 1961, a month before we filed our lawsuit, he became the first Negro given the chance to make an application for registration since Ramsey took office. But getting the application form is only the first rung of the ladder. Filling out an application form is no simple matter in Mississippi. An applicant has to answer 17 questions giving information about himself, filling in the right lines and checking the right places. Then he must interpret one of the 265 sections of the Mississippi constitution selected by the registrar. And finally, the applicant must write a statement setting forth his understanding of the duties and obligations of citizenship under a constitutional form of government. There are no standard, correct answers. The interpretation and statement must be acceptable to the registrar, according to his whim.

Ramsey gave Owens an application form and required him to interpret Section 112 of the Mississippi constitution, a long and difficult section dealing with taxation by the legislature:

> *Section 112.* Taxation shall be uniform and equal throughout the state. Property shall be taxed in proportion to its value. The legislature may, however, impose a tax per capita upon such domestic animals as from their nature and habits are destructive of other property. Property shall be assessed for taxes under general laws, and by uniform rules, according to its true value. But the legislature may provide for a special mode of valuation and assessment for railroads, and railroad and other corporate property, or for particular species of property belonging to persons, corporations or associations not situated wholly in one county. But all such property shall be assessed at its true value, and no county shall be denied the right to levy county and special taxes upon such assessment as in other cases of property situated and assessed in the county.

I asked Ramsey about this:

Q. Mr. Owens was given Section 112.
A. I know.

Q. That's pretty long, isn't it?
A. He's an intelligent man.
Q. So you gave him a bigger one?
A. He is capable.
Q. You knew he was capable of passing it?
A. Yes, sir.

* * *

Q. Is Section 112 a difficult section?
A. Not too much.
Q. Is it a long section?
A. It is, fairly long.
Q. Fairly long?
A. Yes, sir.
BY JUDGE COX: The Supreme Court of Mississippi has had considerable difficulty with it.[7]

After completing the form, interpreting Section 112, and writing a statement of the duties and obligations of citizenship, Owens was told he would be notified if he passed, though Ramsey admitted Owen's form looked "O.K." In fact, Owens's interpretation of Section 112 was so good that it was apparently copied verbatim by two white applicants who registered a year later.*

Owens was not registered the day he completed the form. Only nine white applicants had been required to fill out forms before Owens. These nine were permitted to register the same day they filled out their forms. The next four white applicants who received forms after Owens was given a form were all registered by Ramsey on the same day they completed their forms. In fact, until September 12, 1961, all white applicants were registered the same day they applied. But Owens had to come back again—the fifth time in 1961—the seventh time since 1958, before he became the first Negro registered to vote in Clarke County in at least thirty years.

Sylvester McRee is 71 years old. He is a retired plumber. He's been a member of the NAACP for 25 years and, for part of that time, president of the small Clarke County branch.

---

* See the three interpretations on p. 183.

He had tried to register with each registrar in office for the past thirty years, except for one registrar who only held office for about nine months. Each registrar, including Ramsey, had refused to permit McRee to apply for registration. I will always remember my talks with him. He would lean back in his cane chair, puff on his pipe, smile a bit and tell me he'd been reading the papers and seeing on television that things were changing a bit elsewhere, and he knew it wouldn't be long before things eased a bit in Clarke County. He'd received many threats; bricks had been thrown at his house from cars speeding by on his dusty road, and many a night he sat up with a shotgun in his lap to protect his wife and home from rumored harm.

George Cotton is 53 years old. He owns his own farm and is president of a Negro Benevolent Insurance Association, which collects money to ensure that Negroes get a proper burial. He had only a fourth-grade education, but the white people and Negroes know him to be a very intelligent businessman and farmer. He'd been scared off from an earlier hearing in this case but came to the trial "because I wanted to tell the truth." He testified that Ramsey would not let him register. He later told me, "I knew the government would back me up and prosecute the men who would do something to me." After the trial he finally talked freely with me as we laughed over my efforts to win his confidence. I had once subpoenaed him to come to a second hearing after he had allegedly fallen from his tractor and missed our first hearing. He said he'd try and come. I looked him in the eye as we sat on his porch, grinned a bit, and told him I really wanted him to come. He put his hands in the pockets of his overalls, looked my way, and said "I'll try and be there." I finally told him, "Mr. Cotton. Let me read this subpoena to you. It says 'You are hereby commanded to appear'— It doesn't say please." He laughed—and came. He now told me, "I didn't feel I could trust you at first, but about the second time after you gave me that subpoena I knew I could rely on you. It made me feel better each time you came by."

George Haynes is 53 years old. He is a high-school graduate and an Army veteran with 4 years and 3 months of service. He is another one of the Negroes "sent home" by "Judge" Ramsey when he went in to register to vote.

The other two Negro witnesses Ramsey refused to register were Andrew Kendrick, Jr., and Reverend W. G. Goff. Andrew Kendrick is 57 years old. He has been a janitor at the blue-jean factory in Stonewall, Mississippi, for 41 of his 57 years. He is one of the few Negroes in the county with a steady job, and though the pay is minimal he was able to educate all his children, who are now school teachers, one in Clarke County, one in Meridian, and one in Chicago. He reads the paper every night, is well liked at the plant, and is a very religious gentleman. He always invited me to stay for dinner or have some coffee and cake before I'd go back on the dusty roads to interview other witnesses. Always a cheerful man, he never grumbled. He once told me not to worry about the delays and frustrations we were facing, and said, "I don't care when I get registered to vote as long as it is time enough to vote for President Kennedy in 1964."

Reverend Goff is 47 years old. He is a farmer, builder and minister. He had two years of college in addition to ministerial training. I would usually find him working on someone's house, as the Negro neighbors took turns building each other new houses. He has received his share of threats, and on one occasion his house was fired into by persons driving by on the highway. But no one was hit by the shotgun blast or the broken glass that shattered into the living room.

These witnesses and others testified to their many attempts to register. There was also testimony about the names of five Negroes that mysteriously appeared on the registration books of the county in early 1961. These five Negroes told the court they did not know their names were on the registration books. They did know they had been called for jury duty in 1961, when there was a case against a Negro who killed a deputy in Clarke County. Since jurors are chosen from the registration rolls and since no Negroes were registered to vote, this seemed a bit unusual. Negroes had never been called for jury duty before in Clarke County. Even more unusual was the mathematical coincidence of it all. Jury panels are chosen by taking 200 names from the registration rolls. Surprisingly, the only five Negroes on the registration rolls were included in this list of 200 names. The panel is then picked at random from these 200, and though you might not have thought it possible, all five were drawn to be on the panel actually called for jury duty. They showed up at the courthouse, but there was no trial. Tally Riddell, the lawyer defending "Judge" Ramsey in this voting case, was also the lawyer appointed to defend the Negro, and as Riddell explains it, no trial was necessary because his client decided to plead guilty. Had he chosen to stand trial, the county wanted to make sure that any jury verdict returned against him would not be reversed by the Supreme Court. Ramsey explained the problems facing the county and their neat solution:

> After the murder of a white man by a colored man, we didn't expect any trouble but in case something did show up, why, we wanted to be prepared for it to avoid any controversy or any trouble between anyone, because there had been so many places where they had all-white juries and they had some controversy over it and there was always some trouble about it.[8]

The relevance of this sham is that "Judge" Ramsey and the county officials knew they had been systematically excluding Negroes from the registration rolls, and thus from the jury rolls. This meant that any conviction of a Negro could be reversed as unconstitutional. However, rather than solve the problem by permitting Negroes to register and vote, they secretly placed five Negroes on the registration books. It is doubtful whether the Negroes would have actually served on the jury, since they certainly would have been challenged by the prosecutor.

However, the sham was all wasted effort. Any conviction that would have resulted after such a packing of the jury panel would still have been reversible[9] if the Negro defendant would have known to ask for an appeal. I imagine the county was pleased when the defendant pleaded guilty.

After the voting trial was over and both sides had filed

briefs, Judge Cox made his findings. He found that at least 1500 white persons had been illegally registered to vote, but he found that the registrar also illegally registered Negroes. For this astounding conclusion, Judge Cox cited the example of the five Negroes placed on the rolls for jury service. This evidence which seemed to prove conclusively that the registrar knew that Negroes had systematically been denied the right to register was used to show that they were given the same opportunities that whites received. Judge Cox said of this evidence:

> It was shown that some negroes were registered on the registration books of this county who did not apply for registration according to law; that they were needed for jury service in 1961 by the Circuit Court in a criminal case and some of them were subsequently stricken from the rolls presumably by the election commissioners. The registrar knew little about this important fact.[10]

Of course, the important fact was not whether they were taken off the rolls, but why the registrar felt he had to put them on the rolls in the first place.

Judge Cox also found that "several white citizens appeared before the Court who were registered to vote but who could neither read nor write. Amazingly, one of them said that he had a ninth-grade education but was substantially illiterate."[11]

At least half of the white witnesses could not read or write and yet had been registered to vote. Judge Cox solved this problem by ordering that the registrar not register any more illiterates, white or Negro. Judge Cox then ruled that the registrar must apply the tough Mississippi voting laws requiring applicants to interpret any section of the Mississippi constitution. However, in order to be fair, the registrar was ordered to place the first fifty sections in a jar and have each applicant draw out a section.

Almost all the white people in the county and almost none of the Negroes were now registered to vote. Requiring the registrar to use the interpretation test would keep the illiterate whites on the rolls and the literate Negroes who are unable to interpret the Mississippi constitution off the rolls.[12]

Judge Cox did find that there had been discrimination against Negroes seeking to register in Clarke County. But the key to the Federal voting referee provisions is a finding that Negroes have been denied the right to register to vote pursuant to a "pattern or practice of discrimination." We asked Judge Cox to find that such a pattern existed in Clarke County. The evidence showed no Negro had been registered in thirty years until a week before our case was filed; the registrar admitted telling Negroes to go home when they came in to register; he told them to go home again when they returned; the most respected Negro in the county, the school principal, had to go to the registrar's office seven times and interpret a section of the constitution that even the Mississippi supreme court has trouble with; white people did not have to take tests or even go to the registrar's office to take the trouble of signing their names in the registration books; and white people were registered even if they could not read or write. Judge Cox found there was no pattern or practice of discrimination.

The U.S. Court of Appeals reversed Judge Cox on appeal and said his finding that there had been no pattern or practice of discrimination was "clearly erroneous."[13]

When the case was sent back to Judge Cox, he still refused to find a pattern or practice of discrimination. To avoid the opinion of the Court of Appeals, he withdrew his finding that there had been *no* pattern or practice and decided in his discretion not to decide whether or not there had been a pattern or practice. The case is again on appeal.

After the Clarke County trial, "Judge" Ramsey and the local county officials apparently decided to be fair. Most of the Negro witnesses at the trial had been registered to vote before Judge Cox's opinion came out. I went around to see the people I had visited so often before, and was told: "Well it's like heaven around here. The politicians have been around putting gravel on our dirt roads and asking us to vote for them."

But fear keeps many Negroes from trying to register. Most of the school teachers in Clarke County are afraid to try. And Judge Cox's reaction during the trial to the testimony of Andrew Kendrick, Jr., and Reverend W. G. Goff has had its effect on Negroes in Clarke County. The headline in the Meridian paper the last day of the trial was: "PERJURY CHARGE FACES NEGROES IN CLARKE COUNTY VOTER CASE—Judge Says He Thinks Minister, One Other 'Lied' Against Ramsey."

Kendrick and Goff had testified that they were working at the blue-jean factory in Stonewall one day about seven years ago when they noticed that "Judge" Ramsey had set up a table under a tree across from the plant and was registering voters. They had been thinking about once again trying to register to vote, so they went home after work, changed into clean clothes and went back to Stonewall to try to register. They testified they went up to Ramsey and asked to register to vote, but he told them he could not register them and turned them away. They testified that they saw the registrar registering white persons that day, and that they saw B. Floyd Jones sign the registration book. Ramsey testified that he was registering white people that day, that Jones was there, and that he shook hands with Jones. But Ramsey and Jones also testified that Jones had already registered the year before and did not sign the registration book that day.

Judge Cox exploded at the mistake made by the witnesses as to what had happened seven years ago, even though there was no dispute about the material facts that whites were registered that day and Negroes were not, and that Jones was one of the white persons there that day. Judge Cox said from the bench:

> I want to hear from the Government about why this court shouldn't require this Negro, Rev. W. G. Goff and his companion Kendrick to show cause why they shouldn't be bound over to await the action of a grand jury for perjury . . . I think they ought to be put under about a $3000 bond each to await the action of a grand jury. Unless I change my mind, that is going to be the order.
>
> *   *   *
>
> I just want these Negroes to know that they can't come into this Court and swear to something as important as that

was and is and get away with it. . . . These two witnesses are completely discredited as far as I am concerned. . . . I think they are fit subjects for the penitentiary.[14]

Compare this episode with the following, which happened during the Clarke County trial when I asked a white witness to explain how his interpretation and that of another white person who applied on the same day happened to be verbatim copies of the interpretation given by Samuel Owens a year before they applied. These three interpretations of Section 112 of the Mississippi constitution are as follows:

Samuel Owens—Negro—June 1, 1961

In fairness to all citizens of the State taxes leveed shall be the same. However, all property shall be assessed and tax collected, according to the value thereof. The legislature may impose a tax to be paid by the owner of any animal that may be destructive to other property.

General state laws provide for the uniform rules by which property may be assessed according to its true value. The legislature, by law, may provide in a special manner for valuation and assessment of property belonging to railroads and other persons or corporations etc not situated wholly in one county. Yet all such property shall be assessed at its true value. Each county has the right to levy and collect taxes in cases where property is situated in the county.

Willard Roberts—White—June 9, 1962

In fairness to all citizens of the State taxes leveed shall be the same. However, all property shall be assessed and tax colected [sic] according to the value thereof. The Lesagter [sic] may impose a tax to be payed accountant of [sic] any animal that may be destructive to other property.

Earnest Harold Turner—White—June 9, 1962

In fairness to all citizens of the state, taxes leveed shall be the same. However, all property shall be assessed and tax collected according to the value thereof. The legislature may impose a tax to be paid by the owner of any animal that may be destructive to other property.

Willard Roberts's explanation of this coincidence was: "I couldn't tell, I mean I don't know." At this point Judge Cox interjected:

This witness in following this procedure, is not enlighten-
ing me at all about what he knows about this case and that
is all I am interested in, Mr. Stern. If you've got some applications that have got the same things on them I don't
believe this witness could possibly enlighten me about that.
You may make whatever observation in argument you may
wish to make about it but I wouldn't assume it would be
very fruitful to ask this witness about something he couldn't
possibly know about.[15]

Following the Clarke County trial, the Federal Bureau
of Investigation investigated the possible perjury violations
against Goff and Kendrick. After this investigation, the
Criminal Division of the Justice Department advised Judge
Cox that the matter presented no basis for any prosecution.

The judge still felt the matter was one for the grand jury
and told the Justice Department he would be inclined to
appoint a special prosecutor to present the matter to the
grand jury. The Justice Department concluded Judge Cox
had no authority to appoint a special prosecutor, and as the
judge persisted, the then Deputy Attorney General, Nicholas
Katzenbach, flew to Jackson to explain the department's
position. Judge Cox finally decided not to instruct the
Federal grand jury concerning the perjury charge.

However, the next month Goff and Kendrick were indicted by a state grand jury and arrested on charges of lying
to a Federal court. The state's prosecution was based on
affidavits filed by Tally Riddell, the attorney who had represented the Clarke County registrar.

The Justice Department then filed a suit in Federal court
to enjoin the state prosecution on the ground that the state
has no authority to prosecute for perjury in a Federal
court. Judge Sidney Mize, the other Federal district judge
in Judge Cox's district, granted the injunction, thereby
stopping the state prosecution.

In October, 1964, a Federal grand jury met to hear testimony involving alleged violations of civil rights of Negroes
in Neshoba County, Philadelphia, Mississippi. This grand
jury returned indictments against Sheriff Rainey and Deputy
Price and others of Neshoba County for beating and forcing

confessions from Negroes in Neshoba County. At the end of the grand jury proceedings the foreman of the jury told the government attorney that Judge Cox, who was then away on vacation, had asked the foreman to hear a couple of witnesses on matters unrelated to the Neshoba County matters. One of these witnesses was Tally Riddell. Since Judge Cox was away, the grand jury decided to adjourn until he returned.

When Judge Cox returned, Acting Attorney General Katzenbach again told him of the Department of Justice's position, but the judge said Tally Riddell would probably go ahead and appear before the grand jury. Katzenbach then instructed the United States Attorney, Robert Hauberg, of Jackson, Mississippi, that the cases against Goff and Kendrick (and some other cases that another witness was going to present to the grand jury) should not be prosecuted and that the U.S. Attorney should not prepare or sign any indictments which the grand jury might vote.

Judge Cox ordered the U.S. Attorney to disregard the Acting Attorney General's instructions and, when Hauberg refused, the judge ordered him held in contempt of court. He also ordered Katzenbach to show cause why he should not be held in contempt of court. Judge Cox then allowed the government five days to appeal to the court of appeals, which immediately enjoined his contempt orders until the case could be heard on the merits. On January 26, 1965, the court of appeals reversed Judge Cox's contempt order.

There were about seventy Negroes registered to vote in Clarke County, at last count, three-and-a-half years after the government filed its suit. Many others are afraid to try, and many feel they can't interpret the constitution of Mississippi. Judge Cox's order requires each new applicant to draw one of the first fifty sections of the Mississippi constitution out of a jar and give an interpretation of it. In Panola County in the Northern District of Mississippi, Federal District Judge Claude Clayton entered a strong injunction against the local registrar after being reversed by the court of appeals. As a result, over 1600 Negroes are now registered to vote, although there were only two registered Negroes when the suit was filed. Judge Clayton's order in Panola County provides that new applicants do not have to interpret the constitution to register to vote, since white people were not required to do so in the past. When the government brought suit in Bullock County, Alabama, a rural county like Clarke, there were only one or two Negroes registered to vote. After a strong injunction from District Judge Frank Johnson, over 1000 Negroes were registered to vote. In Macon County, Alabama, Judge Johnson enjoined the board of registrars from discriminating against Negro applicants, and now the Negro voters outnumber white voters. (This is one of the few counties in the South where it happened— Macon County is the home of the famous Tuskegee Institute.) In the last election six Negroes were elected as county officials. There are other places throughout the South where Negroes are now being registered to vote—some with the help of court orders, others after negotiations with the local officials.

Now there will be a new voting rights law to expedite the registration of Negro voters. In his testimony before the Senate Judiciary Committee in support of the new voting rights bill, Attorney General Katzenbach cited the Clarke County case as an example of the delays and frustrations the government has met under the prior Civil Rights Acts. It appears that Judge Cox will no longer be the judge of Clarke County's future.

L E O N   F R I E D M A N

The Federal Courts of the South: Judge Bryan Simpson and His Reluctant Brethren

═══════
═══════

There is no more important figure in the civil rights move-ment than a Federal district court judge. As a practical matter, he is the most immediate interpreter and enforcer of Federal law. Since most of the claims of Negroes against the authorities of the southern states are based on violations of their constitutional and Federal rights—in terms of voting restrictions, segregated schools, discriminatory treatment in public accommodations or other public facilities—a Federal district court judge has the power to correct a wide range of discriminations and abuses. More important, he can act swiftly and effectively to protect the constitutional rights of those bringing suit, in a matter of days if he chooses.

The actual performance of some southern district court judges in civil rights cases has been astonishingly bad. A national magazine recently noted such judges may be "the

The editor of *Southern Justice*, Leon Friedman is a 1960 graduate of the Harvard Law School. He is an attorney in New York.

greatest obstacle to equal rights in the South today."[1] A number of them—although by no means a majority—have again and again ignored ruling precedents of their superior courts which are squarely in point, and have denied Negro plaintiffs the rights to which they are clearly entitled. On being reversed, some have "misinterpreted" the opinion of the appeal courts and entered orders directly at odds with a decision they are obligated to enforce, producing another fruitless round of appeal and remand. Through their control of their court calendars, they have delayed hearing motions or cases for months and, after trial, have refused to decide cases for even longer periods, depriving Negro plaintiffs of even the opportunity to appeal an adverse decision to a higher court. Some have engaged in open warfare with the Justice Department in civil rights suits brought by the government.

Judge William Harold Cox (a Kennedy appointee in Mississippi), for example, has consistently opposed the government's voter registration suits. He has actually written to voter registrars, criticizing the Justice Department for bringing such actions.[2] In one case he refused all the government's requests to order a Mississippi registrar to produce voting records (which were necessary for successful prosecution of the case), although such records are ordinarily made available to the government without question.[3] In another case he found that while some discrimination existed, there was no "pattern or practice of discrimination" in registering voters in Clarke County, Mississippi, despite the fact that of the 3000 voting-age Negroes in the county, only three were registered to vote at the time of trial.[4] Judge Cox ordered a United States Attorney to jail for refusing to prepare indictments for perjury ordered by a "run-away" grand jury, because he believed two Negro witnesses were lying when they testified before him.[5] He issued an injunction against CORE, restraining it from encouraging Negroes to use the McComb, Mississippi, bus terminal, on the grounds that the publicizing of its intent to desegregate the terminal was for the purpose of "provoking the tempers of the community . . . and to taunt and tantalize the community."[6] He also refused to stop Mississippi's prosecution of John Hardy, unlawfully arrested during a voter registration drive in Walthall County, Mississippi, where no Negroes were registered to vote among the 2490 of voting age.[7] In every one of these cases, his decision was reversed on appeal. He once remarked that a group of Negroes in a case before him were "chimpanzees," who "ought to be in the movies rather than being registered to vote."[8]

Judge Sidney C. Mize*—Judge Cox's fellow judge in the Southern District of Mississippi (appointed by President Roosevelt in 1937)—twice dismissed a suit to desegregate the schools in Jackson and Biloxi, Mississippi. He did so first on the ground that the Negro pupils had not applied for assignment to a white school, even though this excuse had been rejected as insufficient numerous times by the Fifth Circuit Court of Appeals.[9] When he was reversed on this point, he again refused to order desegregation, stating that "the learning traits which are characteristic of Negro children do differ to an educationally significant degree from those which are typical of white pupils; . . . [and] differences between Caucasians and Negroes are genetically determined and cannot be changed materially by environment. . . ."[10] He also refused to enjoin the placing of signs by city officials in the Jackson bus terminal—which read "Waiting Room for White," "Waiting Room for Colored"—since such signs only encouraged "voluntary segregation" and were a "valid exercise of the police power of the State."[11] Judge Mize successfully delayed James Meredith's admission to the University of Mississippi from May 1961 until September 1962, by a series of questionable procedural moves that the court of appeals—in typical judicial understatement—later characterized as "of doubtful propriety."[12] In the process he completely disregarded direct orders from his superior court.[13]

The third Federal judge in Mississippi, Judge Claude F. Clayton (appointed by President Eisenhower in 1957), whom civil rights lawyers consider an eminently fair judge in comparison to Judges Cox and Mize, nevertheless joined

---

* Judge Mize died on April 25, 1965.

with Judge Mize to abstain from passing on the constitutionality of Mississippi laws requiring segregation on common carriers and passenger terminals within the state, and
remanded the case to the state courts to determine "the full
meaning of their respective statutes."[14] This decision was
reversed unanimously by the Supreme Court, with the statement that the question of the constitutionality of laws providing for segregated transportation facilities was "foreclosed
as a litigable issue" and that the issues raised by the state
of Mississippi were "wholly insubstantial, legally speaking
non-existent."[15] Although the illegality of segregated bus
terminals was clearly established many years before, Mississippi's Federal judges effectively delayed a specific order
desegregating the Jackson terminal by these and other devices from June, 1961, until September, 1963, two-and-one-
half years after the Freedom Riders first came to Jackson.[16]

In Alabama, Judge Seybourn H. Lynne (appointed by
President Truman in 1946) dismissed a complaint requesting desegregation of the Birmingham railroad station, since
the "dispute [was] of a hypothetical or abstract character."[17]
He refused to desegregate the Birmingham school system
until the "good faith" of the school authorities to desegregate
voluntarily had been tested.[18]

Judge Daniel Holcombe Thomas (a Truman appointee in
1951) of Mobile, Alabama, sat on a motion to desegregate
the municipal golf course for fourteen months before he
found an "opportune" time to issue an appropriate order.
He defended his delay by saying it was necessary to avoid
"unfortunate incidents."[19] The Fifth Circuit, however,
thought that his delays in ordering school desegregation in
Mobile could not be justified, and twice ordered him to speed
up implementation of a desegregation plan.[20] During the
Selma, Alabama voting drive in 1965, he refused to order
the Dallas County voting registrars to open their office
more than two days per month or to process more than 100
Negroes each day the office was open.

Judge Harlan Hobart Grooms (appointed by President
Eisenhower in 1953 to the district court in Alabama) joined
with Judge Lynne and Judge Gewin of the Circuit Court to

declare the public accommodations section (Title II) of the Civil Rights Act of 1964 unconstitutional. The judges claimed that if Congress had "the naked power to do what is attempted in title II of this act, there is no facet of human behavior which it may not control . . . and rights of the individual to liberty and property are in dire peril."[21] The Supreme Court unanimously reversed their decision.

In Louisiana two of President Kennedy's district court appointees, Judges E. Gordon West and Frank B. Ellis, held it was proper for Louisiana to compel disclosure of a candidate's race on the ballot in an election.[22] The Supreme Court reversed unanimously on appeal. Judge West called the Supreme Court's original school desegregation case "one of the truly regrettable decisions of all time" and said that the "trouble" resulting "from that decision . . . has been brought about . . . by the agitation of outsiders."[23] When the government moved to have the voting registrar of East Feliciana Parish open his office—which had been closed to all applicants for six months—Judge West, in a "doublethink" decision reminiscent of *1984*, refused to do so on the grounds that the Louisiana state laws establishing voter qualifications had been found unconstitutional by a three-judge Federal court and the registrar therefore had no "usable criteria" to apply.[24] In point of fact the decision of the three-judge court—in which Judge West cast a dissenting vote—had enjoined the registrars in 21 counties from further discriminatory use of specific voter qualification requirements and compelled the registrars to open their rolls to everyone who *otherwise* qualified.[25] Judge Ellis, although certainly not of Judge West's caliber, still showed great solicitude for problems of "overcrowding," in the New Orleans schools and refused immediate implementation of a desegregation plan.[26]

In Georgia, Judge J. Robert Elliott (appointed by President Kennedy in 1962) delayed decisions in two cases arising out of the Albany civil rights movement until nine months after a hearing had been held, and his decisions were thereafter reversed by the Fifth Circuit.[27] He thought it proper for the state of Georgia to hold four civil rights workers without bail on capital charges of "syndicalism" arising out of their activities in Americus, Georgia.[28] Before he was appointed to the bench, he had defended rural domination of Georgia politics, saying "I don't want these pinks, radicals and black voters to outvote those who are trying to preserve our segregation laws and other traditions."[29]

Judge Frank M. Scarlett of Savannah, Georgia (appointed in 1946 by President Truman) in a school desegregation case found that there were significant differences between white and Negro students in learning capabilities, ". . . that these differences . . . [are] attributable in large part to hereditary factors, predictably resulting from a difference in the physiological and psychological characteristics of the two races . . . [and] must be dealt with . . . as an unchangeable factor. . . ."[30] He further found that "patterns of racial preference are formed and firmly established at a pre-school age . . ." and integration would produce "inter-group tensions and conflicts . . ." which would impair the educational process.[31] Even if some superior Negro children could keep up with whites at first, they "would be inescapably conscious of total social rejection" and inevitably "tend to fall further back."[32] His decision against integrating Savannah's schools was unanimously reversed on appeal.

Some judges have resisted the pressures in their home states and have followed their duty to uphold the Constitution as interpreted by their superior courts. Judges Frank A. Hooper (appointed by Truman in 1949) and Lewis R. Morgan (a Kennedy appointee) upheld the Civil Rights Act in its first court test in Atlanta, Georgia.[33] Judge Frank M. Johnson (appointed by President Eisenhower in 1955) ordered extensive and immediate desegregation of schools in Alabama, without being pushed every inch of the way by the Fifth Circuit,[34] and Judge Johnson enjoined the Ku Klux Klan from interfering with the Freedom Riders' trip through Alabama in 1961.[35] He dissolved Governor Wallace's ban on the Reverend Martin Luther King's 50-mile march from Selma to Montgomery in March, 1965, and ordered Alabama officials to give the marchers adequate police protection. Judges Herbert W. Christenberry and Benjamin C.

Dawkins of Louisiana (appointed by Truman and Eisenhower, respectively) have consistently upheld the government's voter registration suits.[36]

But this is one district court judge who has excelled all others in his speed in enforcing the law and in his willingness to embark on new legal territory to protect Negro rights. He is Judge Bryan Simpson, chief judge of the United States District Court for the Middle District of Florida, sitting in Jacksonville.

Judge Simpson is a handsome, aristocratic white-haired southern gentleman, with a personal charm and friendliness that never interfere with his decisiveness and quick intellect in the courtroom. A descendant of an old and wealthy Florida family, he attended Florida schools, and worked as a Jacksonville lawyer before he was elected a Florida criminal court judge and then a circuit judge. Harry Truman appointed him to the Federal bench in 1950. The bar knew him as a competent, hard-working judge, seldom reversed by the court of appeals.

The civil rights struggle which Judge Simpson passed upon took place in St. Augustine, the oldest city in the United States. It began in 1962, when Dr. Robert B. Hayling formed an NAACP Youth Council in the city. Dr. Hayling, a dentist and former Air Force lieutenant, went to St. Augustine from Tallahassee in 1960 and soon decided something had to be done about St. Augustine's segregated schools, restaurants, hotels and beaches. Sheriff L. O. Davis of St. Johns County, the chief law enforcement officer in St. Augustine, easily suppressed a number of sit-ins and demonstrations Hayling organized in 1962 and 1963, under a Florida law making any undesirable patron of a restaurant an "uninvited guest" and a trespasser.[37] Like so many other southern sheriffs, Davis weighs over 250 pounds and is extremely popular in the county for his vigorous opposition to civil rights. As ingratiating and gentle as a complacent bull, Davis sees St. Johns County as his private domain and resents any interference, even from the governor, into local law enforcement.

In September, 1963, Dr. Hayling and three of his associates wandered too close to a Ku Klux Klan meeting in St. Augustine and were brutally beaten by robed Klansmen. In keeping with the peculiar form of justice in force in St. Johns County, it was Dr. Hayling who was arrested for assault. Soon after, Hayling instituted a suit in Federal court in 1963 against Sheriff Davis and other officials in St. Augustine, alleging that their interference with civil rights demonstrations was a violation of the Constitution. Federal Judge William A. McCrae of Jacksonville dismissed the action with the following words:

> Plaintiffs [the Negroes who brought suit] did not come into court with clean hands. Their leadership and particularly Robert B. Hayling have displayed a lack of restraint, common sense, and good judgment, and an irresponsibility which have done a disservice to the advancement of the best interests of all the plaintiffs and others in St. Augustine who are similarly situated. Problems which might well have been solved by intelligent action have been handled with deliberate provocation and apparent intent to incite disorder and confusion.[38]

Having lost in the courts, Dr. Hayling went back into the streets. The violence grew in St. Augustine and reached a peak when a Klansman was shot through the head and killed during an armed raid through the Negro quarter. A few months later Dr. Hayling sought help from the Southern Christian Leadership Conference, headed by Reverend Martin Luther King. The immediate result of the S.C.L.C.'s entrance into St. Augustine was a full scale sit-in during the spring of 1964. Mrs. Malcolm Peabody, mother of the Massachusetts governor, was one of a large group of white and Negro civil rights workers who attempted a massive sit-in of St. Augustine's restaurants and motels. Hundreds of those workers—including Mrs. Peabody—were arrested.

To meet the spring emergency, Sheriff Davis deputized a large number of special deputies, including one Holsted Richard Manucy—"Hoss" Manucy—who was to figure prominently in the events of the summer of 1964. Manucy, a longstanding friend of Sheriff Davis, weighs about 220 pounds, drives around St. Augustine wearing a battered black cowboy hat—his trademark—and keeps a loaded gun on the front seat of his car. He was once convicted of running an illicit whiskey still in St. Johns County. Manucy is the head of the Ancient City Hunting Club (also called the Ancient City Gun Club), composed of a large number of hard-core segregationists. One of its functions is to provide bail for whites arrested during racial demonstrations. Many of the members have citizen-band two-way radios which they used to call for assistance whenever Negroes tried to "test" motels and restaurants or use local beaches. Reinforcements were quick in coming and Negroes were immediately threatened, harassed or beaten. The police, who had much more efficient radio communication, had, oddly enough, nowhere near the speed of "Manucy raiders" in responding to calls of help from Negroes under attack. Even though a contingent of the club marched in a large Ku Klux Klan demonstration in a neighboring county in 1963, Manucy claimed that he himself does not belong to the Klan (since he is a Catholic), but no one has any doubt of the club's sympathy with Klan objectives.

The spring demonstrations produced much publicity but no important changes. The rest of the country may have been shocked at the conflict that existed in what everyone believed was a sleepy tourist town, but the demonstrations had little impact on segregation in St. Augustine. A few of the restaurants that integrated had their windows broken and quickly reverted to their former policy. Others closed down altogether.

Late in May, 1964, a series of marches began again. Large numbers of Negroes and S.C.L.C. staff workers marched through the narrow streets from the Negro churches to the famous slave market in the center of town. Once they arrived there, the leaders would speak to the assembled group and then all returned to the Negro quarter.

The participants had been carefully instructed in nonviolence before the marches. "No individual or group need submit to any wrong, nor need they use violence to right the wrong."[39] By resisting the evil, but resisting nonviolently, the group retains its dignity but does not return evil with evil. As Reverend King and Gandhi before him said, nonviolence does not seek to defeat or humiliate the opponent but to win his friendship and understanding. The opponents are not evil but are themselves victimized by evil. They can be reached by having their sense of moral shame awakened, and it can be awakened by the example of love, strength, courage and discipline shown by nonviolent demonstrators. The unearned suffering of the demonstrators is redemptive for both them and their opponents.

The theory of nonviolence was put to a crucial test during the summer. From all corners of the state, thugs and criminals gathered for a chance to express their sadism on defenseless Negroes. The Negroes would neither resist nor fight back. Initially, there was no danger of the police stopping these hoodlums. This meant they had a clear opportunity to violate other human beings without fear of retaliation or punishment. There was no discernible effect upon their consciences.

By the end of May, large groups of white toughs—many of them from the Ancient City Hunting Club—began attacking Negro testers at restaurants and motels. The authorities had also readied themselves for the new push. Davis had his officers arrest all the Negro testers as uninvited guests and trespassers. Instead of setting bail at $100 (the bond ordinarily required for violation of a misdeameanor of this type), he set bail at $1,500 for demonstrators who had never been arrested and at $3,000 for demonstrators who did have previous arrests, even if they had not been convicted.

When asked why he ordered this increase, Sheriff Davis answered: "I raised them because I wanted to." In addition, he set up a makeshift open-air pen in his jail, with inadequate toilet facilities shared by both men and women. The demonstrators were put in the pen, exposed to the broiling summer sun and left to stand in the rain. He ordered nine or ten Negro men into a seven-by-eight-foot "sweatbox" overnight. He crammed 21 Negro women (including one polio victim who was unable to stand without crutches) for an hour into a padded cell, ten feet in diameter. This punishment was imposed because the prisoners sang religious songs and prayed in their cells. In addition, juvenile demonstrators were not released to their parents, as is usually done when children are arrested for misdemeanors. The local county juvenile judge, Charles C. Mathis, refused to do so unless their parents promised not to allow them to take part in civil rights demonstrations in the future. (At an earlier time he ordered two young Negroes to reform school for participating in demonstrations at a drugstore.)

On May 28, 1964, a vicious attack was made on the Negro night marchers by white hoodlums gathered around the slave market. The attack was well covered by the press and television and brought so much national attention that public officials, alarmed at the potential loss of tourists, agreed the violence must cease. The easiest way to keep the peace was to stop the demonstrations. Sheriff Davis thereupon declared that an emergency situation existed. On that basis he banned all further night marches by the Negro groups.

It seemed as if the St. Augustine push were over before it had begun. The S.C.L.C. had nowhere to turn but to the Federal courts. Civil rights lawyers filed two suits, one to force Davis to lift the ban on night marching, the other to do something about the conditions in Davis's jail, to have the bond requirements reduced and to get the juvenile demonstrators released.

The two suits were referred to Judge Simpson. It took him just ten days to decide for the civil rights demonstrators on all counts.

In an unusual move Sheriff Davis was called as witness for the plaintiffs on June 2, 1964. Tobias Simon, their attorney, tried to show that the reason for violence during the night marches was that white toughs were given a clear opportunity to attack the Negroes, without intervention of any kind by Sheriff Davis's officers. He tried to show that the deputies themselves were part of "Hoss" Manucy's group. Davis's attorney moved to have all these questions ruled out as irrelevant, but Judge Simpson refused his request. Indeed, Judge Simpson asked questions himself about Sheriff

Davis's recruiting of deputies with a vigor and pointedness that no southern sheriff has ever suffered at a Federal judge's hands:

> THE COURT: Do you recruit them from the Ku Klux Klan there in St. Augustine?
> THE WITNESS: No, sir.
> THE COURT: Are some of them Klansmen, some of these special deputies?
> THE WITNESS: No, sir, not to my knowledge, if they are.
> THE COURT: Are you a Klansman?
> THE WITNESS: No, sir.

*   *   *

> THE COURT: Are you a member of the Ancient City Gun Club?
> THE WITNESS: No, sir.

After Davis admitted he had deputized a number of members of the club, Judge Simpson asked:

> THE COURT: I ask you this, isn't the Ancient City Gun Club just the local name for the Klan down there?
> THE WITNESS: I . . . I don't think it is, your Honor. I questioned everyone that I've had any contact with. . . .[40]

Judge Simpson ordered Davis to supply a list of his special deputies to the court. Davis read off a list of his deputies the next day. When he came to the name of "Holsted Richard Manucy," Judge Simpson asked him, "Isn't he a bootlegger?" Davis admitted that he was.

> THE COURT: He is a convicted felon in this court. . . .
> Has he had his rights of citizenship restored?
> THE WITNESS: Not that I know of, I don't know.
> THE COURT: He's good enough to be a deputy sheriff?
> THE WITNESS: No, sir. . . .

*   *   *

> THE COURT: You have given them cards saying they are Deputy Sheriffs and asked them to help you keep order in your Easter parade; is that correct?
> THE WITNESS: Yes, sir.[41]

Judge Simpson then remarked:

> I think, Sheriff, as a law enforcement officer, you can appreciate the danger in a situation like this when you have members of the Klan and allied organizations in your organization as deputies.[42]

On June 9, 1964, Judge Simpson rendered his opinions on the night marching ban and Davis's jail conditions. His first opinion carefully described the night marches and pointed out that the trouble did not come from the Negro demonstrators but from the white toughs who tried to stop them from asserting their constitutional rights. Under those conditions, effective law enforcement, not banning the demonstrations, was the way to rectify the situation. But effective law enforcement was not forthcoming:

> Further it is convincing on this record that the Police . . . made no effort at close inspection to determine whether the white people were armed, and no attempt to learn their identity or the nature of their business in the market.[43]

Judge Simpson described the number of law enforcement officers at Davis's disposal. He found that while "some disorder existed, considerable annoyance and inconvenience were caused by the Negroes' decision to conduct their marches during the evening hours,"[44] there was sufficient police power available to protect them, and no clear and present danger existed sufficient to justify stopping the marches.

In his second opinion, Judge Simpson described the motive for the high bail requirements:

> The Defendant Sheriff L. O. Davis, or the Defendant County Judge Charles C. Mathis, or the two of them acting in concert, apparently with the motive of discouraging similar attempts to integrate local places of public accommodation (the Defendant Davis stated under oath that the action of raising the amount required for appearance bonds was solely his and that "I raised them because I *wanted to*" and for no other reason) raised in less than sixty days the amount required for appearance bonds from $300 to $1500, or from $450 to $3000.

* * *

The conclusion is inescapable that the appearance bonds in these cases were arbitrarily and capriciously fixed in grossly excessive amounts by the Defendants Davis and Mathis, either or both. No regard was given to the legitimate purpose of appearance bonds in criminal cases, the insuring of the Defendants' appearance to stand trial. Rather, the financial harassment of Defendants, or perhaps of Southern Christian Leadership Conference, which sponsored the sit-ins, appears to be the purpose.[45]

He then described the conditions in Davis's jail:

The Defendant, L. O. Davis, as Sheriff, has inflicted cruel and unusual punishments upon each of the Plaintiffs in connection with their detention awaiting trial. These actions included forcing them outside their cells to remain exposed to the elements in an open unshaded fenced compound through the midday hours, and sometimes all day. This place contained makeshift, exposed and inadequate toilet facilities, which were a source of humiliation, degradation and shame to the mixed group of males and females, juveniles and adults, whites and Negroes forced to share their use. This was used only for these Plaintiffs, not for other jail inmates.

The use of this compound, in Florida's 90-degree plus June temperature, and in one severe storm, was sought to be justified by the Defendant Davis as compliance with three successive Grand Jury reports that the jail must be equipped with an exercise yard so that inmates could get exercise outside their cells.

Further punishment devised by the Sheriff was the crowding of 9 or 10 male plaintiffs together overnight into concrete "sweatboxes," 7' x 8'. The females, 21 in number, on the other hand, were forced on one occasion for an hour and eighteen minutes into a circular padded cell 10 feet in diameter. This group included one polio victim, Mrs. Georgia B. Reed, on crutches and unable stand without them. Both the sweatboxes and the padded cell were so small that the occupants had to sit or lie down in relays. These latter practices were imposed as punishment for singing religious songs or praying in the jail. As to the use of the compound the good Sheriff said further that this was to make the Plaintiffs tired and ready for sleep at nightfall, to discourage singing in advance.

More than cruel and unusual punishment is shown. Here is exposed, in its raw ugliness, studied and cynical brutality, deliberately contrived to break men, physically and mentally.

Regardless of their race or color, regardless of divergent political viewpoints, these were Sheriff Davis' fellow Americans, indeed his fellow townsmen.[46]

Judge Simpson ordered bail reduced for all the demonstrators from $3,000 to a maximum of $300. He ordered all the children in jail released to their parents. Finally he ordered Davis to stop placing any of his prisoners in an open pen, a sweatbox or any padded cells.

The immediate effect of Judge Simpson's orders was to release hundreds of Negro demonstrators who, until that time, could not post the required high bond set by Sheriff Davis. Reverend Martin Luther King returned to St. Augustine to lead further demonstrations, and the civil rights drive began again.

However, the segregationists' side was also strengthened by the arrival of J. B. Stoner, one of the leaders of the National States' Rights party. Stoner thought up the bright idea of having the Klan march through the Negro quarter just as the Negroes had marched through the white quarter. Instead of facing hostile crowds, bricks, bats and stones, the Klanners saw only a group of frightened Negro teen-agers holding signs that read: "We would like to meet eye to eye" and "Welcome."

It became obvious to the state authorities that the Negro demonstrations would continue. The presence of a large number of newsmen and television cameramen would make further violence very embarrassing to them. For the next six weeks they tried again and again to halt the Negro demonstrations, particularly the night marches. In response the civil rights lawyers brought new suits, contempt applications and motions for injunctions before Judge Simpson. Invariably the state took the position—in court—that regardless of who started the violence, the narrow streets of

St. Augustine made it impossible for the police to give Negro demonstrators adequate protection, no matter how many law enforcement officers were in the area. Thus, the only way to stop the violence was to stop the marches. The civil rights lawyers argued that the violence was always initiated by the white counterdemonstrators and that the state made no effort to prevent these attacks beforehand or to provide even a minimum amount of protection. Therefore, the state's defense was made in bad faith since state officials had not tried to see what effective law enforcement could do. Judge Simpson put both sides to their proof in an effort to find the truth of the events. Necessarily this meant defeat for the state of Florida.

On June 13, 1964 the state of Florida—in the person of the state attorney general—intervened in the suit against Davis and urged the court to reverse its order allowing the marches to continue. The attorney general said matters had so deteriorated in the four days following Judge Simpson's order that a banning of demonstrations was in order. In trying to produce evidence to prove this, one of the state's witnesses—a former FBI agent who acted as the governor's special investigator—described a scene in which four armed state-policemen stopped two or three counterdemonstrators from beating a white minister marching with the Negroes. When asked what happened to the attackers, he said they ran off before they could be arrested.

The state authorities were pressed on how many arrests of the attackers were made (very few), what efforts were made to investigate the identity of the counterdemonstrators (none), and what preventive measures to disarm them were taken (practically none). There was testimony that one state trooper did, in fact, search one of the cars in the downtown area and found one loaded shotgun, five pistols and half a bushel of ammunition. Although the identity of the owners of the weapons was known to the police, no arrests were made and the guns were returned to the owners the next day. When asked by Judge Simpson why this was done, a state police officer tried to explain that no law had been violated. Judge Simpson's comment was: "I can't believe that the State has no authority to seize weapons in that kind of situation."[47] He later said to the state attorney general, who offered the same explanation as the major: "The law isn't that big a boob."[48]

Judge Simpson refused to change his order with the following comments:

> I suggest rigid and strict law enforcement and some arrests and some real charges to be placed against those hoodlums that everybody down there seems to be afraid to move against and I make that [suggestion] with deadly seriousness. If the local law enforcement people are willing to let them come in there and take over the downtown section of the city without taking steps against them, maybe it's time for the State to step in and take charge of it.[49]

The state did step in and at first actually followed Judge Simpson's advice. On June 15, 1964, Governor Ferris Bryant issued an executive proclamation establishing a special new law enforcement area in St. Johns County and dispatched a number of state troopers to the area to provide assistance to the local law enforcement groups. The immediate result was that no violence attended either of the night marches on June 16 or 17. On June 17 the first effort was made to integrate the St. Augustine beaches and, because of the presence of state officers, there was no violence.

On June 18, 1964, however, a new crisis began. The civil rights groups had been reinforced by a number of rabbis, who planned to accompany Negroes to the various restaurants and motels in St. Augustine and to be arrested with the Negroes as uninvited guests. One group went to one of the large downtown motels—Monsons Motor Lodge.

Two white S.C.L.C. workers had registered the night before at Monsons. As the rabbis and Negroes who accompanied them were refused service and turned back to the main street, one of the S.C.L.C. guests at Monsons, Charles A. Lingo, Jr., leaped into the pool along with five Negro teen-agers from St. Augustine. The owner, James Brock, in an absolute fury tried to drive the group out by pouring muriatic acid into the pool. The acid, which is used only to clean impurities out of the water, was harmless. A special deputy dived into the pool to get the people out, and photographs of the event appeared nationwide. Everyone involved was arrested. The next day a number of police with dogs and electric prods were assigned to protect the pool.

The state senator from St. Augustine, one of the important real estate brokers in the area, publicly appealed for help from the governor to stop the increasing violence. Governor Bryant responded, on Friday, June 20, 1964, by his second executive order, which banned all demonstrations after 8:30 p.m. until morning because of "certain lawlessness and utter disregard for the laws of Florida exhibited *by the demonstrators* and counter demonstrators." (The attorney general was later to admit before Judge Simpson that he had heard of not a single act of violence emanating from the Negro demonstrators.)

On Sunday, June 22, the white thugs drove right onto the beach, opened up their trunks, took out large wooden clubs, walked over to the Negroes gathered at the beach and started clubbing them in plain sight of state troopers. The state troopers did nothing to stop them until the Negroes were seriously beaten. On the night of June 25, 1964, the Negro demonstrators decided to disregard the governor's ban and marched again. Connie Lynch, a Ku Klux Klan agitator, incited the largest group of whites yet gathered, into an extremely violent attack on Negro demonstrators. All these events were well covered by press and television.

The state continued to insist that both sides were to blame. Judge Simpson's comment about this argument was:

> It's a question of taking the view that, when somebody gets socked in the eye, he's just as guilty as the man that's on the fist.[50]

At another point he said:

> If one group is entitled to march peacefully and to the right of freedom of assembly and to the right of freedom of speech and the right of petition guaranteed by the First Amendment, it doesn't seem to me at all that a corresponding freedom to attack with physical violence goes to another group.[51]

The governor and the attorney general could not have enjoyed telling Judge Simpson how powerless they were to stop the violence. No state official wants to defend a lawsuit on the basis of his own incompetence and inability to perform his constitutional functions. The state's witnesses finally had to admit that Negroes were not responsible for the disorder and had a legal right to march and use the beaches. Under pressure from Judge Simpson, the state acknowledged that the trouble came from the "lawless elements," the "counterdemonstrators," "Manucy's raiders," and no solution was possible until these groups complied with the law. Judge Simpson continued to press this point during the hearings. He said:

> Well, you know what everybody knows and what the newspaper prints every day for weeks, there comes a time when, as insulated and as cotton-wrapped as Courts are, that Courts almost get to know it. I mean, there comes a point when general knowledge may be equated with judicial knowledge, or the other way around, and I think there's no real secret involved as to the source of what have been called the anti-demonstrators or counter-demonstrators, whether you call them the Klan, the Ancient City Gun Club, the Citizens Band Radio or Manucy's Raiders, or whatever name you give them. And I won't draw any conclusions from the nomenclature that counsel uses but, whatever tag you give the group, it's pretty clear on this record, made in this and other hearings, that there is this violent resistance to any attempt by this plaintiff and the class that he represents to assert [their constitutional rights].[52]

He further stated:

> I can't learn that anybody has been willing to do any more than hope that these demonstrations of what have been called here at various times Manucy's Raiders. . . . that any responsible official has made any appeals to them.[53]

At another point he said:

> There was no restraint by this Court on whatever action the law enforcement officers wanted to take with respect to this lawless element.[54]

It became clear to the state authorities that Judge Simpson was not going to order the demonstrations halted. Perhaps because of pressure from the White House, or because of the damage to the local economy, or because they were tired of the mess in the Ancient City, the state began to change its position. Before Judge Simpson the attorney general said:

> . . . the people arrested won't be put into the jail by the State Officers through the front door and released out the side door by the Local Officials; and . . . the evidence won't be turned in by the State Officers and released back to the offenders by the Local people.[55]

The local state attorney said:

> This man "Hoss" Manucy and his marauders are not going to be the influence in law enforcement in St. Johns County so long as I am State Attorney.[56]

The attorney general later said:

> I have informed our local officials and State law enforcement officials as well that they do have an overriding responsibility to maintain peace and order. . . .[57]

An additional force of eighty state troopers was sent into St. Augustine. This brought the total to about two hundred. On the beaches they solidly flanked the Negro bathers. The white hoodlums could not get near them. State police came to the aid of Negro testers at motels and restaurants. The state pressed a vigorous investigation to find the hoodlums that beat and knifed an S.C.L.C. worker who was quietly fishing off a pier. The white toughs suddenly had to deal with the law. They gradually left town or went back to their old pursuits.

Judge Simpson was in large part responsible for these changes. An unsympathetic judge could have found many ways of blocking the civil rights efforts in St. Augustine. He could have delayed hearings on each of the suits for days or even weeks. He could have restricted the questioning of the state's witnesses, so that the truth of the events in St. Augustine would never appear on a court record. He could have delayed giving a decision for a long period, so that even if an order were entered on behalf of the Negroes, it would be meaningless by the time it could be enforced (as, in the *Jackson Bus Terminal* case).

Judge Simpson took none of these courses. Instead he followed what he saw were the clear dictates of the Supreme Court and the Constitution. However brief it might be, a new era had begun in St. Augustine.

Judge Simpson adhered to the same course in the difficult days following passage of the Civil Rights Act. On July 2, 1964, the act was signed into law by President Johnson. The restaurant and motel owners of St. Augustine had met late in June and announced that they would comply with the new act, as distasteful and offensive as it was to them. Following that announcement, many owners received bomb threats over the phone or through the mail, telling them their business would be destroyed if they admitted Negroes. Nevertheless after passage of the act, Negroes were served in most of St. Augustine's restaurants and motels.

"Hoss" Manucy and his cohorts then decided to put the motel owners to the test. James Brock (the manager of the motel where the acid was thrown) did a complete about-face and admitted a group of Negroes to his motel on July 8, 1964. On July 9, pickets appeared outside Brock's motel with signs stating "Delicious food. Eat with Niggers here." and "Niggers sleep here: Will you?" Brock did what he could to get the pickets "off his back." He spoke to "Hoss" Manucy, who told him that his people had as much a right to demonstrate as the Negroes did, and his group didn't want Brock "to serve Niggers." Brock gave in to the pressure and reverted to his previous segregated policy. The other restaurants followed suit. (When asked who the pickets were during later court hearings, Brock started to name them and then hesitated. He said: "You know you put me in a very unpleasant position when you ask me this up here. . . . Because I recognize that you're not going to be too happy—too interested in my safety and welfare, and I'm a little bit frightened to be talking like this." Judge Simpson stopped any further questioning.[58])

The civil rights lawyers went back to Judge Simpson to

force the restaurant to serve Negroes. Seventeen restaurants and motels were named as defendants in three separate suits filed under the Civil Rights Act on July 15, 1964. A series of hearings were held later in the month. After the first hearing, when a number of the restaurant owners stated that they would agree to any order issued by the court, Brock's restaurant was bombed by a Molotov cocktail.

There was no difficulty in showing the two prerequisites for relief under the Civil Rights Act: the restaurants catered to interstate travelers and refused to serve Negroes. Once again Judge Simpson acted quickly to enter an appropriate order. His first orders were entered on July 24, eleven days after suit was filed, to be made effective thirty days later.[59] Early in August, when it was apparent that the constitutionality of the Civil Rights Act was to be put to its first test in Atlanta, Judge Simpson amended his orders to make them effective as of the time the Atlanta restaurant order went into effect, August 8.[60]

The real problem was not with the restaurant owners who had agreed initially to follow the Civil Rights Act. The trouble lay with "Manucy's raiders," who were putting pressure on the restaurant owners and intimidating the Negroes and civil rights workers. The lawyers therefore named a group of "Class II" defendants in the original suits. They asked that an order be directed against them—"Hoss" Manucy, his four brothers, the entire Ancient City Hunting Club, the Ku Klux Klan and a number of other known troublemakers in St. Augustine—to stop them from intimidating, threatening, or coercing anyone asserting rights under the Civil Rights Act. Judge Simpson's order was not only directed against these named defendants (with the exception of the Klan, which was not served in the case), but it also was directed to "any other person to whom notice or knowledge of this order may come."[61] All of them were ordered not to interfere with, "molest, threaten, intimidate or coerce any person of the Negro race with the purpose of interfering with such person's right to seek, use and enjoy" the facilities of the restaurants who were named as defendants in the suit.[62]

On August 12, 1964, Negro civil rights workers went around to a number of the restaurants to see whether they were complying with Judge Simpson's order. Arthur Funderberk and two other Negro workers went to one of the restaurants, were served, ate, and then started back to their car. Charles O. Lance, Jr., a special unpaid deputy of Sheriff Davis, saw the three Negroes leaving the restaurant and started to curse and shout at them. Later, the same day after Funderberk had driven two white civil rights workers to another restaurant, he noticed he was being followed in a car by Lance. Two days later Funderberk saw he was being followed by Lance again.

There was no doubt that Lance knew the terms of Judge Simpson's order. He was a good friend of William Chew, one of the most adamant segregationists among the restaurant and motel owners and the only one who continued to refuse service to Negroes. It was the view of the lawyers that Lance also was in contempt of Judge Simpson's orders. His cursing at Funderberk as he left the restaurant and following him afterwards were clear methods of intimidating him into giving up a right which he was afforded under Judge Simpson's order. The lawyers therefore moved to have both Lance and Chew held in contempt. A series of hearings were held later in August. Lance rationalized his actions as an attempt to "protect" Funderberk and the other civil rights workers against intimidation by the community. Judge Simpson made short shrift of that contention. He noted that on the day that Lance had cursed the civil rights workers, there were two young toughs present who were also threatening them, and Lance did nothing to stop them. But, Judge Simpson noted, when Funderberk was alone and in no apparent danger, Lance felt it necessary to follow him closely.[63]

Judge Simpson therefore found both Lance and Chew in contempt of his order. Relying on one of the provisions of the 1964 Civil Rights Act, he imposed a fine against both Lance and Chew of $600 for attorneys' fees. It was the first application of the contempt provisions of the act. Since Lance's power to intimidate potential Negro patrons at the restaurants and hence his ability to undermine Judge Simpson's order were based on his position as a deputy sheriff, Judge Simpson required that Lance "get off the Sheriff's force, . . . [turn] in his star" and no longer hold himself out as a peace officer in St. Johns County.[64]

Judge Simpson made it clear, however, that he was not otherwise interfering with Sheriff Davis's conduct of his office:

> Mr. Davis listed as one of his unpaid deputies one Holsted R. Manucy . . . known to Sheriff Davis to be a convicted, unpardoned felon. I conclude that if persons are appointed special or auxiliary deputies, without investigation, simply upon application, that it approaches the ludicrous to assert that the conduct by the Sheriff of his office is being interfered with in any meaningful way when one of such volunteers is required to divest himself of his authority by being required to resign as deputy.[65]

The order made newspaper headlines in Florida and judicial history in the United States. Never before had a Federal judge decided who could or could not be a deputy sheriff. Senator Strom Thurmond immediately labeled Judge Simpson's order the start of Federal "judicial dictatorship."[66] Sheriff Davis was furious. He was asked a week later to send some of his officers to the beach where a group of Negroes were being threatened, and he refused. He said in justification that he had lost one deputy for "protecting" Negroes and didn't want to lose any more. He told the newspapers he was looking into the question of impeaching Judge Simpson. It was the last straw in a summer of frustration for the sheriff.

But it was a summer of advance for the Negroes of St. Augustine. Negro groups were still cursed and threatened when they went to the beaches—and occasionally some fists flew. But one of the hoodlums remarked one day as he walked away from the Negroes without trying to attack them: "You're lucky you have Judge Simpson on your side." Without the presence of marshals or Federal troops, the local whites began to see that law had returned to St. Augustine, and there was authority and power in support of civil rights.

The Negroes saw this too. Throughout the South there are hundreds of abuses each day against Negroes. Many of these take the form of violence, which under any civilized legal system should be prevented or immediately punished. Instead, the authorities either condone them or participate in them. More important, these abuses against a Negro are immediately forgotten by those who have the responsibility to correct them and ignored by the rest of the country. Not only is the legal system the Negro's enemy, but it never even deigns to recognize the abuses he has suffered. They remain only in the minds of the victims, where they breed hatred and contempt of the institutions that allow them.

Witnesses who appeared before Judge Simpson were permitted to testify in detail about what happened to them. Their statements were preserved in the court record, and the court accepted the truth of what they said. In civil rights cases in the South, it is rare for court records to correspond to the facts as the participants knew them. Victims of attack by ten hoodlums find themselves under arrest for assault. School superintendents testify that their rejection of every Negro applicant for fifty years had nothing to do with color. Eyewitnesses to a murder hear five witnesses swear the defendant was miles away at the time. The state courts—and many Federal district courts—seldom accept the version of any incident told by a Negro. This Alice-in-Wonderland world did not extend into Judge Simpson's court. The Negroes of St. Augustine had discovered that the law could be their friend.

Why is Judge Simpson the exception rather than the rule in the South? A district court judge is generally a native of the state in which he sits. He may have fought in the same political wars as the state officials whose actions are under examination and who are often friends of long standing. He either reflects the local community's attitude toward national law or at least is most susceptible to the local opposition to it. He can rationalize his delay in following superior court decisions by waiting for an "opportune" time—as Judge Thomas of Mobile said—to avoid "unfortunate incidents." Public confidence in the Federal judiciary, he may think, will be destroyed by immediate and effective implementation of unpopular Supreme Court decisions. This could lead to disobedience of all its orders. Besides, why should he make himself an outcast in his own community?[67] (When a witness was discussing some of the violence during the summer marches in St. Augustine, he said to Judge Simpson: "I heard a lot of people say they would like for you to come down and march with them." Judge Simpson responded: "I've had a little stronger suggestions than that in some of the letters I've had of what I should do."[68])

But as a recent law review article noted:

> For an inferior court judge to defy the law as declared is for him to undermine the foundation of the very structure entrusted to his care; such conduct may well lead to more basic disrespect of the law as an institution than any momentary acquiescence to "public feelings" can prevent.[69]

Justice Goldberg pointed out that the judicial process "rests upon unreserved acceptance of and compliance with the decisions of the Court of last resort."[70] Prolonged delay in following such orders is the equivalent of direct disobedience.

The answer lies ultimately in appointing judges who will themselves follow the national law and compel obedience to it by the local community. Temporary reassignment of judges to or from the southern states or impeachment creates more problems than it solves.[71] No doubt Robert Kennedy was unpleasantly surprised at the difficulties he created for himself as Attorney General after—at Senator Eastland's urging—he agreed to the appointment of Judge Cox in Mississippi. The appointing authorities cannot bargain on district court judgeships in the South, since nothing they get in return can make up for the problems a recalcitrant judge can create for the government. "Senatorial courtesy" is now an outmoded gesture. A Senate that stopped a southern filibuster on the Civil Rights Act by a four-to-one margin might be receptive to stopping a judicial filibuster as well. The administration must refuse to give a southern senator the last word on judicial appointments in his state if it is to fulfill its obligation to the electorate. Federal judges must be appointed with courage, such as Judge Simpson's, to listen to the Supreme Court and the national voice on civil rights and to ignore the local din that would drown it out. Nothing less than the integrity of the judicial process is at stake.

SHIRLEY FINGERHOOD

The Fifth Circuit Court
of Appeals

One of the new and significant theaters of the civil rights struggle in recent years has been the United States Court of Appeals for the Fifth Circuit. It hears appeals from lower Federal courts—the district courts—in Florida, Georgia, Louisiana, Alabama, Mississippi and Texas. It therefore has jurisdiction over the section of the South that has most bitterly, adamantly, and successfully resisted Federal law on Negro rights in all areas. This resistance has operated not only through state officials from governors to local sheriffs but also through the courts, affecting municipal and state judges as well as members of the Federal judiciary.

Shirley Fingerhood is an attorney in private practice in New York City. She is Legal Research Director for the Law Students Civil Rights Research Council and a cooperating attorney with the American Civil Liberties Union. She is a graduate of the Yale Law School.

When the Supreme Court of the United States held school segregation unconstitutional in 1954,[1] it deeded to the Federal district judges the awesome task of supervising and enforcing compliance with its decision. Its 1955 decree[2] formulated general instructions for the district judges: local school boards had the primary responsibility for effecting the change; the boards were to proceed "with all deliberate speed," considering problems of school administration, districting, transportation and local laws. The district courts were only to permit delay when time was requested in good faith to cope with these complexities.

The effect was to give wide discretion to the district courts and to place them squarely in the center of the storm of hostility to desegregation. The legal maneuvers to obstruct and delay compliance with the Supreme Court's mandates took place in their courtrooms. They were given the responsibility of rejecting or accepting the ingenious defenses designed to thwart integration. And the Supreme Court's directive to consider local school conditions provided an excuse for passivity, particularly as militant segregationists promptly used violence to increase the problems of many school administrators.

The U.S. Court of Appeals for the Fifth Circuit thus presided over a conflict that, with the increasing momentum of the civil rights movement and the mounting opposition to it, threatened the authority of Federal law. It also threatened to split apart the Federal judiciary to which that law has been entrusted. For nearly all Federal judges in the Fifth Circuit area are native Southerners. The few born elsewhere have long since become acculturated to the manners, mores and values of the South. They are men who have attained success in its traditional society, who live in segregated communities, and who are subject to the pressures generated by a universal belief in the customs and institutions of white supremacy. Whether the pressure comes from within, from their own attitudes, or from without, from the blandishments, disapproval and harassment of the community, it is a powerful incentive for giving a sympathetic hearing to the excuses and evasions of state officials, and for seeing "good faith" where there is no intention at all to make a start towards compliance with the law.

But regardless of his personal views, despite the opposition of his peers, each Federal judge in the Fifth Circuit—whether a member of a district court or of the court of appeals—is required to enforce integration. Some district judges have fully accepted the mandate of the national law, some have required only minimal change and some have actively participated in the tactics of obstruction. The members of the Court of Appeals for the Fifth Circuit also have diverse convictions and legal attitudes concerning the proper course and pace of integration. Thus, a study of that court (which will be referred to as the Fifth Circuit) reveals not only the role of the Federal judiciary in implementing civil rights but also a struggle between those responsible for law in a society where local pressures have placed lawlessness in a position of power and respectability.

Four members of the Fifth Circuit, Chief Judge Elbert P. Tuttle of Georgia and Judges Richard T. Rives of Alabama, John R. Brown of Texas and John Minor Wisdom of Louisiana, have firmly and consistently taken the position that their fellow Southerners must be forced to recognize Negro rights, and sooner rather than later. Their actions have been opposed by Judges Ben F. Cameron of Mississippi, and Walter P. Gewin of Alabama, a Kennedy appointee. The other members of the court, Judges Warren L. Jones of Florida, Joseph C. Hutcheson of Texas, and Griffin B. Bell of Georgia, another Kennedy appointee, have mixed records.*

Like most other circuit courts, the Fifth Circuit performs its work through panels of three judges, except for the rare case which presents novel or important issues and is therefore heard by the entire bench. As Chief Judge Tuttle and Judges Rives, Wisdom and Brown almost always stand

---

* Judges Gewin and Bell were appointed by President Kennedy after the membership of the Court was increased from seven to nine by statute in 1961. The number of active judges decreased to eight early in 1963 when Judge Hutcheson became incapacitated, and to seven when Judge Cameron died in April 1964.

together in civil rights cases and from time to time pick up the support of one of the other judges, their attitudes prevail in all panels which include two of them and in some panels which include only one.

Their efforts to force recalcitrant district court judges to follow decisions of the Fifth Circuit and of the U.S. Supreme Court have given rise to the esteem the court enjoys in the North as "courageous" and "trailblazing" and to the opprobrium it has received in the South for "shocking," "unorthodox" decisions which are "unsanctioned by the law"—to note only the kindlier epithets. The four have been accused of performing their obligations in "a crusading spirit." The term was used in July, 1963, by Judge Cameron in a vituperative dissenting opinion, in which he complained that the public—presumably the southern white public—was concerned over the split between "The Four," as he called them, and the others on the bench on the use of "extraordinary" procedures.[3]

Ordinarily, a court of appeals maintains the law by merely reversing erroneous decisions of a lower court. When a litigant appeals, he argues that the judge of the lower court erred in applying the law to his case. If the appellate court agrees with him, it reverses and sends the case back with an opinion delineating the error and prescribing action to be taken by the district court. Because the Supreme Court reviews only a few circuit court decisions, most are final. Each is implemented by the district court that originally judged the case, and followed in analogous cases by all of the district courts in the circuit. Since judges do not invite reversals, district court judges will ordinarily accept and follow the decisions of the higher courts. If, however, a judge refuses to follow binding precedent, or his ruling cannot effectively be remedied on appeal, he can be ordered by the appellate court to take specific action in a specific case by means of the "extraordinary writs" of mandamus, prohibition, or injunctions pending appeal.[4]

In the first years after the *Brown* decisions, the Fifth Circuit reversed a good number of district court judges who were dragging their feet on desegregation orders. However, in recent years, The Four have used extraordinary writs with increasing frequency to thwart the dilatory tactics of recalcitrant members of the lower Federal judiciary whose ranks were increased by four appointments by President Kennedy: Judge E. Gordon West in Louisiana, Judge William H. Cox in Mississippi, Judge J. Robert Elliott in Georgia, and Judge Clarence W. Allgood in Alabama.

Several catalysts induced The Four to adopt a more aggressive course. One is undoubtedly the increasingly impatient mood of the U.S. Supreme Court. In 1958 it rejected the argument that community opposition and violence justified delay in the *Little Rock School* case.[5] In 1963 it added to the mandate to proceed "with all deliberate speed" the more definite and urgent statement that the "basic guarantees of our constitution are warrants for the here and now."[6] In 1964, it delivered the unequivocal warning that "there has been entirely too much deliberation and not enough speed."[7]

In 1960 the sit-ins began, and an increase in civil rights demonstrations followed. This led to demands for acceleration of the tempo of change and for extension of civil rights to the previously unchallenged territories of rural Georgia, Alabama and Mississippi. The violence which Negroes met —mass arrests, police brutality, and flagrant denials of constitutional rights—became known to the world and to the law-abiding white Southerner. The issue was no longer implementing the *School Segregation* cases but the authority of law itself.

Few white Southerners openly supported integration before or after 1954, but substantial numbers were committed to the rule of law and were willing to accept integration when it became the law. The opposition of zealots, many of them in public office, created a social climate in which these moderates could not be heard. White supremacists believed that the Supreme Court's decisions were not the law and would be abandoned if they proved unenforceable. Although some of the district judges in the Fifth Circuit ordered desegregation in no uncertain terms, more of them delayed, vacillated or denied relief.[8] The effect was to encourage the view that resistance and violence paid.[9]

The court of appeals had to take drastic measures to maintain the authority of Federal law. Extraordinary writs were appropriate weapons to prevent recalcitrant district judges from flouting explicit orders of the Fifth Circuit, as Chief Judge Tuttle showed in an opinion written in July, 1964. In granting a writ of *mandamus*, ordering District Judge E. Gordon West of Louisiana to issue an injunction against the School Board of St. Helena Parish,[10] Judge Tuttle quoted from a Supreme Court decision:

> Mandamus, prohibition and injunction against judges are drastic and extraordinary remedies. We do not doubt power in a proper case to issue such writs. But they have the unfortunate consequence of making a judge a litigant, obliged to obtain personal counsel or to leave his defense to one of the litigants before him. These remedies should be resorted to only when appeal is a clearly inadequate remedy. We are unwilling to utilize them as a substitute for appeal. As extraordinary remedies, they are reserved for really extraordinary cases.[11]

"This is such a really extraordinary case," said Judge Tuttle. It was a desegregation action initiated eleven years before against a local school board in Louisiana. In 1960, a district court judge had enjoined the school board from requiring segregation.[12] The Fifth Circuit had affirmed the decision and the Supreme Court had refused to review.[13] The state of Louisiana then passed a law permitting public schools to close if they were ordered to desegregate. This law was declared unconstitutional by a three-judge court and the Supreme Court affirmed that decision.[14] Supported by these decisions, Negro petitioners three times asked the district court for an order requiring the school board to submit a desegregation plan. Judge West neither granted nor denied their requests. Since there was no decision to appeal, the lawyers for the Negro school children finally petitioned the Fifth Circuit for a writ of *mandamus* requiring Judge West to act.

In his new position as litigant, Judge West left his defense to the attorneys for the school board. They argued that *mandamus* was an inappropriate measure since a district court judge has the power to control his docket; also, time was necessary to work out the problems that arise in a difficult racial situation. The problems were being discussed by Judge West at conferences with members of the school board and its attorneys with a view to arriving at an amicable solution to the problem.

To Judge Tuttle this defense demonstrated a "startling, if not shocking, lack of appreciation of the clear pronouncements of the Supreme Court and this Court . . . which make it perfectly plain that time has run out. . . ." Judge Tuttle went on to observe that "it is plain by cases which it is an affectation to cite, that if the district court in these circumstances fails to perform its duty . . . then it falls to the lot of the Court of Appeals to require it to do so." Finally, Judge Tuttle noted that no explanation had been given to justify the "unusual procedure" of a judge holding a conference with one party without inviting the attorneys for the other party.

Judge West's reaction was one of cool and measured fury. He would, of course, scrupulously obey the order of the Fifth Circuit. But Judge West remarked that the opinion was "so extraordinary as to be termed by the press 'unique in legal annals.' " He found it "so injudiciously couched in personal terms, and . . . so written as to . . . accuse me, personally of refusing to accept my responsibilities . . . of wasting precious judicial time, of acting in an 'unusual' and 'shocking' manner. . . ."[15] "And I must say," he added, "that it is only by the exercise of the restraint so necessary, but so often lacking in the proper performance of judicial functions, that I am deterred from responding in kind."

Judge West did relax his restraint long enough to suggest that the Fifth Circuit applied one standard for civil rights cases and another for ordinary litigation. Such a charge had been made the previous summer by Judge Cameron in an internecine quarrel between members of the court of appeals itself.[16]

The occasion for Judge Cameron's ire is illuminating in its own right. The Fifth Circuit issued an injunction pending appeal after a district court judge in Birmingham had denied Negro petitioners the injunction they sought, on the ground that they had not exhausted administrative procedures under the Alabama School Placement Law before coming into court.

In granting the injunction pending appeal, Judge Rives, speaking for himself and Chief Judge Tuttle, said flatly, "that ruling was directly contrary to repeated decisions of this court." He went on to point out that the litigation had already been pending for three years and that the schools must now begin desegregation. To avoid further misunderstanding of the intent of the court, Judge Rives's order spelled out the exact language of the injunction that he ordered the district court to grant.

Judge Gewin, the third member of the panel, dissented on the ground that under the guise of staying action during the appeal, the court had really decided the appeal. He complained that although there had been a full trial in the district court the appeals court had not even seen the record, which included evidence of strong opposition from Negroes as well as whites to the mixing of races in the schools of Birmingham and which showed that not one single Negro had applied for transfer to a white school under the Alabama School Placement Law. As for undue delay, Judge Gewin pointed out that the case had begun "only" three years ago and there had been no previous complaints of delay. He objected to the procedure as unorthodox and, perhaps even more vehemently, to calendar precedence given to the Birmingham school case and five others involving racial problems over nearly five hundred cases, some involving "matters of tremendous importance involving business affairs, taxes, property, personal injuries, life and liberty."

In concluding his dissent, Judge Gewin asked that the entire bench assemble to rehear the case. A majority of the active judges then voted against what is known as an *en banc* hearing. Judge Cameron came forward in dissent to that vote and carried Judge Gewin's complaints a bit further.

Charging that the procedure followed by Judges Rives and Tuttle in the Birmingham case was unsanctioned by the law, Judge Cameron attacked "The Four" for inventing special, unorthodox procedures for handling civil rights procedures. The fiats which resulted had to be obeyed by district judges and civil authorities, whether they were legal or not. Winding up an unusually bitter opinion, Judge Cameron accused Chief Judge Tuttle* of misusing his administrative prerogatives by assigning himself and his three crusading colleagues to panels which heard civil rights appeals and to the three-judge district panels which decide the constitutionality of state statutes.**

The gerrymandering charge was denied, but it poses a crucial question. If some Fifth Circuit judges consistently refuse to obey the Supreme Court's directives, assigning them to civil rights cases would permit disregard of the Constitution of the United States. The priority of the Constitution would seem to justify controlling assignments. The chief judge has the authority to make assignments; there is no law which requires them to be made in a particular order. Moreover, it is proper to have a case judged only by those who have no prejudice against any of the parties. However, a judge who is biased against a litigant or a class of litigants is supposed to disqualify himself; it is not customary to use assignment powers to achieve this result.*** And it is not easy to do so when, although bias is clear, it is shown by

---

* Judge Cameron urged the court to forsake special procedures to regain the stature it had owned before Judge Hutcheson laid down the duties of chief judge. As the chief judge is the senior judge under age seventy, Judge Hutcheson held the position until 1959. Judge Rives succeeded him but relinquished the job in 1961 although he was not of mandatory age. Judge Tuttle, at 67, is presently the chief judge; Judge Brown is next in seniority.

** Panels of the Fifth Circuit ordinarily include two court of appeals judges and a third judge who may be a local district judge or a judge from another circuit temporarily assigned to reduce docket congestion. The chief judge of the circuit appoints two-thirds of the panel of a three-judge district court; the third member being the local district judge. One of the appointed judges is always an appellate judge; the other may be either an appellate judge or a district judge, but is most often the latter.

*** Others have the power to keep those who are prejudiced off the bench: the President appoints Federal judges, he may also reassign them; the Senate may impeach those guilty of flagrant misbehavior.

technical rulings. Denial of prompt and effective remedies is attributed to immaterial mistakes in papers, crowded dockets, and the misinterpretation of traditional doctrines such as those which require litigants to contest state statutes in state courts and to exhaust administrative remedies before coming into Federal court. Use of the Chief Judge's administrative powers to restrict prejudiced judges under such circumstances can provoke countercharges of bias—of partiality to Negro litigants. There is a danger that the Federal bench may appear to be a group of squabbling men instead of the voice of Federal authority.

Judge Cameron does not appear to be concerned with this danger. In the summer of 1962 he issued a curious, if not unique, series of orders[17] which reveal an indifference to this problem and give perspective to the accusation of irregularity and unorthodoxy he leveled against The Four. After prolonged litigation, a panel of the Fifth Circuit ordered the University of Mississippi to admit James Meredith.[18] Though Judge Cameron was not even a member of the panel, he availed himself of the quite extraordinary tactic of staying the court's mandate until the university could ask the U.S. Supreme Court for a reversal, and, incidentally, until after the commencement of the next semester. Speaking for the panel that had granted the order, Judge Wisdom vacated the stay on the ground that it violated the court's rules. "And," he wrote, "it is unthinkable that a judge who was not a member of the panel should be allowed to frustrate the mandate of the court."

Judge Cameron promptly issued another stay; without giving any reason, he asserted that the panel's proceedings were void. Again the panel set it aside, and again Judge Cameron reissued it. The panel reaffirmed its two previous orders and declared Judge Cameron's stays erroneous, improvident and void. Another stay followed. The matter was finally settled by Justice Hugo L. Black who vacated Judge Cameron's stay and indicated that the entire Supreme Court concurred in his view that the university would not be granted review.[19]

Similarly, there is a sharp contrast between Judge Gewin's

reaction to the "impropriety" of an injunction pending appeal and his failure to notice the injudicious behavior of Judge West in participating in a meeting with the attorneys for one side in a litigation. Judge Gewin is experienced and competent and, one can surmise, would immediately object to such judicial behavior in cases involving business affairs, taxes, property, etc.

Since decisions in civil rights cases often depend on whether or not a judge sees an "emergency," or "irremediable injury" or "good faith," they are affected by even the most subtle bias. Each judge's value system inevitably conditions these almost personal determinations. Judge Gewin found there was no delay in Birmingham, where litigation had been pending "only" three years. Three years constituted intolerable delay to Judge Rives. Judge Tuttle has expressed his belief that there is irremediable harm to Negro children when they graduate from school without being part of an integrated classroom. Last August, promptly after the Supreme Court ordered a change of pace, he explicitly designed an injunction so that each Negro child in a Georgia school district would have the opportunity to enjoy desegregated education before he graduated.[20]

Considering the extraordinary number of cases in which lower court judges have followed their personal reactions, and refused to follow binding precedents, extraordinary writs have been used sparingly. But they have been used with telling effect. These writs have served to prevent judges from flouting explicit orders, to break through the flimsy screen of state statutes to their actual operation in thwarting the constitutional rights of Negroes, to prevent the year-by-year perpetuation of segregation through judicial delay, and to save the time lost by civil rights lawyers, and the courts, in interminable litigation.

Their effect has been most felt in desegregation cases; school desegregation plans have been ordered by district judges in many areas in Alabama, Florida, Georgia and Louisiana including the strongholds of Birmingham, Alabama,[21] Albany, Georgia,[22] and Jackson, Leake County and Biloxi, Mississippi.[23] (In the Mississippi cases, District Court

Judge Mize noted that he was following the directive of the Fifth Circuit, although he believed his decision contrary to the law and the facts.) There is even a school desegregation plan acceptable to Judges Tittle, Rives and Wisdom for St. Helena[24]—formulated by Judge West with the aid of the Community Relations Service.*

The Four's adamancy has also had some impact on voting cases and cases concerning civil rights demonstrations. For example, following a Fifth Circuit opinion, Judge Elliott enjoined the city officials of Albany from interfering with Negro protests against racial discrimination.[26] And during 1963 and 1964, hundreds of demonstrators who were arrested for disorderly conduct, trespass, blocking traffic, etc., were not prosecuted by state authorities in Mississippi, Florida, Georgia and Louisiana because of stays issued by the Fifth Circuit. Their attorneys had removed the prosecutions under a Federal statute which permits the transfer of certain types of civil rights cases to a Federal court.[27] District court judges throughout the South had sent such cases back to state and local courts by finding that they were not covered by the statute. Attorneys asked the Fifth Circuit to decide that these remand orders could be appealed. Although the right to appeal them had not previously been recognized, the Fifth Circuit stayed the prosecutions while it considered the question. Meantime, those arrested were under Federal jurisdiction safe from the brutality and hostility of local jailers and sheriffs.

The Civil Rights Act of 1964 specifically gave the right to

---

* In response to *mandamus*, the District Court Judge ordered the St. Helena Parish School Board to promptly submit a plan of desegregation. The school board, at a special meeting, passed a resolution requesting the court to reconsider, among other reasons, because: "We may be persecuted and misunderstood if we were to comply . . . our respective businesses could and probably would fail . . . we beg of this court to understand . . . the humility with which we present these views as free men in a free society."

Judge West ordered the board to submit a plan within three days, and stated that if it failed, he would presume that it favored complete desegregation and submitted that proposal. The board then requested the aid of the Community Relations Service which was established by the Civil Rights Act of 1964.[25]

appeal;[28] the Fifth Circuit will now decide whether or not the cases were properly removed. In holding these cases until there was a clear right to appeal, the Fifth Circuit sought to decide the key point of law involved, the right to remove civil rights cases to the Federal court.[29] It is probable that the Fifth Circuit will decide that some if not all of the cases on appeal should be tried by Federal courts. These courts will then decide whether the activities for which the arrests were made are protected by the Federal Constitution and law.

Segregationists have been able to count on the short shrift given to constitutional defenses by state courts. They will no doubt also be able to count on similar actions by some Federal judges. For example, Judge West, in giving his personal view that *Brown* was "one of the truly regrettable decisions of all time," also remarked that "even more regrettable" is "the agitation of outsiders from far distant states, who, after creating turmoil and strife in one locality are ready to move on to meddle in the affairs of others elsewhere."[30] But the appeal route from decisions that can be expected from such judges will be short: directly to the Fifth Circuit Court of Appeals, instead of through two or three state appeals and then to the U.S. Supreme Court. And the Fifth Circuit can exact compliance with its decisions, as it has shown.

The burden of these appeals will fall on the already overworked court. The number of appeals in voting cases are increasing. Civil rights litigation is only a small part of its caseload, which is presently heavier than that of any other of the nation's ten circuits.[31] With only seven active members, the Fifth Circuit's backlog constantly grows.

The court saves time by its efficiency: oral argument is shortened by advance preparation. Since the briefs have been read before argument, attorneys are quickly directed to points that interest the judges or need clarification. The judges already know the applicable law.

And in civil rights cases, repeated appeals are eliminated when extraordinary remedies are granted. Chief Judge Tuttle in granting *mandamus* against Judge West in the *St. Helena School* case wrote:

> The courts can ill afford the judicial time required to consider the case of every municipal, county, or parish board of education two or three times, through the whole gamut of litigation from the District Court to the Court of Appeals to the Supreme Court, back to a three-judge District Court, thence to the Supreme Court, with the return visit to the District Court and then back to this court for the granting of an order that it was apparent from the start was already overdue.[32]

Nevertheless, the seven currently active members of the Fifth Circuit cannot cope with an ever increasing number of appeals. In the near future two more judges will be appointed to bring the bench to its full force of nine;* two more appointments may be made if, as has been proposed, its force is increased to eleven.[33]

The character of the men chosen will determine the future of the court. The Four are now the majority; if the new appointees share their dedication to constitutional principles, there is hope that the Federal judiciary will maintain national law even in such states as Mississippi.

If, on the other hand, indecisive or prejudiced judges come to outnumber The Four, the entire complexion of the civil rights movement may change. The dedication of The Four and their acceptance of the implications of the Supreme Court's decisions are, in one sense, no more than should be expected of Federal judges. But they have had to contend with the opposition of their brethren. Their job has not been easy; its effect has just begun to be felt. If they are outnumbered in the court by the opposition, their achievements can easily be undone.

---

* On June 17, 1965, President Johnson appointed former Governor James P. Coleman of Mississippi and Homer Thornberry of Texas to the Fifth Circuit.

HAYWOOD BURNS

The Federal Government and Civil Rights

There is a town in Mississippi called Liberty, there is a department in Washington called Justice. This anonymous legend appeared on the wall of the headquarters of the Council of Federated Organizations in Jackson, Mississippi in the summer of 1964. It expresses much of the frustration and disillusionment felt by many civil rights workers about the role the Federal government has played—or not played—in the administration of justice in the South. The view of these workers is quite simple. It is that under the Constitution of the United States they are possessed of certain First Amendment rights to speak freely, to assemble peacefully and

---

W. Haywood Burns is a third-year law student at Yale. He has worked with both the Civil Rights Division of the Justice Department and with COFO in Mississippi. He is the author of *The Voices of Negro Protest in America,* and his poetry, book reviews and articles have appeared in publications in the United States and England.

distribute literature; that they are possessed of certain Fifteenth Amendment rights that guarantee the right to vote; that under the Fourteenth Amendment no state official may deprive them of these rights or discriminate against them because of their race. These constitutional provisions are the "supreme law of the land" (Article VI) and, in the final analysis, it is the duty of the President of the United States to see that the laws be "faithfully executed" (Article II). Despite the guarantees of the Constitution and Federal law, Negroes and whites in the South have been subjected in countless instances to deprivations of their rights both by private individuals and by state and local officials. However, the executive branch of the government, they feel, and more specifically the President and the Department of Justice, by their lack of effective action have not been fulfilling their obligations under the Constitution and Federal law.

Blessed are the peacemakers, for they catch hell from both sides. So read a sign in the office of the former Assistant Attorney General for Civil Rights Burke Marshall in Washington, D.C. The Department of Justice as the law enforcement branch of the executive has borne the brunt of criticism not only from those who feel the Federal government has not done enough but also from those who feel it has gone too far. Burke Marshall, in his public statements and in his book *Federalism and Civil Rights*, published in the fall of 1964, answers critics from both sides by invoking the delicate balance in Federal-state relations. He recognizes the authority of the Federal government and its executive to act in the area of civil rights but cites the limitations upon their law enforcement powers in the elimination of racial injustice.

Voting

The primary response of the Justice Department to the situation in the South has been in the area of voting. This has been especially true since the Kennedy and Johnson administrations decided to concentrate upon helping the southern Negro secure the franchise as an instrument of change. In the Gino Speranza lectures delivered at Columbia University in the spring of 1964, Burke Marshall said, "Only political power—not court orders or other federal law—will insure the election of fair men as sheriffs, school board members, police chiefs, mayors, county commissioners and state officials." In keeping with this theory of the primacy of political power as a means to correct the inequities existing in the South, the Justice Department under the Civil Rights Acts of 1957 and 1960 filed more than forty suits to end voting discrimination and intimidation. And the recent 1965 voting bill is a far-reaching effort along the same lines.

The work that went into the preparation of each voting case under the earlier Civil Rights Acts was long and arduous. The Justice Department would ask to inspect and photograph the voting records of a certain area and, if the registrar of that area would not willingly permit, obtain a court order granting such access. Copies of voting application forms, sometimes numbering thousands, must then be examined and a "pattern and practice of discrimination" established. Only then would the case go to a Federal court —where it would be heard by a Federal judge who might have been hostile to the suit from the outset. There were many evasionary and dilatory tactics followed by those opposed to the purpose of voting suits. Despite difficulties the department succeeded in winning broad relief in several cases. For example, two cases, in Panola and Tallahatchie counties, Mississippi, were decided in the summer of 1964, and in both the Federal government convinced the Federal courts of its "freezing" argument. According to this argument, a registrar may not, after a suit for discriminatory practices has been filed against him, apply equally to Negroes and whites a higher standard for the purpose of forever "freezing" out those who had been effectively disfranchised under the previously administered discriminatory standard. The court decisions allow those who have been discriminated against previously to register simply by going to the registrar's office and filling in the personal information on the registration application—without having to undergo the writing and interpretational tests otherwise required in Mississippi.

The 1965 Voting Rights Act attacks the problem directly and, instead of providing for individual suits against discriminatory practices, sets up a uniform standard for registration. In areas where qualifying tests, discriminatorily applied, prevented more than half the Negro citizens from registering, Federal referees would register Negro voters for all elections. This approach obviates the need for cumbersome court procedures.

But experience under the earlier system suggests that the new law alone will not solve all the problems. Even after the earlier government voting suits had been won and the registrars enjoined from further discriminatory practices, the change in the number of people voting has not been encouraging. The reasons for this disappointing result in the past are likely to apply in the future also. Scores of suits against registrars who are discriminating—even the new voting bill—are of little practical value if there is not at the same time some kind of correlative action to protect the exercise of that right which the court or Congress has declared is being abridged. James Forman, executive secretary of the Student Nonviolent Coordinating Committee, outlined the civil rights workers' plight in these words in a recently published interview:

> It is hard to describe the irony of the situation. Voting is a constitutional right. We take the time out of school, take all sorts of risks and try to register folks. When you get no help, that's pretty demoralizing. Take Mississippi. The government has filed suits. O.K. But people are still scared. They tell us, "All right, I'll go down to register, but what are you going to do for me when I lose my job and they beat my head?" And we can't do anything. The local folks are beginning to doubt that it's worth the risk.[1]

As long as people are beaten, their homes bombed, their economic lifelines cut, their family's lives threatened, their attempts at political organization thwarted—all with the purpose of keeping them from realizing their power at the ballot box, the process of change through the franchise will be severely restricted. On the other hand, a vigorous protection of the exercise of these rights would give confidence to the intimidated and hasten the day when participation in the democratic political process will have real meaning for Negroes in the South. With the election of fair sheriffs, school board members, police chiefs, mayors, county commissioners, and state officials, the Justice Department could withdraw from the scene and again play the restrained role that it has assumed until now.

The 1965 Voting Rights Act provides for Federal prosecution of those who interfere with the rights granted under the act. But similar laws providing for prosecution of those who intimidate voters or potential voters have existed for some time in the United States Code. Under Title 42, Section 1971 (b) of the U.S. Code, the government can enjoin anyone, "whether acting under color of law or otherwise," from intimidating those who are attempting to exercise their franchise in a Federal election. Under Title 18, Section 594, there are criminal penalties of up to $1,000 fine and one year in jail for "whoever intimidates, threatens, coerces or attempts to intimidate, threaten or coerce any other person for the purpose of interfering with the right of such other person to vote or to vote as he may choose. . . ." Yet those provisions were rarely invoked by the Justice Department, with the result that potential voters knew they were taking substantial risks in asserting their rights.

The fact that these broad powers to deter intimidation of voters have not been fully exploited is due at least in part to the narrow view of "voting" taken by the Justice Department. In the Mississippi or Alabama context, it is not only the registration process *per se* and the casting of the ballot *per se* which constitute "voting," but the whole gamut of activity involved in making a deliberately disfranchised and intimidated group of people aware of their political rights and introducing them to their use. It is not difficult to show that much of the violence perpetrated on would-be voters and on civil rights workers has the conscious purpose of discouraging the exercise of the ballot by Negroes. The nexus between much of the work of the civil rights groups in the South and the exercise of the franchise is close enough, and the intent of the statutes involved is clear enough to give good grounds for applying the intimidation-of-voters statutes in cases involving attacks on and intimidation of workers in this field.

Similarly, in the future the widest possible protection must be given by the Federal government to Negroes trying to register under the new voting bill and to workers assisting them in doing so. Otherwise the rights given by Congress will be completely vitiated by local authorities using all their power to maintain the status quo.

Violence and Lawlessness

The mandate for Federal action in this area comes from a failure of a state to protect its citizens and to live up to its responsibilities under the Constitution. As long as these responsibilities are being fulfilled, there are no grounds for wide-scale Federal action, but when they are being disregarded, the Federal government must step in to fill the vacuum. The alternative, to let the lawless hold sway, is unpalatable; it is also at odds with an appreciation of the true nature of federalism. The basis for wider Federal action in Mississippi is apparent. The catalog of violence and lawlessness in that state is a matter of record, and for every deed of cruelty and crime of violence in Mississippi, there are others that never come to light. This fact was dramatized by the discovery of two half-bodies of Negro men in the Pearl River during the summer of 1964, when a search was being conducted for the three missing civil rights workers. Until the gruesome find, there had been no popular knowledge, interest or concern about the two missing Mississippi black men. But Negroes in Mississippi will tell you that the murky waters of the Pearl have hidden many secrets beneath their surface.

The U.S. Commission on Civil Rights, the branch of the

Federal government chiefly responsible for research and fact-finding in the area of civil rights, in January, 1963, published the findings of its Mississippi Advisory Committee, made up of prominent local citizens, concerning conditions obtaining in the state. Among the findings were the following:

> . . . justice under law is not guaranteed for the Negro in Mississippi in the way that it is for the white man. . . . We find that terror hangs over the Negro in Mississippi and is an expectancy for those who refuse to accept their color as a badge of inferiority . . .
>
> . . . the state government of Mississippi is not sufficiently concerned with the task of protecting the rights of all the citizens of Mississippi. . . . A firm position . . . would reduce the tendency of lesser officials to abuse their authority and would enhance the respect of the people for the State Government . . . [The] attitude of the State Government, rather than being one of protection, has been one of obstruction. . . . The Committee finds that the Federal Government has not provided the citizens of Mississippi the protection due them as American citizens. The Department of Justice has acted in good faith, but the present interpretation of the function of the Civil Rights Division of the Justice Department is unduly and unwisely narrow and limited.

In April, 1963, the Civil Rights Commission made an interim report to the President and Congress in order to describe further the situation in Mississippi and elsewhere in the South:

> Citizens of the United States have been shot, set upon by vicious dogs, beaten and otherwise terrorized because they sought to vote. Since October, students have been fired upon, ministers have been assaulted and the home of the Vice-Chairman of the State Advisory Committee to this Commission has been bombed. Another member and his wife were jailed on trumped-up charges after their home had been defiled. Even children, at the brink of starvation, have been deprived of assistance by the callous and discriminatory acts of Mississippi officials administering Federal funds.

Before the summer of 1964 the Council of Federated Organizations had sought protection of its constitutional rights as it carried out its work in Mississippi. The wide-scale Federal action they had hoped for was not forthcoming. At the end of the four months of the Summer Project, *The New York Times* reported a total of 3 dead, 83 persons injured, 35 churches burned, 31 bombings and over 1,000 arrests of civil rights workers.

Federal Intervention and Civil Rights

Both former Attorney General Robert Kennedy and former Assistant Attorney General Burke Marshall have answered pleas for a greater show of Federal force with the reply, "We have no national police force." It has been a standard practice for representatives of the executive branch of the government to disclaim responsibility for the protection of citizens' rights on these grounds. The then Deputy Attorney General Nicholas Katzenbach told a Boston College audience in April, 1964, that civil rights workers would have to depend upon state and local officials to protect their rights and that "to do anything else would be making major changes in the Federal system." Katzenbach also echoed a view which he shares with Burke Marshall about civil rights workers' lack of understanding of the nature of federalism and the failure of the nation's educational institutions to give them such an understanding. He said that civil rights groups "through despair or ignorance of the Federal system seek to invoke the power of the Federal government to enforce personal rights." In November of 1964, Katzenbach, serving then as Acting Attorney General, told a University of Miami group, "There is no answer which embraces both compassion and law."

In June of 1964, John Doar, who was to replace Burke Marshall as head of the Civil Rights Division upon Marshall's resignation in December of that year, told a group of students at Oxford, Ohio, in an orientation program for the

Mississippi Summer Project, that they could not expect to receive protection from the Federal government. "We simply do not have the necessary tools to cope with the problem," said Doar.

J. Edgar Hoover, Director of the Federal Bureau of Investigation, was sent on a special mission by President Johnson to Mississippi, in the wake of the disappearance of the three civil rights workers in the summer of 1964. He held a press conference in Jackson at which he said that the FBI does not "and will not give protection to civil rights workers. . . . The protection of individual citizens . . . is a matter for the local authorities. The FBI will not participate in any such protection."

On June 24, 1964 Attorney General Robert Kennedy told an NAACP delegation that the situation in Mississippi was a "local matter for law enforcement" and declared to them that his power to act in this area was "very limited."

Kennedy's view was challenged almost immediately by twenty-nine law school professors in six of the nation's leading law schools. Their statement pointed up the misleading effect of the comments made by the Attorney General. Their criticism is one that applies to many of the postures assumed by the Federal government on the crucial question of Federal protection of civil rights in the South—the failure to distinguish *power* from *policy*. It is honest for Federal officials to tell the public that they do not think a certain course of action is wise under the circumstances, but dishonest to tell them that they do not have the power to exercise under the circumstances. In the former case there can at least be some kind of dialogue on the question of whether the existing situation justifies a certain course of action; in the latter, the only result is to mislead a trusting public and to arouse those in the legal profession with a knowledge of the arsenal of power at the disposal of the executive branch of the government. The Attorney General's decision in the summer of 1964 not to take further action in Mississippi was based upon a policy, and not a power, consideration. In reply to Kennedy the professors cited Title 10, Section 333 of the U.S. Code, which says in part:

The President, by using the militia or the armed forces, or both, *or by any other means,* [my emphasis] shall take such measures as he considers necessary to suppress, in a state, any domestic violence, unlawful combination, or conspiracy, if it—

(1) so hinders the execution of the laws of that State, and of the United States within the State, that any part or class of its people is deprived of a right, privilege, immunity, or protection named in the Constitution and secured by law, and the constituted authorites of that State are unable, fail, or refuse to protect that right, privilege, or immunity, or to give that protection; or

(2) opposes or obstructs the execution of the laws of the United States or impedes the course of justice under those laws. . . .

The professors were highly critical of the misleading nature of what the Attorney General had said:

Doubtless some creditable considerations of expedience could be cited to support a decision against now taking vigorous presidential action under Section 333 in Mississippi. Surely, however, the Attorney-General's position would be less misleading and therefore less perilous if he would acknowledge that the President today has power to act but believes that police action under Section 333 of Title 10 is inadvisable.

The professors concluded that:

It is at once disappointing and ironic, that the Department of Justice, which has been bold beyond precedent in successfully urging the Supreme Court that the judiciary possesses the broadest powers to enforce the constitutional assurances of equality, should now discover non-existent barriers to executive action.[2]

Only after the Selma crisis in March, 1965, did Attorney General Katzenbach begin to talk of the *desirability* instead of the *power* of the Federal government to send troops if necessary to protect the rights of Alabama's Negro citizens.

That the executive branch of the government possesses the power to act and needs only to make the pertinent policy decision was made abundantly clear by the late President Kennedy in a telegram that he sent to Governor Wallace of Alabama during the Birmingham crisis of May, 1963; it said in part:

> Under this section [Title 10, Section 333] which has been invoked by my immediate predecessor and other Presidents as well as myself on previous occasions, the Congress entrusts to the President all determinations as to (1) the necessity for action; (2) the means to be employed; and (3) the adequacy or inadequacy of the protection afforded by state authorities to the citizens of that state.

Under Title 10, Section 333, there is clearly scope for the widest possible action.

The situation in many parts of the South makes the Federal government's emphasis upon local control appear misplaced. Good constitutionalists will readily accept the need for "local control" but also ask the question "subject to what?" The answer can only be, "to the requirements of the Constitution." In all situations the supremacy of the Federal law and Constitution should be made plain. To leave protection entirely in the hands of local authorities can be cruelly insensitive to the problems at hand, for in many instances it is these very local authorities themselves who are the source of the difficulty. The victims of reckless disregard of the Constitution are in effect asked to depend upon their victimizers for their deliverance.

The statement, "We have no national police force," is frequently given in response to pleas for Federal protection as if this concluded the matter. It does not. The plea for protection is not predicated upon the existence of a national police force—nor is one advocated. What *is* known is that we have what is, in effect, a Federal police force in the form of the FBI, which makes arrests for violation of Federal law in other areas. The disclaimer that it is only an "investigatory" body will not stand even the most superficial analysis. The FBI makes arrest for Federal bank robbery, espionage, kidnapping, narcotics violations, and other crimes. There is no legitimate reason why it cannot make on-the-spot arrests for violations of the Federal civil rights statutes. Title 18, Section 3052 allows the FBI to make arrests without warrant for any offense against the United States committed in their presence, or for any felony cognizable under the laws of the United States if they have reasonable grounds to believe that the person to be arrested has committed or is committing such felony. Under the following section, 3053, Federal marshals' arrest powers are outlined, and under Title 28, Section 549, marshals "may exercise the same powers which a sheriff of such state may exercise in executing the laws thereof." In 1963 the Notre Dame Conference on Congressional Civil Rights Legislation rejected the notion that delicate considerations of federalism were at stake or that a radical change in the existing law was needed to meet the problem. A statement from the conference maintained:

> New and more refined legislative remedies are not required to reach this blatant disregard of rights. To contain and disarm lawlessness, a clear federal presence is required at the first outbreaks. We think that the Attorney General has the power, in the face of determined lawlessness supported by an acquiescent or conspiratorial community, to send federal marshals and agents of the Federal Bureau of Investigation for on-the-spot protection of the exercise of federal rights. Such marshals and federal agents should be deployed in accordance with principles normally governing in law enforcement, in numbers and with authority adequate to deal with all anticipated exigencies, including authority and instructions to enforce compliance with federal law and to make arrests for violations.

The succession of events in Selma, Alabama, leading up to the bloody Sunday of March 7, 1965, provides a good example of where early preventive action by the Federal government might have averted violence and bloodshed. The Justice Department did not intervene vigorously in the Selma crisis until *after* 26-year-old Negro Jimmie Lee Jackson was killed by a state trooper; until *after* hundreds of Negro men, women and children had been tear-gassed, bull-whipped, and billy-clubbed; until *after* a white Boston minister, the Reverend James J. Reeb, had had his skull crushed and was left dying on a Selma street. The situation in Selma had deteriorated long before these events took place. The extent of the interference, violence and intimidation by private persons and state and local officials had been great enough to justify Federal intervention under Title 10, Section 333, and the general powers of the Chief Executive. It certainly was great enough to make arrests of Selma authorities for violations of Federal law.

The nature and the scope of the interference with Negroes by Governor Wallace and those working under his direction merited the Justice Department's asking for an injunction against their interference with the right to vote and the right to demonstrate. But it was only after the brutal events of that Sunday and what followed immediately in their wake that the Justice Department took steps to bring charges against private citizens and state and local authorities for Federal violations. It was only then that the Justice Department sought a Federal injunction against Governor Wallace, Director of Alabama Department of Public Safety Albert Lingo, and Sheriff of Dallas County James Clark, to prevent them from interfering with the Negroes' right to register, vote and demonstrate peacefully. The language of the injunction sought asked that these men be enjoined from interfering with "lawful, peaceable demonstrations on behalf of the rights of Negroes by attempting forceably to disperse the demonstrators or seeking to impose unreasonable conditions on the demonstrators." An injunction in exactly these same words, running against these very same people, backed by whatever Federal force necessary to make it effective, had it been drawn *prior* to the proposed march, would have provided the type of protection that previous events had shown was so necessary in that Alabama city.

Federal Presence

Reluctance on the part of the Federal government to play a larger role in the Deep South can be attributed at least in part to its fear that to do so might lead to an abdication of responsibility by those local officials charged with keeping the peace, and might bring about a situation of such violence and chaos that nothing less than a Federal occupation would be necessary. Robert Kennedy has asked, "Should the role of the Federal Government be merely to stand by and let these activities [wide-scale violence and deprivation of constitutional rights] continue?" The answer he gives is that: "The decision to use marshals or troops against the wishes of a state government and a substantial proportion of the citizens of the state is one of the most difficult decisions that an Attorney General must recommend and that a President must make." Burke Marshall contends that Federal marshals do not enjoy the respect of the local people and are not thought of as law enforcement officers by them; an increase in their presence and duty would not be strong enough in the face of local opposition. He cites as an example the Meredith-Ole Miss case, in which the marshals were almost overwhelmed by the local people before the troops came in as reinforcements. Because the need for the use of force is found to escalate, in Marshall's view a decision to use marshals in Mississippi is much more than just that. It is a decision to occupy the state, since this would be the inevitable consequence of the use of Federal marshals.

Some civil rights advocates have favored just that—"a marshal on every porch"—if this is ultimately what it takes to bring law enforcement to Mississippi. They reason that, however distasteful and disruptive a large-scale Federal intervention might be, to choose not to act is to surrender to the forces of lawlessness that hold sway in some parts of the South. Such intervention may be the only answer in a place like Neshoba County, Mississippi, where a county official bluntly told a group of NAACP officers, "In Neshoba County you haven't got any civil rights."

The difficulty with so much of the discussion of this question is that it has been considered in either-or terms. There are ways of approaching the problem which embrace neither a large-scale take-over of what are properly state functions nor a policy of refraining from action in the interest of federalism. As Hazel Brannon Smith, courageous Pulitzer Prize-winning publisher of Mississippi's *Lexington Advertiser*, has pointed out on a number of occasions, most of the people in Mississippi are law-abiding and the forces of violence that are in control do not represent the majority of the community. If a situation of law and order could be established, she says, then most of the people would go along with it.

What is needed at this stage at least is not a Federal occupation, but what is called in the civil rights movement a greater "Federal presence." That is, there is a distinct need for a highly visible Federal government to be seen enforcing law and creating a just as well as an ordered atmosphere. An example of Federal concern and a show of Federal power would help to create a climate in which law and order could operate as they should. The role of the Federal government within the state should be one of guidance; a mere presence would inhibit acts of official and private violence. And where this is not sufficient, injunctions against law enforcement officials who abuse their authority, coupled with more arrests under the civil right statutes, would serve notice that the Federal government is not content to stand by while the rights and dignity of American citizens are being violated with impunity.

Burke Marshall's example of Oxford, Mississippi, is atypical. A specific instance in which the Federal government has been called in to integrate a university is quite different from a more general, but less blatant, course of action in which Federal officers go about their duty on a day-to-day basis, enforcing Federal law and protecting the rights of individuals. Rather than precipitating violence, this approach prevents it. Marshall's approach is one of neutralizing— to maintain a modicum of order. It depends upon the non-violence of Negroes and civil rights workers; as long as Negroes and civil rights workers continue to endure the violence as they have until now, this approach will seem to be working; but if ever they begin to answer violence with violence, the situation will deteriorate into one of much worse lawlessness than now prevails. This can be avoided by the proper kind of preventive action which yet falls short of occupation.

The Justice Department has been equivocal on the use of its injunctive powers to prevent violence and the interference with the exercise of constitutional rights. In his Gino Speranza lectures Burke Marshall declares, "There is nothing to do unless something happens." Other authorities on constitutional law, among them Professor Charles Black of the Yale Law School, have said that this position is unsound, and that the Justice Department may seek injunctions against "massive and widespread violations of fundamental law." They assert that the government could go into the Federal courts and secure injunctions to enjoin policemen or other officials from interfering with the right of free speech, the right to distribute leaflets, the right to picket peacefully, the right to hold peaceful demonstrations, or the right to vote and register without intimidation. Marshall contends that: "The problem is that legal concepts have developed in terms of individual personal rights, but the rights of masses of an entire race are affected all at once. The solution is more within the control of the states than anywhere else." Whatever validity this argument may have in other realms of law, it flies in the face of the historical and legislative background out of which many of the civil rights statutes have arisen. These statutes were designed specifically to prevent the kinds of violence, night-riding and intimidation of Negroes—as a class—that still exist today.

Since the Hayes-Tilden compromise of 1876, the United States government has been derelict in living up to the constitutional mandate of the Reconstruction laws drafted to ensure that the Negro would not have to wear the badge of servitude in any form after attaining his new status of free man and citizen. Indeed, since 1876 the situation toward which this legislation was directed has remained substantially the same. Marshall further invokes the reluctance of Federal courts to interfere with the state criminal process when it is at work. He says that the courts will not enjoin a *pending* or *future* state criminal proceeding. But later in the same lecture he admits that this has been done, that there is no *constitutional* inhibition that prevents its being done, only certain "notions" or "concepts" about Federal-state relations. Once again what started as an argument about the lack of power becomes a statement of policy, of preference.

A Federal court in a recent Louisiana case stated that where a complaint "is based upon a state law which is contrary to the superior authority of the United States constitution, the Nation, as well as the aggrieved individuals, is injured." Marshall's assertions that he needs special statutory authority for injunctions in other than voting cases is contrary to what the Supreme Court has said on this issue. The Court's convoluted reasoning in *In re Debs*[3] has been questioned, but the case nevertheless points up the fault in Marshall's position. In that case the government secured an injunction against a railroad strike, although Congress had passed no statute giving it the right to ask for an injunction in such a case. The Supreme Court in the *Debs* case said:

> Every government, entrusted by the very terms of its being with powers and duties to be exercised and discharged for the general welfare, has a right to apply to its own courts for any proper assistance . . . whenever the wrongs complained of . . . are in respect of matters which by the Constitution are entrusted to the care of the nation. . . .

This is argument from major purposes. Any government is expected, by the very terms of its existence, to have the authority to enforce its own law upon its own territory. There is ample statement of this enforcement power in both U.S. statutory and case law. Justice Bradley, writing for the Supreme Court in the case of *Ex Parte Siebold*[4] in 1879, described the broad range of Federal power in these words:

> We hold it to be an incontrovertible principle that the government of the United States may, by means of physical force exercised through its official agents, execute on every foot of American soil the powers to command obedience to its laws and hence the power to keep the peace to that extent.

In spite of the constitutional arguments to the contrary, the Justice Department has generally denied that it has the power to seek injunctions unless statutorily granted; this has been one of the leading arguments against wider Federal action in the South. However, a look at the record almost makes it appear that the Federal government does not *want* such power. A subcommittee proposal to include a section in the new Civil Rights Act to broaden Justice Department powers in this area was dropped at the insistence of the then Attorney General, Robert Kennedy, who claimed that increased power of this nature would damage Federal-state relations and the restriction of police power to state control. The Justice Department has taken action which deviates from this general disclaimer, however: in 1961 it enjoined the prosecution of a Mississippi Negro registration worker on the grounds that such a prosecution would intimidate other Negroes in the area who were attempting to vote. And in 1964 it sought an injunction against Sheriff Jim Clark of Selma, Alabama, after he and other officials had followed a long and especially abusive course of harassment of Negroes attempting to register and vote in that city. However, both of these cases involved voting rights, and the power to seek injunctions in voting cases has been specifically granted by statute; thus the problem of injunctions in cases for which there has been no specific authorization for the Justice Department to seek injunctive relief is still open for contention.

The preventive advantages of an injunction are considerable and the sanctions for disobeying it are more certain of being applied than in a criminal situation where a jury trial is required, since trial for contempt of an injunction does not require a jury. It thus alleviates some of the problems involved in obtaining convictions of those accused of civil rights crimes under the jury system.

In addition to statutes supporting broad statewide Federal action in cases of emergency, there are many statutes that provide a legal basis for day-to-day Federal action. Title 18, Section 241 is one of the main civil rights criminal statutes. This makes it a crime for

. . . two or more persons to conspire to injure, oppress, threaten, or intimidate any citizen in the free exercise or enjoyment of any right or privilege secured to him by the Constitution or laws of the United States, or because of his having so exercised the same.

The background of this statute shows that it was directed mainly at *private* acts of violence which were being used as a means of keeping the Negro from voting. The statute was drafted, during Reconstruction, with the Ku Klux Klan specifically in mind. Though potentially an extremely powerful weapon, the Federal government had virtually ignored it in recent times until the FBI arrested three men on the spot in Itta Bena, Mississippi, on June 26, 1964, when they were interfering with voter registration workers. This was a distinct departure from the usual policies the Federal government had been following. Such on-the-spot, rather than after-the-fact, action can save much bloodshed and many lives. Other Federal statutes could be used tellingly in dealing with the problems of violence and lawlessness in the South, in view of the burnings and church bombings of the summer of 1964. Under Title 18, Section 1509, it is a Federal crime to interfere with the "due exercise of rights or performance of duties under any order, judgement, or decree of a court of the United States." Title 18, Section 837, covers the illegal use of explosives and threats to damage or destroy "real or personal property by fire or explosives." Title 18, Section 1074, makes "flight to avoid prosecution for damaging or destroying any building or other real or personal property" a Federal crime.

The other major civil rights statute with criminal sanctions is Title 18, Section 242, which deals with deprivation of civil rights under color of law. This statute is directed towards violations of constitutional rights by policemen and other public officials. However, the simple fact of deprivation of a civil right under the color of law—and there have been thousands—is not enough under this statute. Because of the way the Supreme Court interpreted it in the case of *Screws v. United States*[5] in 1945, it must be shown that this deprivation was "willful." It is not enough that the officer was acting with bad purpose. He need not be thinking in "constitutional terms," however; and a "reckless disregard" of civil rights may be enough to sustain a conviction under this statute. But the limitations of the requirement of "willfulness" imposed by the *Screws* case, make convictions under Section 242 very difficult. This difficulty could be alleviated in part by pressing for a more liberal construction of the *Screws* case in the courts, but in order for this to happen, several events would have to take place in sequence. The department would have to ask for a broader interpretation of Section 242 at the trial court level, and if it were accepted, the losing defendant would then have to appeal it up through the appellate level to the Supreme Court for its decision whether to strike it down or to sanction it—if rejected, the government would have to do the appealing.

Generally in applying Federal criminal statutes, grand jury indictment is required before a case can be brought to trial. One way of avoiding this problem with Section 242, however, is to use a procedural device known as an information. A charge under Section 242 is a misdemeanor, and misdemeanor cases do not need grand jury indictments before they can be heard. A U.S. Attorney has only to file a sworn statement, or information, setting out the charges against the defendant, and with this the case can be brought. This is, in fact, what happens with most criminal misdemeanors handled by the Justice Department, but an exception seems to be made for charges under Section 242. Recently the department has used the information in some cases, but this represents a departure from past practice and cannot yet be regarded as general policy. Aside from the use of the information, more prosecutions under Section 242 might arise if the Justice Department did not rely so heavily on the decision made by the local U.S. Attorney on whether to prosecute. Most U.S. Attorneys come from the area where they serve. The Civil Rights Commission has pointed out in its 1961 report that although most U.S. Attorneys can be counted on to do their job regardless of the prejudices of their local community, some have "consistently opposed the prosecution of police brutality cases" on matters involving deprivation of civil rights under color of law.

The number of instances in which the Justice Department is asked to take some action under Section 242 is large; the number in which they do so is quite small. This comes from an overcautious policy in the face of the *Screws* case and southern juries, and also, it seems, from a desire to prosecute only when convictions are reasonably certain. Underlying all of this there seems to be a reluctance to use this criminal statute to help correct the situation that obtains in the South. The department seems to hope that it can educate the local officials out of their practices and believes it will not help their growth to responsibility to arrest them; it also hopes that the concentration on voting will eventually change both the situation and the type of man who holds office in the South to such an extent that the current emphasis on local control will not be misplaced. It is this policy of caution now, in the hope of a better future, that is misplaced. The department puts too much faith in time as a panacea. Time is neutral. It is the scope and nature of action in time that makes the difference, and the Federal government has not initiated sufficient action to achieve the kind of change it advocates. It is not necessary that an attitudinal change precede a behavioral change. Behavior often conditions attitudes. The crucial goal at this moment should be to assert the supremacy of the law of the land, not make lawfulness depend upon a change in the "hearts and minds" of the lawless.

There are indications that because of the difficulty of obtaining convictions from a southern jury in cases of persons accused of civil rights crimes, the Federal government has chosen to rely more upon a community-education, almost a public-relations, approach than upon a wide use of the criminal statutes. A great deal of the time of Roy K. Moore, head of the FBI in Mississippi, is spent in giving after-dinner speeches designed to educate the local population to the functions and role of the FBI in the state. He seeks to remove from their minds the image of the FBI as "outsiders" or "invaders," to let them see that the FBI's interest is in the lawless element, and to show them how different are the interests of this element from those of the law-abiding members of the community. The arrests made of bombers during the reign of terror in McComb is used as an example: here, among those arrested were not only opponents of civil rights but also a bank robber. The "educational" approach is important, but it is no substitute for prosecutions. In most cases no bank robbers are involved; instead, there may be some of the "pillars of the community"—an elected official, a small businessman, a yeoman farmer, or even a minister of the gospel. Moral suasion alone is inadequate to meet the needs in Mississippi. But suasion coupled with civil action, such as voter suits, has been put forward as the best approach to the problem by many who feel that repeated failures by the Federal government to obtain indictments or convictions in civil rights cases would have a deleterious effect on the prestige of the Federal government, on its effectiveness, and on the respect with which it is regarded by local people.

However, the mere bringing of cases and exposure of government evidence have an educational effect—on those of the local community still able to be educated, and on the wider community outside. Not to prosecute makes it appear that the government is unconcerned and that there has been little change from the decades of Federal inaction in the Deep South. On the other hand, there is value to requiring persons accused of civil rights crimes to answer charges in court. As a result, they might be less hasty in taking the courses of action that would lead to their prosecutions.

In the long run, if nonconviction continues, the government will have to re-evaluate its basic approach to trial by jury, and find creative ways to meet this systematic denial of equal justice. The constitutional right to jury trial in certain types of criminal cases is regarded almost as sacrosanct, but also in the Constitution are guarantees of "equal protection of the law" designed specifically for the abolition of a double standard of justice. The jury system is not so sacrosanct that it cannot at least be re-examined in

the way it operates in Mississippi. Here in civil rights
cases, Negroes and civil rights workers do not receive fair
trials under the jury system. In these kinds of cases, and in
cases of local whites on trial for civil rights crimes, a systematic study both of the cases that have been brought and
of those that have not been brought shows that the jury
system in Mississippi works as an arm of the state in perpetuating a white supremacist society. Resignation to these
facts is not appropriate to the Federal government. The approach suggested to Acting Attorney General Katzenbach in
a letter from twenty-one congressmen in December, 1964,
concerning the case of the men accused of conspiring to
violate the rights of the three COFO workers killed near
Philadelphia, Mississippi, that summer, was to have the
chief judge of the circuit appoint a different judge to sit in
the case and require that a new panel for jurors be selected
which would include Negroes. This is a step in the right
direction. It represents an appreciation of the nature of the
situation and turns away from a blind reliance on a historic
system—a reliance that, in this context, is hostile to the
purposes of that system.

This, in and of itself, will not be sufficient, however. Of
course, ultimately the aim is to bring the state to a level
of law and order where Federal intervention will be unnecessary, but until that day a more creative approach by
the Justice Department is vital. In addition to having the
supervision of the chief judge of the circuit in Federal cases,
a change in the laws with regard to venue might be found
to be useful. At present it is the *defendant's* right under certain circumstances to ask for such a change. Machinery
is needed which would enable the aggrieved party, or the
government when bringing the action, to move for a change
of venue to an area where the jury system could be expected to operate without undue bias. The power to "remove" cases from the state to the Federal system already
exists in civil rights cases—where the defendant has legitimate reason to believe that he will not receive a fair trial
in the state courts—and as a result of the Civil Rights Act
of 1964, an order from a judge refusing to grant removal

is appealable. These special provisions in the legal code will eventually become vestigial organs of the law, but in the interest of justice now they could be of significant value. Beyond these measures, greater care in the selection of Federal judges in the South is an absolute necessity.

The FBI, like the Justice Department, has been harshly criticized for its role in the South. Civil rights workers have often found the FBI "cold, unresponsive and at times hostile." Based upon statements made by J. Edgar Hoover and former agents of the FBI, the Civil Rights Commission report of 1961 concluded that there is a certain reluctance on the part of the FBI to become involved in civil rights matters. In the fall of 1964, J. Edgar Hoover called Nobel Peace Prize winner the Reverend Martin Luther King "the most notorious liar in America" as a result of remarks King had allegedly made concerning FBI performance in Albany, Georgia. But criticism of the FBI-men for their biased racial attitudes and for their inaction is echoed throughout the South. Randolph T. Blackwell, program director of the Southern Christian Leadership Conference, for example, recounts that he was in a car blasted by fourteen shots during a voter registration trip in March, 1963, near Greenwood, Mississippi. His co-worker, Jimmy Travis, was hit in the head and neck. According to Blackwell, "The FBI investigated, but I felt as if I was talking to a member of the Ku Klux Klan. He was suggesting, 'Are you boys sure you didn't shoot up this car?' "[6] The resident Greenwood FBI agent, George Everett, in August of that year, retired and ran successfully for District Attorney of Leflore Country. In his campaign he contended that: "The South has no friends in the legal staff of the Justice Department."

From the report of the Civil Rights Commission it would seem that at least part of the difficulty for the FBI arises from the Bureau's need for close cooperation with and its great dependence upon the local police to help them do their job in areas other than civil rights. For example, an agent in the South may find himself in the embarrassing position one afternoon of having to investigate the officer with whom he had been working on another case that morning. With adequate manpower, this should present no problem, and there were 6,140 agents, as of 1964. However, if the link between FBI-men and local authorities is a problem, Professor Howard Zinn of Boston University has made an interesting proposal to meet it. He advocates the creation of a force of "E" (Emancipation) Men—a group of Federal agents to work in the Deep South and any other part of the country where they are needed to protect the constitutional rights of persons against unlawful private or official action. They would be present at all civil rights demonstrations, be subject to immediate calls for help, and have the power to make on-the-spot arrests. They would be trained in the use of persuasion and mediation. In addition, every local police station in the country could have a "hot line" direct to the regional Federal agent's office, so that a person arrested could get immediate help if needed.

There is much the Federal government can do, quite apart from statutes and executive action in the way of establishing a Federal presence in Mississippi and other states where similar conditions prevail, and providing the kind of atmosphere and guidelines the Southern Regional Council in its report, *Law Enforcement in Mississippi,* has pointed out are needed. In an open letter to President Johnson in October, 1964, eighteen congressmen called on the Federal government to "take all necessary steps to prevent further violence and bloodshed" in the civil rights struggle in Mississippi. They set forth a multi-point program for a greater Federal role which, they felt, would help obtain this end. The program asked for consisted of: more permanent FBI agents in the state; branch offices of the FBI throughout the state—especially in the southwest; an FBI report on the violence in Mississippi in the summer of 1964, on the lines of their report on the northern urban riots of the same summer; enforcement of Sections 241 and 242; the convening of a Federal grand jury to investigate possible connections between rights violations, bombings, etc., and law enforcement officers; establishment of a branch of the Civil Rights Division of the Justice Department and of the newly created Federal Community Relations Service there; and finally hearings conducted there by the Civil Rights Commission. The Civil Rights Commission has, in fact, attempted to hold hearings in Mississippi before but for a while was prevented from doing so by the Department of Justice. And all these proposals would be of value in the Mississippi situation.

The Politics of Justice

The Federal government now, when compared to its performance in the past, is making great steps forward in the effort to guarantee for all persons their fundamental civil rights under the Constitution. But this is relative: its performance falls far short of what it could and, it is contended here, should be doing. Those at the head of the Civil Rights Division have a hard brief to hold. They have the responsibility for directing the affairs of the division, keeping in mind not only the fervor of today's crisis but also the lasting structure of our government in the years to come. This, however, should lead them to conclude that in the present situation more, not less, action is needed. But department officials continue to talk in terms of *adequacy of power*, when the crucial issues now are matters of *policy*: the question in most situations should be not "Can the Federal government do it?" but "Should the Federal government do it under the circumstances?"

There are, of course, questions of politics behind the department's posture. These in essence amount to: "What will be the effect on this administration in the political arena of such and such a course of action?" The answer has been and will be different, depending on what administration is asking the question and what kind of goals it had set out for in the first place. Federal agencies are expected to be influenced by political considerations. However, decisions with regard to the fundamental rights of citizenship are of a different order than those concerning, for example, antitrust activities. Such rights are not negotiable.

The Department of Justice is at present bound by the political considerations involved in appropriations—while Mayor Thompson of Jackson, Mississippi may request with assurance and receive the 2.2 million dollars he wants for an armored tank and stronger police force, Burke Marshall dare not be so confident in asking for the modest sum of one million dollars to meet the division's increased needs under the augmented responsibility of the Civil Rights Act of 1964. The department is also bound by the amount of public support it can muster in the execution of its programs. But these should not be overriding limitations or accepted as justifications for inaction. The President of the United States, in the face of his constitutional duty and a growing national consensus on civil rights, has it in his power to make a profound contribution to the realization of the American promise despite present obstacles. Many of those involved in the civil rights movement are becoming disillusioned about the response America has made when challenged with its own credo, and have begun to question seriously the efficacy of nonviolence and dependence upon the judicial process. The hour is late, but it is still not too late, for the President and those under his direction to use the powers at their disposal in taking the kinds of bold affirmative action necessary to complete the unfinished business of democracy.

L O U I S L U S K Y

Racial Discrimination and the Federal Law: A Problem in Nullification

—

[ED. NOTE: This article first appeared in the November, 1963, issue of the *Columbia Law Review*. Since that time there have been further developments with respect to a number of the matters discussed. In September, 1964, secondary schools in three separate locales in Mississippi were integrated for the first time and 58 Negro children constituting 0.02 per cent of the total Negro school population attended integrated schools. The Prince Edward County school system also opened on an integrated basis in September, 1964. The Twenty-fourth Amendment to the Constitution forbidding the imposition of a poll tax in any Federal election went into effect in February, 1964. One of the five legislative proposals advanced by Professor Lusky—allowing appeal of remand orders in cases removed from a state court to a Federal court—has been enacted into law under

Louis Lusky is a Professor of Law at Columbia University. He is the author of numerous articles which have appeared in *Harper's* and in many legal and scholastic journals.

a specific provision of the Civil Rights Act of 1964. However, Professor Lusky's analysis of the various legal problems incident to the civil rights movement has as much application today as it did when the article first appeared. Because it ties together a number of different points discussed in earlier articles and puts them into a larger context, the article is reproduced as originally published.]

Gradualism has come to be regarded as a dirty word among Negroes. Ever louder is their demand for equality *now*. Consider the Negro father whose nine-year-old child attends the same Mississippi school he himself attended, and his own father before him. In the year in which the child was born, the Supreme Court unanimously declared that racial segregation in the schools is an unlawful and destructive badge of Negro inferiority, and that the child had a constitutional right to be free of it.[1] Yet not a single grade school or high school in Mississippi has been integrated; and for all that appears, the child (and indeed the child's children and grandchildren) will go through school without ever seeing a Caucasian face there. How can this Negro father be expected to regard litigation as a meaningful process?

Patience is a virtue which belongs to Negroes at least as much as to their fairer-skinned brothers. No general outcry was heard during the long years between 1938, when the Supreme Court began to search out the practical effects of public school segregation,[2] and 1954, when in *Brown v. Board of Education* the Court declared broadly that it violates the equal protection clause. But there is a difference between waiting for the establishment of a right and waiting for its enjoyment after it has been established. It is important to understand the exact nature of that difference and the consequences of ignoring it.

1. *Legitimate Delay and Obstructionism*

Substantial delay is to be expected in the creation of new legal rights. If occasioned by the need for full and careful deliberation or by the time required to convince the law-maker of the merit of the claim for redress of grievances, it is a not unwholesome aspect of our lawmaking system. But delay for its own sake—obstructionism—violates the pivotal compact of the open society, the terms of which are: ungrudging acceptance of the present law in return for effective access to the processes of orderly change.[3] Such violation destroys faith in those processes and constitutes a direct invitation to "self-help," that is, the achievement of desired objectives by force or illegal pressure tactics. Self-help is the negation of civil order; and if employed on a broad scale, it brings on the pervasive coercion of the police state.

Ordinarily, new legal rights are created by the legislature rather than the courts. The legislative process does not purport to be systematic in the sense of providing an articulate response to all demands for action. It is primarily (if not entirely) a means for achieving a fair compromise between the competing needs of the various segments of the community rather than settling specific disputes between particular parties.[4] Unlike courts, which are supposed to press forward to some explicit disposition of the litigated dispute as soon as the litigants have had their say, legislatures are under no formal compulsion to act quickly—or, indeed, to act at all. Whatever a majority of the legislators do or omit is ordinarily accepted by the constituent community without great protest, provided only that the legislature comprises a fair cross-section of the community, and that the community is reasonably homogeneous, in the sense that there is no deep estrangement between substantial segments of the population.[5] It might be said that *inaction* is a standard form of legislative action.

Therefore, legislative inaction cannot rightly be called obstructionism except in the special situation in which the legislature permits itself to be frustrated by a minority of its members—as by a filibuster or arbitrary committee action. When the legislature *has* acted to create new legal rights and the courts deny them expeditious enforcement, obstructionism does occur; but this is rather a rare phenomenon, since a measure so controversial that judges are constrained to ignore or emasculate it (despite their oath to uphold the law) will usually fail of enactment in the first place.

Another way that legal rights are created is by judicial development of new doctrine. This kind of lawmaking demands special attention here, for two reasons: (a) recent changes in the law of racial discrimination have mainly come about in this way; (b) the likelihood of overt obstructionism is much greater than when the legislature has acted, because strongly felt opposition has not had a chance to translate itself into legislative delay or to become reconciled in the process of legislative compromise.

While there is often an indignant charge of judicial usurpation whenever the Supreme Court revises its views as to what the Constitution requires or forbids, it is now pretty well recognized that—under certain circumstances and within certain limits—the Court is entitled and indeed obligated to change the law.[6] Its conception of the *broad objectives* of constitutional provisions such as the due process clauses, the equal protection clause, and the commerce clause has remained remarkably stable over the years. But the rules whereby those objectives are brought to bear upon particular fact situations are always subject to re-examination in the light of (a) changed social conditions,[7] (b) deeper insights into the existence and nature of the public interests that the constitutional provisions are designed to serve,[8] and (c) better understanding of the operation, in actual practice, of rules previously announced.[9]

The process of judicial lawmaking is not a rapid one. Frequently it takes a long time—a period of years or even decades—for a particular issue to reach the stage of generalized and articulate resolution.[10] This is the way the system works, and should work. The slow process of judicial accretion has proved itself to be a relatively sure avenue to ultimate expression of the deep-laid values of the community by our courts—notably the United States Supreme Court—in terms consistent with the real needs, desires, ideals and aspirations of the people as a whole.

These delays often work great hardship. Unless they bear the stamp of obstructionism, however, they provide no justification for repudiation of the process. The alternative road, which is self-help, may in some cases be quicker; but the final result is less secure. Whether the self-help takes the extreme form of revolt, or the milder form of civil disobedience or passive resistance, the objective thus realized by force or coercion or organized lawbreaking lacks the legitimacy and compelling power of a final and official affirmation of legal right.

There are, however, two corollaries to this position: (a) Those who claim new rights can be induced to resort to the courts and legislatures rather than the streets only if they believe that no delays will occur that are not reasonably necessary to the effective operation of our lawmaking system. And, (b) if those claimants are to wait until the lawmaking process is complete before receiving full judicial protection of their interests, they must have confidence that they need not wait *longer* than that. In short, there must be an objectively determined end to the process, as well as something worth waiting for when the end is reached. Lacking this confidence, the claimants will shun litigation as an illusory hope.

The relationship between the claimants and their government has the aspects of an implicit bargain: You wait till the grist is properly ground; we will grind it as fast as our centuries-old millstones can do it, and will give it to you, in form ready to use, as soon as it is done.

Quite clearly, the inevitable consequence of breaking this bargain—let us say this bargain with Negroes, since they are the people whose claims for redress of grievances comprise our present subject matter[11]—is Negro repudiation of the legal approach, and resort to self-help. Should anyone doubt the ineluctable connection between breach of the bargain and election of self-help, the Black Muslims stand ready to remind him.[12]

And yet there are those who, opposing racial integration, claim the normal and necessary delay and then reject the corollaries. Not only do they resist prompt appraisal and disposition of claims for new rights; they also resist or withhold enforcement of legal rights even after they have been confirmed as fully and finally and explicitly as is possible under our system, namely, by unanimous decision of the Supreme Court. Obstructionism in the lawmaking process is sometimes hard to identify (the normal process being itself so slow). But denial of rights *after they have been established* is easy to see and understand. And being not a tactic of delay but a strategy of permanent resistance, it strikes immediately and destructively at the integrity of the whole lawmaking process.

II. *The Techniques of Local Resistance*

We have seen the hazardous game of nullification played in its most dramatic form at Little Rock and Oxford. An abortive effort along the same line took place in the spring of 1963 at the University of Alabama, and at this writing a similar effort with respect to the public schools at four cities in that state has just been defeated. But these experiences, spectacular as they have been, were doomed to failure by their very candor. When the governor of a state openly defies federal law, he creates an issue on which he cannot win. The prestige of the United States itself is automatically challenged, and it cannot back down or compromise.

There are, however, other methods, less flamboyant but far more effective, which have been and are being used. Although they are employed not by private rebels but by public officials acting outside the law, they are essentially similar to guerrilla activities and can rightly be described as such. Basically, these methods shun open defiance of federal law and, paradoxically, take advantage of one of the basic modern improvements in judicial administration: the *discretionary leeway* upon which our legal system has come to rely more and more. Most of the recent advances in the application of legal principles to an increasingly complex subject matter have involved the broadening of official discretion, both in regulatory agencies[13] and the courts,[14] so that the sharp corners of the law can be rounded off to meet the exigencies of particular situations.

This development, wholesome as it is in its primary aspect, carries with it a new danger of abuse. It makes each official—whether a policeman, a justice of the peace, an insurance examiner, a school board, a voting registrar, or whatever—a potential resistance point for frustration of laws disapproved by the local community. Such officials need no formal, centralized direction. They can take their guidance—as effective guerrilla fighters usually do—from the general public pronouncements of some acknowledged leader (whether a private person, such as a retired general, or a public official, such as a governor) uttered in terms of broad policy and general objective for each subordinate official to implement in specific situations.

These guerrilla methods fall into two main types, exemplified by the divergent reactions of Alabama and Mississippi to the so-called Freedom Rides which took place in the spring of 1961. The Alabama method was to withhold official protection of claimed federal rights, and thus to expose the claimants (most, but not all of them, Negroes) to the fury of the local mobs. The Mississippi method was to prosecute the Freedom Riders on plainly unfounded criminal charges.[15]

Well before 1961, the right of unsegregated interstate travel on common carriers was clearly established by the Supreme Court.[16] Nevertheless, the enjoyment of this right has been systematically frustrated in the Deep South, through enforcement of local customs backed up by official action where necessary. The Freedom Riders, by ignoring the custom whereby Negroes were expected to sit in the rear of buses and use separate waiting rooms, made a demand for payment of a constitutional debt long overdue, and provided a clean-cut test of the solidity of the due process, equal protection, and commerce clause guarantees—i.e., a test of the efficacy of legal adjudication in the area of racial discrimination.

When the Freedom Riders arrived in Alabama in May, 1961, the police initially defaulted and the Klans burnt a bus at Anniston and mobbed the Freedom Riders at Birmingham and Montgomery. Then limited martial law was declared, and the federal district court, at the instance of the U.S. Department of Justice, ordered the Montgomery police to do their duty.[17] One group of eleven Freedom Riders was prosecuted in the state court during the martial-law period, but this was an isolated occurrence.[18] From June 2 on, the federal district court was in effective control, and thereafter the issues were litigated there.[19]

In Mississippi there was little or no physical violence; but, beginning on May 24, when the first Freedom Riders arrived, the local authorities arrested them as a matter of course and prosecuted them by the hundreds in the state courts. On June 9 the NAACP Legal Defense office brought a class action for an injunction in the federal district court, but that court adopted a hands-off policy, and even now the substantive issues have not been finally resolved.[20]

Fundamentally, the Alabama reaction was based on the established proposition that the due process and equal protection clauses of the fourteenth amendment apply only to official action by the state or local government and not to purely private action.[21] This has turned out to be an inadequate means of forestalling federal intervention, for two reasons: (a) for some years the federal courts have been whittling down this limitation on the scope of the fourteenth amendment and have been applying it in cases in which the official action is of a passive character;[22] and (b) insofar as interstate commerce is involved, the "state action" rule is inapplicable since the commerce clause prevents private as well as public interference with interstate commerce.[23]

In Mississippi reliance was placed instead on the traditional reluctance of the federal courts to interfere with state *court* proceedings.[24] With the cooperation of the state courts, it was possible to place a very heavy procedural burden upon the Freedom Riders; unless the federal courts could and would prevent it, each Freedom Rider could be made to endure great expense, and a delay of years, in order to obtain vindication of his rights.[25] This approach has thus far been quite successful, for reasons to be explored presently.

The Freedom Ride experience is an apt vehicle for illustrating the two major resistance techniques (action and inaction on the part of the local officials) because it presents the issues in unusually clear form, unvexed by secondary considerations which usually intervene to complicate and befog the primary issue—which is "Why not now?": such considerations as (a) uncertainty as to the legality of the Negroes' actions under existing law (compare the New Orleans sit-in cases[26]); (b) doubt whether official discrimination has in fact occurred (compare the question of school segregation resulting from neighborhood patterns[27]), or is immediately remediable (compare the Brooklyn job demonstrations[28]); (c) the alleged personal unacceptability of a particular Negro (compare the James Meredith case[29]); or (d) collateral problems of public policy (compare the use of juveniles as demonstrators[30]). The Freedom Rides offer the spectacle of obstructionism in its baldest form—clear legal right opposed by naked power.

In other aspects of Negro-white relationships the issues are ordinarily more complex but analysis will reveal the same basic pattern. Obstructionism in each field of activity is accomplished either by lawless official *action* against the Negro and those who espouse his cause, or by official *inaction* that exposes them to lawless private force, or—as is more often the case—by a resourceful combination of the two techniques. Observable throughout is a primary preference on the part of the nullifiers for broad, explicit, and unself-conscious measures.[31] As these laws are held unconstitutional, there is a tendency to switch over to laws fair on their face but adaptable to guerrilla-type administration that imposes on each Negro the burden of proving discrimination in his own particular case.[32] Then, as the emerging pattern of official discrimination condemns these laws in their turn, more emphasis is placed on techniques of official inaction,[33] which, though devastating in their effect on the social fabric, are the hardest for the federal government to reach.

Detailed review of obstructionism in all its protean forms, which together add up to an effort at nullification thus far remarkably successful, would carry this article beyond its proper scope. But mention must be made of one essay in obstructionism that has the special dimension of being nominally under the aegis of the Supreme Court itself.

In all fields other than public education (at the primary and secondary levels), the Court has taken pains to invest its judgments with the finality traditionally accorded to an adjudication of constitutional rights. But in this one field, an excess of devotion to principles of comity and a mistaken faith in the intrinsic force of the supremacy clause have led it to extend an invitation to resistance by inaction. Under the "deliberate speed" formula, which was promulgated upon issuance of the *Brown* mandate in 1955, implementation of the decision is left to the local school authorities with the district courts standing by to supervise.[34] In these circumstances, simple inaction by the school boards has sufficed to hold the line. In most of the Deep South, no integration has taken place at all.[35] By the end of 1962, 0.4 per cent of all Negro students in the eleven states of the Confederacy had been brought into schools also attended by whites, and 2013 biracial school districts out of 2283 were still fully segregated.[36] When, by dint of years of litigation, an occasional school board finally has come up with a "plan," it has usually been one that would keep integration on a token basis for years to come. The time has come for the Supreme Court to recognize that the "deliberate speed" formula involves an unprecedented and dangerous postponement of established legal rights, and to write it off and bury it as a sad mistake.[37] There is some basis for hope that it will do so.[38]

Until now we have confined attention to resistance devices that are used to deal with a single problem or a narrow range of related problems. They might be called narrow-spectrum devices. In order to complete the picture, reference should be made to the arsenal of broad-spectrum devices that supplements and backstops them.

The primary thrust of the narrow-spectrum devices is

to keep the Negro "in his place" in some particular relation-ship—as student, voter, neighbor, passenger, customer—and while there has been an attendant implication of *generally* inferior status, this is not the main objective. So long as the Negro does not seek entry to "white" schools, to the voting booth, etc., he is not molested by these devices.[39]

The broad-spectrum devices, on the other hand, are not thus limited. They deal with the Negro as a whole in-dividual, and their primary thrust is to remind and con-vince *him* that he is an intrinsically inferior order of being who cannot justly claim equal treatment. These broad-spectrum devices include action techniques, such as sys-tematic inequalities in administration of the law: for example, exclusion of Negroes from jury panels and juries,[40] courtroom segregation,[41] unduly light punishment of Ne-groes convicted of crimes against other Negroes,[42] and cruel and unusual punishment of Negroes convicted of crimes against whites, and of convicted whites who have aided Negro protests.[43] Another action technique is the suppres-sion of constitutionally protected speech, press, and as-sembly by local legislation directly restricting parades, picketing, and public meetings.[44] An approach that com-bines action and inaction in a sophisticated and effective manner is: to "investigate" the question whether Negro protest is identified with Communism; to require disclosure of the names and addresses of protesting Negroes, pur-portedly on the ground that this information is essential to the "investigation"; to publicize these names and ad-dresses; and thereby to set up the named individuals as clay pigeons for hostile employers, creditors, landlords, and potential lynchers.[45] This approach will very probably re-main in vogue until the Supreme Court expressly overrules its amazing decision in *Uphaus v. Wyman*,[46] which seems to sanction it. The Court itself appears to have ignored the *Uphaus* decision in a recent Negro protest case,[47] but one can hardly expect Southern lawyers and courts to ignore it so long as it remains nominally in good standing.

Backstopping all these relatively subtle broad-spectrum devices is the old reliable direct remedy, lynch law—assault, arson, and murder (and the threat thereof) as a means of social control. Although lynch law is ordinarily administered by a mob, an individual can also dispense it. The killer of Medgar W. Evers appears to have acted alone,[48] but the killing stands as a warning to tens and hundreds of thousands that active work in the NAACP (Evers was its Mississippi Field Secretary) may be a capital offense. The essential attribute of lynch law is that it is intended as a deterrent to deviant behavior and is so understood.

For any community that contains enough willing murderers, thugs, and arsonists, lynch law provides a solution of a sort. Since the police play no part except to stay away and let the lynchers do their work, it involves little public expense, preparation, or manpower. The trouble with it is that it is relatively difficult to channel and control. The mayor or governor who invites resort to lynch law—whether by direct incitation, or by disparagement of the law, or by the time-honored technique of predicting violence in a thitherto peaceful situation—resembles the camper who builds a roaring fire in a dry forest swept by a high wind. Maybe he can confine it to the job he wants it to do, but the odds are that he cannot. Violence, incited by prediction or otherwise, has not infrequently reached a degree of barbarism which has dismayed even those whose defiance of the law may have triggered it.[49]

With respect to the absence of criminal liability of a public official for acts predictably leading to violence that he does not desire, a curious paradox exists. He is not protected by his official status as such, since public officials are amenable to the normal criminal processes. The practical immunity flowing from the right to a jury trial may be only temporary, since the temper of local opinion may change (and felony prosecutions, particularly for homicide, are normally subject to long statutes of limitations or none at all). What does protect him is the commendable reluctance of modern courts to penalize conduct which, though it encourages others to commit crimes, is not intended to have that effect.[50]

The paradox results from the fact that Southern prosecutors seem to be bent on destroying this very principle. Negroes are being prosecuted on charges ranging from breach of the peace to anarchy and insurrection, on the theory that their conduct—entering a "white" waiting room, or picketing and parading, for example—is likely to bring on violence even though the defendants cannot be shown to have desired it, and even though the anticipated violence has not in fact occurred.[51] Should such prosecutions be successful, a foundation will unwittingly have been laid for criminal prosecution of public officials who sow the wind.

Difficult as it is to punish the encouragement of lynch law, enthusiasm for its use is tempered by the awareness that it brings deterioration in community values for whites as well as Negroes; and there have been some cases in which local juries (usually functioning in the somewhat detached atmosphere of the federal district courts) have either convicted the lyncher[52] or, by disagreeing and reaching no verdict, have given notice that the limit of community tolerance has been approached or reached. Even a few such cases serve as a substantial deterrent to potential stoners, bombers, cross- and barn-burners, pistol-whippers, and murderers.

There is a temptation to generalize about the interplay of the various techniques of action and inaction. Patterns doubtless exist and may provide grist for the mill of the social scientist. For present purposes, however, a single observation is sufficient: all the techniques of official action being reachable by federal power, resistance comes to depend ever more heavily (as federal intervention becomes increasingly effective) upon techniques of official inaction, such as lynching, that are not fully controllable without creation of a state of federal siege.

This brings us to the fundamental issue. The states of the Deep South lack the physical power to resist the federal law by force, but they can create a real dilemma. They can put the federal government to the choice of acquiescing in continued disregard of constitutional requirements or of imposing police state conditions. Nobody was very happy with the steps taken at Little Rock and Oxford.

While protection of minority groups from invidious discrimination is a very important part of the constitutional package which secures and enhances the openness of our society, it is not the whole of it. Maximization of the areas of individual freedom must take account of many freedoms, including at least some freedom to adopt and persist in stupid and wrong-headed and neurotically prejudiced attitudes. The Negroes themselves would suffer, along with the whites, if racial equality were purchased at the price of the broader freedom. They are entitled to as good a society as the whites now enjoy—not to a police state society or anything approaching it.

The only really satisfactory way of dealing with the dilemma created by Southern resistance to federal requirements is (as in the case of any true dilemma) to avoid it. It is by no means certain that this can be done, but there is good basis for hope. The key to the problem is destruction of the stereotype of the Negro which lies at the root of the trouble. But this will take a generation or so, at the least; and meanwhile it is essential to keep the problem in the courts (and legislatures), and away from the devices of Negro separatism and self-help, insofar as it can be done. To accomplish this we must at all costs forestall legalistic delays, typified by the Mississippi reaction to the Freedom Rides, which in effect tell the Negro that his constitutional rights are without value unless he grasps them by force or coercion.

III. *Proposals for Federal Legislation*

In building an effective legislative program, three basic propositions should provide the groundwork. The first is that, while state and local legislation is preferable to federal if it really does the job, and while some Southern cities have made a serious attack on such problems as discrimination in privately owned places of public accommodation, the hardening of resistance in the Deep South during the past decade has made clear the need for federal action. The second is that preservation of the openness of our national society is a national problem that the federal government has constitutional power to deal with.[53] And the third is that the limiting factor on the effectiveness of federal law is the ability and the readiness of the federal judiciary to enforce it—so that activation of the federal courts, and particularly the district courts, must be the leading congressional objective.

It is sometimes forgotten that the principal, if not the only, reason for establishment of the lower federal courts was the need for dealing with local opposition to, or disregard of, the federal law.[54] Unless they perform this function adequately, there is little reason to have them at all. The question was mooted in the 1787 Convention. Pierce Butler and Edward Rutledge, both of South Carolina, opposed the creation of lower federal courts. It would be enough, they said, to obligate the state judges to uphold the federal constitution and laws and to provide for appellate review of their decisions by the Supreme Court.[55]

James Madison, Jr., of Virginia disagreed:

> MR. MADISON observed, that, unless inferior tribunals were dispersed throughout the republic . . . appeals would be multiplied to a most oppressive degree; that, besides, an appeal would not in many cases be a remedy. What was to be done after improper verdicts, in state tribunals, obtained under the biased directions of a dependent judge, or the local prejudices of an undirected jury? To remand the cause for a new trial would answer no purpose. . . . An effective judiciary establishment, commensurate to the legislative authority, was essential. A government without a proper executive and judiciary would be the mere trunk of a body, without arms or legs to act or move.[56]

The Madison view prevailed. Congress was authorized to ordain and establish "inferior" courts.[57] And it is quite clear that the reason Congress was given such power, and presumably the basic reason for the existence of the federal courts which Congress did establish forthwith,[58] was the need for national tribunals to enforce the national law in the teeth of local resistance.

The lower federal courts have only partially performed this function. During the last ten years they have repeatedly suffered the federal law to be flouted. The "dependent judge" of the state court and "the local prejudices of an undirected jury" have not infrequently prevailed over the mandates of the federal constitution and laws as interpreted by the United States Supreme Court.[59] And in too many cases, the lower federal courts have declined to interfere.

Legislation in the fields of federal jurisdiction and procedure must be undertaken cautiously and with full comprehension of the long history of careful efforts at mutual accommodation between the state and federal courts. The proposals about to be made are therefore presented more in the spirit of outlining the areas in which remedial action is needed, than of dogmatically asserting that the particular remedies suggested are the only means to the desired objective. It may be possible to devise other measures that would involve less recasting of existing forms but would be equally effective to re-establish the supremacy of federal law. No apologies are offered, however, for the underlying value judgment that the need for effective enforcement of established federal rights should take precedence over considerations of courtesy, comity, and delicacy toward state courts that are manifesting a growing contempt for the requirements of federal law.

With this disclaimer of finality and perfection, five legislative recommendations are made as the minimum steps which must be taken if the federal courts are to be counted on for the job they were created to do: (1) affirmation of their power to halt obviously groundless state court prosecutions and injunction proceedings whose only purpose can be to effectuate racial discrimination or stifle protest against it; (2) abolition or strict limitation of the so-called "abstention" doctrine, under which federal courts have been prone to defer action (sometimes for years) until pertinent state statutes have been interpreted by the state courts; (3) provision for intermediate review by the courts of appeals of all district court decisions, including those of three-judge courts, in cases involving racial discrimination or protest against it; (4) affirmation of the right to remove to the federal district court any state court proceeding, civil or criminal, involving racial discrimination or protest against it, at any time before final judgment in the trial court, upon a showing that state court denial of federal rights is reasonably to be anticipated and, (5) in such cases, affirmation of the appealability of district court orders remanding removed cases to the state courts.

As it happens, the Jackson Freedom Ride litigation, which has already been used to illustrate one major mode of resistance, also affords a convenient reference point for discussion of the need for these changes in the law. On May 24, 1961, the first Freedom Riders reached Jackson, debarked from their interstate bus, entered the "wrong" waiting room at the terminal, were politely asked by Police Captain J. L. Ray to leave it, ignored the request, and were arrested on charges of breach of the peace and conspiracy to breach the peace. There was no dispute over the material facts, nor was there a claim that the Riders had been disorderly in any way.[60]

It was therefore quite clear that the charges against them were groundless and that any conviction would ultimately be reversed on due process grounds, provided they did not abandon the litigation.[61] Actually, a number of them did abandon their defenses because of their inability to cope with the procedural burdens imposed upon them by the state courts. These burdens included counsel fees, stenographic fees, travel expense, loss of working time, and—most important—the need to raise *cash* bail (since no individual bondsman and none of the 304 licensed surety companies would write bail bonds for them) in the amount of $1500 apiece. The over-all cash requirement can be estimated conservatively at $2000 per case. Some of the defendants, unable to raise this much money, pleaded *nolo contendere—* accepting a suspended jail term and a $200 fine. The rest of the cases are now working their way up through the state courts (except for those of fifteen white Protestant ministers who, on testimony not materially different from that in the other three hundred cases, were given a directed acquittal at retrial in Hinds County Court). At present writing all the cases have gone through Municipal Court and have been retried before juries in County Court; a number of them have been decided (and affirmed) by Circuit Court; a few of them have been briefed in the Mississippi Supreme Court; and the first two cases, having been argued there, may be decided within the next few months. If affirmed, they will probably reach the United States Supreme Court for reversal some time in 1965, unless there is unexpected delay.

An effort was made to avoid this heavy expense and delay, but it proved vain. On June 9, 1961, after nearly a hundred arrests had taken place, three local NAACP members brought a class action in federal district court to enjoin enforcement of the Mississippi travel segregation statutes. Injunction was sought against all methods of enforcement, including further breach-of-peace prosecutions designed to compel obedience to the segregation statutes.[62] Simultaneously, the plaintiffs applied for a preliminary injunction. A three-judge court, convened because the attack on the state statutes included a demand for injunctive relief,[63] simply failed to adjudicate the preliminary injunction motion.[64] After a full trial on September 25-28, the court on November 17 ruled that it should abstain from adjudicating the merits until the Mississippi Supreme Court had interpreted the state statutes involved.[65] (One of them had been interpreted and applied by the highest state court as early as 1889[66] and another in 1912.[67])

An appeal was promptly taken to the United States Supreme Court, which has exclusive appellate jurisdiction over rulings of three-judge courts.[68] On February 26, 1962, it summarily dismissed the appeal on the basis of novel legal principles and an apparent misconception of the state of the record, but vacated the order of the district court and remanded the case for "expeditious" disposition by a one-judge district court (whose decision would be reviewable by the court of appeals).[69] Forty days later the district court denied injunctive relief, though (in compliance with the Supreme Court's directions) it declared the questioned Mississippi statutes to be void.[70] An appeal from this ruling was taken to the Court of Appeals for the Fifth Circuit which held on September 24, 1963, that injunctive relief should be granted.[71] Within a year or so the Supreme Court may have its second opportunity to decide in this case the important question whether injunctive relief against the state court prosecutions is precluded by Section 2283 of the Judicial Code, which provides:

> A court of the United States may not grant an injunction to stay proceedings in a State court except as expressly authorized by Act of Congress, or where necessary in aid of its jurisdiction, or to protect or effectuate its judgments.

This statute, which has been on the books in one form or another since 1793,[72] is somewhat indistinct in its scope. It has been held inapplicable to actions brought by the United States.[73] It has also been held not to prevent the federal courts from enjoining future (as opposed to pending) state prosecutions.[74] But it is not clear whether Congress, by enacting the Civil Rights Act, has "expressly authorized" federal injunctions against state court proceedings in private actions brought under that act.[75] Nor is it clear whether a federal injunction can be deemed to be "in aid of" the federal court's jurisdiction if directed against state court prosecutions begun after commencement of the federal action (and after application for a preliminary injunction) but before the federal court has decided the case.[76] Eventually the Supreme Court may resolve these questions. But Congress can and should act now to affirm the power of the federal courts to halt any state court proceedings that can be explained only as an effort to impede or harass the enjoyment of a federal right to be free of racial discrimination or a federal right of peaceable protest against it.

Success of the Jackson formula has already led to its proliferation throughout the Deep South.[77] Its message to the Negro is that litigation is not a meaningful avenue to the enjoyment of federal rights. It is incumbent upon Congress to disavow that message without delay.

The abstention doctrine which the district court relied on should likewise be repudiated or sharply limited. Originally devised as a judge-made rule of self-restraint designed to give the state courts primary jurisdiction over difficult problems of interpreting local legislation,[78] it has enjoyed a considerable vogue in Southern race discrimination cases.[79] It has tended to paralyze the federal courts in doing the job they were primarily designed for—enforcement of locally unpopular federal law. More than one justice of the Supreme Court has criticized it as an evasion of judicial responsibility.[80] The doctrine has undergone a cancerous growth in recent years, and now bids fair to make it a betting proposition (for each prospective plaintiff) whether the federal courts will, in any particular case, exercise jurisdiction that they admittedly have.[81] Whatever value the doctrine may have in other cases, it only provides an occasion for disastrous delay in racial discrimination and racial protest cases.

There may be some question whether congressional abrogation or modification of the doctrine would violate the constitutional requirement of separation of powers. But the Constitution does give Congress power to regulate the jurisdiction of the lower federal courts,[82] and there may be a cognate power to prescribe rules as to when that jurisdiction shall be exercised. In any event, the courts could hardly ignore an express congressional finding that the abstention doctrine, as presently applied, is subject to grave abuse and is conducive to dangerous uncertainties and delays. Whether the situation is to be remedied by Congress or the Supreme Court, one of them should promptly see to it that the federal courts remain open for business in cases where their services are needed as desperately as they are in situations of the type discussed here.[83] For present purposes it is unnecessary to express an opinion whether restriction of the abstention doctrine to diversity cases, or even its outright repudiation, would deprive us of anything very useful.[84]

The third of the five legislative recommendations is to abolish (at least with respect to racial discrimination and racial protest cases) the direct appeal procedure whereby the Supreme Court alone can review the actions of three-judge district courts.[85] In appraising this proposal, it is appropriate to consider the extremes to which the Court went in summarily disclaiming jurisdiction over the Jackson Freedom Riders' appeal.[86] The Court proceeded from the premise "that no State may require racial segregation of interstate or intrastate transportation facilities"[87] and that this was so well-settled that "the constitutional issue is essentially fictitious."[88] Then—without receiving full briefs or oral argument—it broke new ground by extending the rule that an application to convene a three-judge court will be denied when the *plaintiff's* constitutional position is frivolous,[89] to the wholly different case presented by the frivolousness of a *defendant's* position. It is one thing to say that the three-judge procedure, which was designed to protect state laws from ill-considered interference by a single district judge, need not be utilized when the attack is based on a clearly untenable ground. It is quite another to say that if the plaintiff's ground is clearly tenable, a state statute can be invalidated without resort to the three-judge procedure erected by Congress for its protection. Such a holding requires the plaintiff to make a very difficult election, based on a judgment whether the state statute is *arguably* invalid or *obviously* invalid.

The effect of this ruling was to render impossible an immediate interpretation of Section 2283 of the Judicial Code. Such an interpretation was urgently needed; even if existing law had been held to afford no effective remedy for the dismal failure to protect established federal rights, the need for congressional action would at least have been made clear. The importance of the issue had been underscored by the unusual action of the Department of Justice in filing an amicus curiae brief in support of the plaintiff's application for a stay—in order to prevent the smothering of the defenses in state court by mounting cash requirements, which were estimated at $372,000 for bail alone.[90]

Moreover, the Court held that the plaintiffs had no "stand-ing to enjoin criminal prosecution under Mississippi's breach of peace statutes, since they do not allege that they have been prosecuted or threatened with prosecution under them."[91] The plaintiffs, after listing the breach of peace statutes and others, had in fact alleged: "Plaintiffs . . . have suffered and shall continue to suffer irreparable injury as a result of the enforcement or threat of enforcement of the state statutes referred to herein."[92]

The case cried out for decision. Yet the appeal was dis-missed, and on doubtful grounds. Until some better explan-ation comes along, it seems reasonable to view the case as an index of the great need of a frightfully busy Court to channel cases of this type through the courts of appeals.

The Supreme Court in recent years has magnificently per-formed its primary function, which is to declare the mean-ing of our basic law in the context of today's society. But it is limited by simple considerations of time; it is not equipped to handle the heavy case-load that would be in-curred if it took jurisdiction of each case that arises, and must therefore depend heavily on the courts of appeals to serve as its sympathetic coadjutors, which will dispose of the bulk of the appeals in accordance with principles laid down by the Supreme Court. Without such aid, the Court might easily be swamped.

If, as seems likely, the need for intermediate appellate review has impelled the Court to find new and unpredictable ways of limiting its jurisdiction of direct appeals, the time has come to face the problem squarely. Congress should provide for intermediate appellate review of all judgments and orders of district courts, at least in racial discrimination and racial protest cases.[93]

The fourth and fifth legislative recommendations relate to removal jurisdiction. Affirmation of an adequate injunc-tion power would suffice in cases such as the Jackson Freedom Ride litigation, in which there were no factual is-sues as to the conduct of the Riders. But an issue of fact can be created by any willing perjurer, and perjury is pun-ishable only by the verdict of a local jury.[94] Had there been

testimony that the Freedom Riders threw bricks, brandished
weapons, or even were boisterous or profane, the federal
court might have rightly hesitated to adjudicate these issues
in a civil rather than a criminal proceeding. And while
the libel laws make it unwise to name names, it would not
be hard to list cases in which such perjury has occurred.
Of course, perjury is possible in federal as well as state
courts (though the formidable investigatory resources of the
Federal Bureau of Investigation make it a more hazardous
occupation there).[95] But procedural abuses such as excessive bail requirements are subject to plenary and quick control by the higher federal courts.[96]

The remedy here is to make better use of the removal
power. Congress can authorize removal of cases from state
to federal courts, for trial and appeal there, when necessary
to protect federal rights.[97] Statutes now on the books permit
such removal of various types of cases, such as prosecutions of federal officials or military personnel for acts
in line of duty,[98] and actions affecting property on which the
United States claims a lien.[99] Section 1443 of the Judicial
Code also authorizes removal of the following civil actions
or criminal prosecutions:

> [1] Against any person who is denied or cannot enforce
> in the courts of such State a right under any law providing
> for the equal civil rights of citizens of the United States,
> or of all persons within the jurisdiction thereof.
> [2] For any act under color of authority derived from
> any law providing for equal rights, or for refusing to do any
> act on the ground that it would be inconsistent with such
> law.

After the first few convictions of Freedom Riders in
Jackson Municipal Court, it became entirely legitimate to
make a circumstantial inference that the remaining defendants—whose cases were indistinguishable on their facts
from those which had already been decided—would be denied equal civil rights secured by federal law, or be unable
to enforce them in the Mississippi courts.[100] Indeed, it was
clear that enjoyment of the federal right to travel unsegregated in interstate commerce was being substantially frus-

trated by the systematic program of arrests, detention, and prosecution, even if all the charges were prompty dismissed as soon as they reached judicial hearing.[101] But an effort to remove several of the prosecutions to the federal district court was rejected on grounds which have been deemed well-settled ever since the 1879 decision in *Virginia v. Rives*.[102] In that case the Supreme Court, holding that a murder prosecution was not removable by the Negro defendant even though Negroes had been systematically excluded from the grand jury that indicted him and from the panel from which his trial jury was to be selected, said it could not assume that the state courts, if demanded, would deny the defendant redress for these constitutional deficiencies. It is hard to tell from the opinion whether the Court intended to apply a factual test under which the probable effectiveness of state remedies would be open for consideration in each case,[103] or whether it "conclusively presumed" that the state remedies would be effective.[104] Later cases, however, appear to have adopted the latter interpretation and have therefore denied the right to removal unless the infringement of federal rights is threatened by a state *statute* (which the Court assumes, somewhat illogically, will be enforced by the state courts despite the supremacy clause).[105] The wording of Section 1443 strongly suggests that Congress intended the section to apply more broadly, and opportunity for reconsideration of the question may be presented by a set of cases now pending in the Fourth Circuit, in which an overwhelming factual showing has been made that equal rights secured by federal law are likely to be overridden in the state trial court.[106] But here again, there is no reason to wait for the Supreme Court to settle the question. Congress has undoubted power to authorize removal upon a reasonable showing (a) that the state trial court, in closely similar cases involving racial discrimination or racial protest, has wrongly (or perhaps arbitrarily) rejected federal claims, or (b) that pendency of the state court cases is in itself of such a nature as to involve frustration of federal claims no matter how the state courts ultimately decide the cases.

But even this will not be enough unless the appealability of remand orders, at least in racial discrimination and racial protest cases, is confirmed. The remand orders in the Jackson Freedom Ride cases were not appealed because of the very general belief at the bar that Section 1447 (d) of the Judicial Code means what it says: "An order remanding a case to the State court from which it was removed is not reviewable on appeal or otherwise." Considering the tremendous community pressures under which the Southern district courts operate in racial cases,[107] and the consequent desirability of enabling the courts of appeals to assume the onus of locally unpopular decisions, such a restriction is most unwise in cases of this type. A determined effort, based on respectable historical grounds, is now being made in the Fourth Circuit to establish the proposition that Congress intended Section 1447 (d) to be inapplicable to civil rights cases.[108] But here again it is preferable for Congress to take the initiative and establish clearly the appealability of remand orders in cases removed under Section 1443.

It is not suggested that legislation should be limited to the five proposals outlined above. But they cover the large deficiencies which are visible to the naked eye, and can rightly be regarded as a minimum program. Their primary effect would be to deal with the new resistance technique that was perfected in the Jackson Freedom Ride litigation —mass arrests on petty charges wholly lacking in legal foundation. The principles developed over the past 174 years for regulation of the relationships between federal and state courts have proved inadequate to deal with this phenomenon, and need to be revamped to accommodate it.

Confirmation of the federal injunction power and abolition or containment of the abstention doctrine would equip the federal courts to deal with state prosecutions that, on the admitted facts, are constitutionally defective. Rehabilitation of the removal power would equip them to deal with mass-produced groups of substantially identical cases—except perhaps the *first* case of the group (if the right to removal depended on inferences drawn from the state trial court's handling of the first case. Revision of the appeal procedures on remand orders and in three-judge-court cases would permit assumption of greater responsibility by the courts of appeals, which are best able to accept it—better able than the Supreme Court, because of their greater manpower and less demanding dockets, and better able than the district courts, because of their relative insulation from local pressures.

The proposed changes would have little effect on the usual case, in which one or a few defendants are prosecuted or sued on grounds that are at least arguably sound. Federal control of such cases would continue to be exercised, for the most part, by way of appellate review of final state court judgments. Therefore, it cannot be said that all opportunities for abuse of judicial process would be denied to the state courts. But there would be an effective remedy for the major abuses which have so far appeared.

Presentation of the foregoing legislative recommendations is not intended to disparage the importance of the Administration's Civil Rights Bill which is now pending in Congress.[109] It contains salutary proposals concerning, for example, voting rights, public education, discrimination in employment and in places of public accommodation, and cessation of federal grants in aid of discriminatory activities. Particularly valuable are the provisions for increased assumption of the litigation burden by the Department of Justice, since they are addressed directly to the problem that is believed to be most basic and most urgent: the elimination of obstructionism that frustrates the exercise and enjoyment of *established rights*.

But improvements of the substantive law, even though the full resources of the Department of Justice are brought to bear, will be fully effective only if the federal courts— and particularly the lower federal courts—assume the task that Madison and the 1787 Convention envisaged for them. The first task of Congress in the civil rights field is to do all it can to activate these courts. Federal rights, once established, must be enforcible.

Notes

F O R E W O R D

1. Charge to the Grand Jury, Fed. Cas. # 18260 at pp. 1006–1007.
2. McCulloch v. Maryland, 4 Wheat. 316, 421 (1819).
3. Civil Rights Cases, 109 U.S. 3, 48 (1883).

I N T R O D U C T I O N

1. Edmond Cahn, *The Sense of Injustice* (Bloomington, Indiana 1964) p. 13.
2. *Ibid.*, at p. 22.
3. Cooper v. Aaron, 358 U.S. 1, 18 (1958).
4. *Ibid.*, at p. 24.
5. Fried, "Moral Causation," 77 *Harv. L. Rev.* 1258, 1269 (1964).

L O U I S I A N A   U N D E R L A W

1. See United States v. State of Louisiana, 225 F. Supp. 353, 363 *et seq.* (E.D. La. 1963). The history that follows is taken in large part from Judge Wisdom's excellent opinion in that case.
2. *Ibid.*
3. A. J. Liebling, *The Earl of Louisiana* (N.Y., Simon and Schuster 1961) p. 29.

4. United States v. State of Louisiana, 225 F. Supp. at p. 380.

5. *Ibid.*, at p. 379.

6. *Ibid.*, at p. 384.

7. Liebling, *op. cit.*, pp. 29–31.

8. Edward B. Williams, *One Man's Freedom* (N.Y., Atheneum 1962) p. 231 *ff.*

9. Erwin N. Griswold, *Law and Lawyers in the United States: The Common Law Under Stress* (London, Stevens 1964) p. 125.

10. United States v. State of Louisiana, 225 F. Supp. at p. 381.

11. From an article entitled, "Armed Negroes Make Jonesboro an Unusual Town," appearing in *The New York Times* on February 21, 1965.

12. Williams, *op. cit.*, p. 162.

13. Jelks v. Perez, Civil Action No. 3028.

14. Sir Frederick Pollock and Frederick W. Maitland, *History of English Law* (Cambridge, The University Press 1911) pp. 138–139.

15. At pp. 126–127.

C L I N T O N ,   L O U I S I A N A

1. 83 U.S. 36 (1873).

2. 92 U.S. 542 (1876).

3. 163 U.S. 537 (1896).

4. Garner v. Louisiana, 368 U.S. 157, 174 (1961).

5. Cox v. Louisiana, 379 U.S. 536, 551, 558 (1965).

6. Lombard v. Louisiana, 373 U.S. 267, 273 (1963).

S O U T H E R N   A P P E L L A T E C O U R T S :   A   D E A D   E N D

1. McLaughlin v. Florida, —Fla.—, 153 So. 2d 1 (1963), rev'd, 379 U.S. 184 (1964) (overturning statute prohibiting nighttime cohabitation between whites and Negroes not married to each other, but failing to reach question of constitutionality of anti-miscegenation laws.)

2. Act of March 1, 1875, 18 Stat. 336, revised and codified as 18 U.S.C. §243.

3. Strauder v. West Virginia, 100 U.S. 303 (1880).

4. *1961 Commission on Civil Rights Report: Justice*, p. 90.

5. Jones v. Georgia, 219 Ga. 848, 136 S.E.2d 358 (1964), cert. denied, 379 U.S. 935 (1964).

6. Hamilton v. Alabama, 275 Ala. 574, 156 So.2d 926 (1963).

7. *Ibid.*

8. 376 U.S. 650 (1964).

9. See, e.g., Robinson v. Alabama, —Ala.—, 168 So.2d 491 (1964).

10. 1 Race Relations Law Reporter 707–709 (1956).

11. *Ibid.*, pp. 917–18 (1956).

12. NAACP v. State of Alabama ex rel. John Patterson, 265 Ala. 699, 91 So.2d 221; 265 Ala. 349, 91 So.2d 214 (1956).

13. NAACP v. State of Alabama ex rel. John Patterson, 357 U.S. 449, 456 (1958).

14. *Ibid.*, 357 U.S. 462.

15. Ex parte NAACP, 268 Ala. 531, 109 So.2d 138 (1959).

16. NAACP v. Alabama ex rel. Patterson, 360 U.S. 240 (1959).

17. NAACP v. Gallion, 190 F. Supp. 583 (M.D. Ala. 1960).

18. NAACP v. Gallion, 290 F.2d 337 (5th Cir. 1961).

19. NAACP v. Gallion, 368 U.S. 19 (1961).

20. NAACP v. State, 274 Ala. 544, 150 So.2d 677 (1963).

21. *Ibid.*, 150 So.2d 679.

22. NAACP v. Alabama ex rel. Flowers, 377 U.S. 288 (1961).

23. *Ibid.*, 377 U.S. 297.

24. *Ibid.*, 377 U.S. 309.

25. See Woods v. Wright, 334 F.2d 369 (5th Cir. 1964).

26. Thomas v. Mississippi, —Miss.—, 160 So.2d 657 (1964).

27. Herndon v. Lowry, 301 U.S. 242 (1937).

28. *Atlanta Constitution*, October 21, 1963, p. 3.

29. Aelony v. Pace; Harris v. Pace, 9 Race Relations Law Reporter 1355 (1963).

30. Lusky, "Racial Discrimination and the Federal Law: A Problem in Nullification," 63 *Colum. L. Rev.* 1163, 1178 (1963).

31. Brief Amicus Curiae of the NAACP Legal Defense and Educational Fund, Inc. in Dombrowski v. Pfister, Supreme Court of the United States, No. 52, October Term, 1964.

S E G R E G A T E D   J U S T I C E

1. 263 F.2d 71, 82 (5th Cir. 1959).

2. Whitus v. Balkcom, 333, F.2d 496 (5th Cir. 1964).

3. 304 F.2d 53 (5th Cir. 1962).

4. Collins v. Walker, 335 F.2d 417, 420 (5th Cir. 1964).

J U D G E   W I L L I A M   H A R O L D   C O X A N D   T H E   R I G H T   T O   V O T E   I N C L A R K E   C O U N T Y ,   M I S S I S S I P P I

1. *New York Herald Tribune*, December 20, 1964, p. 24.

2. *Ibid.*

3. State of Alabama v. United States, 304 F.2d 583, 586 (5th Cir. 1962), aff'd, 371 U.S. 37 (1962).

4. United States v. A. L. Ramsey, Civil No. 1084, S.D. Miss., February 5, 1963.

5. United States v. John Q. Wood, Civil No. 1656, S.D. Miss., October 25, 1963.

6. Transcript, United States v. A. L. Ramsey, Civil No. 1084.

7. *Ibid.*

8. *Ibid.*

9. Collins v. Walker, 329 F.2d 100 (5th Cir. 1964).

10. United States v. A. L. Ramsey, Civil No. 1084, S.D. Miss., February 5, 1963.

11. *Ibid.*

12. In the Walthall County case the Court of Appeals for the Fifth Circuit ordered Judge Cox to enter an injunction against the registrar requiring that the county not use the interpretation test unless there was a complete new reregistration of all voters. United States v. State of Mississippi, 339 F.2d 679 (5th Cir. 1964).

13. United States v. A. L. Ramsey, 331 F.2d 824, 838 (5th Cir. 1964).

14. Transcript, United States v. A. L. Ramsey, Civil No. 1084.

15. *Ibid.*

THE FEDERAL COURTS OF THE
SOUTH: JUDGE BRYAN SIMPSON
AND HIS RELUCTANT BRETHREN

1. *Time Magazine,* November 6, 1964, p. 44.
2. *The New York Times,* October 23, 1964, p. 45, col. 2.
3. See Kennedy v. Lynd, 306 F.2d 222 (5th Cir. 1962).
4. United States v. Ramsey, 8 *Race Relations Law Reporter* 150 (1963), rev'd, 331 F.2d 824 (5th Cir. 1964).
5. *The New York Times,* October 23, 1964, p. 1.
6. Congress of Racial Equality v. Douglas, 318 F.2d 95, 100 (5th Cir. 1963), reversing 6 *Race Relations Law Reporter* 1161 (1961).
7. United States v. Wood, 6 *Race Relations Law Reporter* 1069 (1961), rev'd, 295 F.2d 772 (5th Cir. 1961).
8. *Time Magazine,* November 6, 1964, p. 44.
9. See Evers v. Jackson Municipal Separate School District, 328 F.2d 408 (5th Cir. 1964).
10. Evers v. Jackson Municipal Separate School District, 232 F. Supp. 241, 251 (S.D. Miss. 1964).
11. United States v. City of Jackson, Mississippi, 206 F. Supp. 45, 49 (S.D. Miss. 1962), rev'd, 318 F.2d 1 (5th Cir. 1963).
12. Meredith v. Fair, 305 F.2d 343, 352 (5th Cir. 1962), cert. denied, 371 U.S. 828 (1962).
13. See Note, "Judicial Performance in the Fifth Circuit," 73 *Yale L. J.* 90, 91–92 (1963).
14. Bailey v. Patterson, 199 F. Supp. 595, 603 (S.D. Miss. 1961), vacated per curiam, 369 U.S. 31 (1962).
15. Bailey v. Patterson, 369 U.S. 31, 33 (1962).
16. See Bailey v. Patterson, 323 F.2d 201 (5th Cir. 1963); Lusky, "Racial Discrimination and the Federal Law; A Problem in Nullification," 63 *Colum. L. Rev.* 1163, 1179–82 (1963).
17. Baldwin v. Morgan, 149 F. Supp. 224, 225 (N.D. Ala. 1957), rev'd, 251 F.2d 780 (5th Cir. 1958).
18. Armstrong v. Board of Education of City of Birmingham, Ala., 220 F. Supp. 217 (N.D. Ala. 1963), rev'd, 333 F.2d 47 (5th Cir. 1964).
19. Davis v. Board of School Com'rs of Mobile County, 219 F. Supp. 542, 545–46 (S.D. Ala. 1963), rev'd, 333 F.2d 53 (5th Cir. 1964).
20. Davis v. Board of School Com'rs of Mobile County, Ala., 322 F.2d 356 (5th Cir. 1963), 333 F.2d 53 (5th Cir. 1964).

21. McClung v. Katzenbach, 233 F. Supp. 815 (N.D. Ala. 1964), rev'd, 379 U.S. 294 (1964).

22. Anderson v. Martin, 206 F. Supp. 700 (D. La. 1962), rev'd, 375 U.S. 399 (1964).

23. Davis v. East Baton Rouge Parish School Bd., 214 F. Supp. 624, 625 (E.D. La. 1963).

24. United States v. Palmer, 230 F. Supp. 716 (E.D. La. 1964).

25. United States v. State of Louisiana, 225 F. Supp. 353 (E.D. La. 1963). In the 21 counties in question there were 212,273 whites of voting age and 107,446 Negroes of voting age in 1960. Of the whites, 162,427 were in fact registered while only 10,256 Negroes were registered. White Citizens' Council members successfully reduced the total of Negro voters in the counties in question by 15,000 in a four-year period by challenging their qualifications.

26. Bush v. Orleans Parish School Board, 230 F. Supp. 509, 515 (E.D. La. 1963). See also Bush v. Orleans Parish School Board, 308 F.2d 491 (5th Cir. 1962), where the Fifth Circuit had modified Judge Ellis's earlier decisions and ordered a faster rate of desegregation.

27. "Judicial Performance," *supra*, note 13, 73 *Yale L.J.* at 96–97.

28. Aelony v. Pace, 8 *Race Relations Law Reporter* 1355 (M.D. Ga. 1963).

29. *The New York Times,* July 19, 1963, p. 8, col. 3.

30. Stell v. Savannah-Chatham County Board of Education, 220 F. Supp. 667, 683 (S.D. Ga. 1963), rev'd, 333 F.2d 55 (5th Cir. 1964).

31. *Ibid.*

32. *Ibid.,* 220 F. Supp. at 684.

33. Heart of Atlanta Motel, Inc. v. United States, 231 F. Supp. 393 (N.D. Ga. 1964), aff'd, 379 U.S. 241 (1964).

34. Lee v. Macon Board of Education, 231 F. Supp. 743 (M.D. Ala. 1964); Harris v. Bullock County Board of Education, 232 F. Supp. 959 (M.D. Ala. 1964).

35. United States v. U.S. Klans, Knights of Ku Klux Klan, Inc., 194 F. Supp. 897 (M.D. Ga. 1961).

36. United States v. State of Louisiana, 225 F. Supp. 353 (E.D. La. 1963); United States v. Clement, 231 F. Supp. 913 (W.D. La. 1964).

37. Fla. Stat. 509.141 and Fla. Stat. 821.01. They were also indicated under Florida conspiracy statute Fla. Stat. 833.05.

38. Hayling v. Shelley, No. 63-201-Civ.-J. (M.D. Fla. 1963), decree filed November 15, 1963.

39. Martin Luther King, *Stride Toward Freedom* (N.Y., Harper & Row 1964) p. 83.

40. Young v. Davis, No. 64-133-Civ.-J. (M.D. Fla. 1964), Transcript of Proceedings, June 2, 1964.

41. *Ibid.*, June 3, 1964.

42. *Ibid.*

43. *Ibid.*, Findings of Fact and Conclusions of Law, Filed June 9, 1964.

44. *Ibid.*

45. Johnson v. Davis, No. 64-141-Civ.-J. (M.D. Fla. 1964), Findings of Fact and Conclusions of Law, filed June 9, 1964.

46. *Ibid.*

47. Young v. Davis, *supra*, Transcript of Proceedings, June 13, 1964.

48. *Ibid.*

49. *Ibid.*, June 15, 1964.

50. *Ibid.*, June 27, 1964.

51. *Ibid.*

52. *Ibid.*

53. *Ibid.*

54. *Ibid.*

55. *Ibid.*, June 13, 1964.

56. *Ibid.*, June 27, 1964.

57. Young v. Bryant, No. 64-152-Civ.-J. (M.D. Fla. 1964), Transcript of Proceedings, July 22, 1964.

58. Plummer v. Brock, No. 64-187-Civ.-J. (M.D. Fla. 1964), Transcript of Proceedings, July 28, 1964.

59. Williams v. Connell, No. 64-183-Civ.-J. (M.D. Fla. 1964), Order for Interlocutory Injunction, filed July 24, 1964.

60. *Ibid.* Order Amending Order for Interlocutory Injunction of July 24, 1964, filed August 5, 1964; Plummer v. Brock, No. 64-187-Civ.-J. (M.D. Fla. 1964), Order for Interlocutory Injunction, filed August 5, 1964.

61. *Ibid.*

62. *Ibid.*

63. Plummer v. Brock, *supra*, Transcript of Findings, August 19, 1964.

64. *Ibid.*

65. *Ibid.*, Additional Findings of Fact by the Court in Connection with Civil Contempt Proceedings of August 17, 18, and 19, 1964 —Mr. Charles Lance, Jr., Contemnor, filed September 2, 1964.

66. (Jacksonville) *Florida Times-Union*, August 20, 1964.

67. See generally J. W. Peltason, *Fifty-Eight Lonely Men* (N.Y., Harcourt 1961).

68. Young v. Davis, *supra*, Transcript of Proceedings, June 27, 1964.

69. "Judicial Performance," *supra*, note 13, 73 *Yale L.J.* at 103.

70. *The New York Times*, August 8, 1963, p. 1., col. 8.

71. See generally "Judicial Performance," *supra*, note 13, 73 *Yale L.J.* at 106–122.

T H E   F I F T H   C I R C U I T   C O U R T
O F   A P P E A L S

1. Brown v. Board of Education, 347 U.S. 454 (1954).

2. Brown v. Board of Education, 349 U.S. 294, 301 (1955).

3. Armstrong v. Board of Education of City of Birmingham, 323 F.2d 333, 352 (5th Cir. 1963).

4. These common-law writs are authorized by the All Writs Statute, 28 U.S.C. §1651.

5. Aaron v. Cooper, 358 U.S. 1 (1958).

6. Watson v. City of Memphis, 373 U.S. 526 (1963).

7. Griffin v. County School Board of Prince Edward County, 84 Sup. Ct. 400 (1964).

8. Note, "Judicial Performance in the Fifth Circuit," 73 *Yale L.J.* 90 (1963).

9. For an excellent review of the role of the Federal judiciary prior to 1961, see J. W. Peltason, *Fifty-Eight Lonely Men* (N.Y., Harcourt 1961).

10. Hall v. West, 9 *Race Relations Law Reporter* 668 (1964).

11. Ex Parte Fahey, 332 U.S. 258 (1947).

12. Hall v. St. Helena Parish School Board, 5 *Race Relations Law Reporter* 654 (1960).

13. Hall v. St. Helena Parish School Board, 287 F.2d 376 (5th Cir. 1961), cert. denied, 368 U.S. 830 (1961).

14. Hall v. St. Helena Parish School Board, 197 F. Supp. 649 (E.D. La. 1961), aff'd, 368 U.S. 515 (1962).

15. 9 *Race Relations Law Reporter* 1227 (1964).

16. See footnote 3.

17. Meredith v. Fair, 7 *Race Relations Law Reporter* 741, 742–45 (1962).

18. Meredith v. Fair, 305 F.2d 343 (5th Cir. 1962), cert. denied, 371 U.S. 828 (1962).

19. Meredith v. Fair, 83 Sup Ct. 10 (1962).

20. Gaines v. Dougherty School Board of Education, 334 F.2d 983, 984 (5th Cir. 1964).

21. Armstrong v. Board of Education of the City of Birmingham, 9 *Race Relations Law Reporter* 1163 (1964).

22. See footnote 20.

23. Evers v. Jackson Municipal Separate School System, 232 F. Supp. 241 (S.D. Miss. 1964); Hudson v. Leake County School Board; Mason v. Biloxi Municipal Separate School District, 9 *Race Relations Law Reporter* 1239 (1964).

24. 9 *Race Relations Law Reporter* 1251 (1964).

25. 9 *Race Relations Law Reporter* 1229, 1231, 1233, 1235 (1964).

26. Anderson v. City of Albany, Georgia, 335 F.2d 114 (5th Cir. 1964).

27. 28 U.S.C. §1443. The case is removed and all state proceedings halted upon the filing of the petition for removal and a bond. 28 U.S.C. §1446. Thereafter, the Federal court may remand the case to the state court if it decides that the case was removed improvidently and without jurisdiction. 28 U.S.C. §1447.

28. Section 901 of the Civil Rights Act of 1964.

29. Core v. City of Clinton, Robinson v. State of Florida, Rachel v. State of Georgia, see 9 *Race Relations Law Reporter* 1131–38; Lefton v. Hattiesburg, 333 F.2d 280 (5th Cir. 1964).

30. Davis v. East Baton Rouge Parish School Board, 214 F. Supp. 624, 625 (E.D. La. 1963).

31. Wright, "The Overloaded Fifth Circuit," 42 *Texas L. R.* 949 (1964).

32. 9 *Race Relations Law Reporter* 670–671.

33. Wright, *op. cit.*

THE FEDERAL GOVERNMENT
AND CIVIL RIGHTS

1. John Poppy, "The South's War Against Negro Votes," *Look Magazine*, May 21, 1963.

2. See *The New York Times*, July 1, 1964, p. 1.

3. 158 U.S. 564 (1895).

4. 100 U.S. 371 (1879).

5. 325 U.S. 91 (1945).

6. *The New York Times*, November 30, 1964, p. 24.

R A C I A L   D I S C R I M I N A T I O N   A N D
T H E   F E D E R A L   L A W :   A   P R O B L E M
I N   N U L L I F I C A T I O N

1. Brown v. Board of Educ., 347 U.S. 483 (1954).

2. Beginning with Missouri *ex rel.* Gaines v. Canada, 305 U.S. 337 (1938), the Court enforced with increasing strictness the rule that the separate schools must be equal. In the *Gaines* case, inequality was found in the fact that the Negro applicant would have to go outside the state for a legal education, even though the state would pay his tuition and despite a factual showing that the out-of-state schools were on a par with the domestic law school available to white students. In Sipuel v. Board of Regents, 332 U.S. 631 (1948), inequality was found in the fact that the Negro applicant would have to await the establishment of a separate Negro law school—though her right to have it established promptly was not denied. In Sweatt v. Painter, 339 U.S. 629 (1950), a separate Negro law school was in fact established to accommodate the applicant, but inequality was found in such inevitable differences as the relative smallness of its student body, faculty and library, and its lack of the traditions and prestige of its older white counterpart. In McLaurin v. Oklahoma State Regents, 339 U.S. 637 (1950), the Negro applicant was admitted to graduate study in the same school with whites but was set apart from his fellow students by separate seating in the classroom, library, and cafeteria; inequality was found in restriction of his opportunity to engage in discussion and exchange views with other students. When the equality requirement had been extended to recognize the reality and importance of differences as intangible as this, it was but a short step to the general proposition that separateness and equality cannot coexist in the field of education.

3. See generally Lusky, "Minority Rights and the Public Interest," 52 *Yale L.J.* 1, 2–6 (1942).

4. See Lusky, "Peace . . . the Presence of Justice," 17 *The Humanist* 195, 198 (1957).

5. *Id.*, at 198–204.

6. See East Ohio Gas Co. v. Tax Comm'n, 283 U.S. 465, 472 (1931); Terral v. Burke Constr. Co., 257 U.S. 529, 533 (1922); Pennsylvania R.R. v. Towers, 245 U.S. 6, 17 (1917); Burnet v. Coronado Oil & Gas Co., 285 U.S. 393, 406–08 (1932) (Brandeis, J., dissenting).

7. *E.g.*, the broadening of the reach of the commerce clause that began in 1937 when the Court—after some delay—took cognizance of the great and growing interdependence of our na-

tional economy and the resulting need for a larger degree of centralized regulation. NLRB v. Jones & Laughlin Steel Corp., 301 U.S. 1 (1937); Sunshine Anthracite Coal Co. v. Adkins, 310 U.S. 381 (1940); United States v. Darby, 312 U.S. 100 (1941); Wickard v. Filburn, 317 U.S. 111 (1942).

8. See, *e.g.*, United States v. Carolene Prods. Co., 304 U.S. 144, 152 n.4 (1938) (recognizing the necessity and propriety of judicial intervention to preserve the corrective political processes); Mason, *Harlan Fiske Stone: Pillar of the Law* 470, 491, 512–17, 526, 527, 531, 534–35, 600 n. (1956); Mason, *The Supreme Court, Palladium of Freedom* 151–52, 155–56, 160, 163, 165–67, 171, 173 (1962); Lusky, "Minority Rights and the Public Interest," 52 *Yale L.J.* 1, 20–21, 26, 33–34 (1942).

9. *E.g.*, Brown v. Board of Educ., 347 U.S. 483 (1954), the 1954 school segregation decision, which did little more than recognize that "separate but equal"—initially plausible as an avenue to substantial equality—had proved itself, over a period of more than half a century, to be a contradiction in terms.

10. The process is by no means limited to the development of new constitutional doctrine, as in the cases cited notes 7–9 *supra*. It pervades the common-law system and is perhaps its distinguishing characteristic. For a collection of cases illustrating its operation in a private-law field (manufacturers' liability for defective products), see Dowling, Patterson & Powell, *Materials for Legal Method* 165–217 (2d Jones ed. 1952).

11. The above formulation is adopted for simplicity, despite the resulting danger of misunderstanding as to the existence of a *public* interest in the just treatment of minority groups. See generally Lusky, "Minority Rights and the Public Interest, 52 *Yale L.J.* 1 (1942). Negroes are not the only persons adversely affected by discrimination against Negroes; indeed, a case can be made for the proposition that they are hurt less than the whites.

12. For a perceptive appraisal of the Black Muslim movement, see Baldwin, "Down at the Cross: Letter from a Region in My Mind," in *The Fire Next Time* 25 (1963).

13. The entire paraphernalia of federal and state regulatory agencies witness the pervasiveness of official discretion in modern law. See 1 Davis, *Administrative Law* §§1.06, 1.08 (1958); Elias, "Administrative Discretion—No Solution in Sight," 14 *Baylor L. Rev.* 1 (1962).

14. Developments in procedural law, such as the 1938 Federal Rules of Civil Procedure and their progeny in the states, all favor enlarged judicial discretion. See generally Moore, *Federal Rules and Official Forms* §2 (1956); 1 Moore, *Federal Practice* §0.01 (1938); Address by Nielsen, Twenty-Ninth Annual Meeting, Idaho State Bar, July 7, 1955, in 29 *Idaho S.B. Proceedings* 15 (1955).

15. See text accompanying notes 60–77 *infra*.

16. See, *e.g.*, Boynton v. Virginia, 364 U.S. 454 (1960); Gayle v. Browder, 352 U.S. 903 (1956), affirming per curiam 142 F. Supp. 707 (M.D. Ala.); Morgan v. Virginia, 328 U.S. 373 (1946).

17. United States v. U. S. Klans, Inc., 194 F. Supp. 897 (M.D. Ala. 1961).

18. Their convictions were affirmed by the Court of Appeals of Alabama, Abernathy v. State, 155 So.2d 586 (1962), and the Alabama Supreme Court denied certiorari, 155 So.2d 592 (July 25, 1963). Petition for certiorari has been filed in the U. S. Supreme Court, October 22, 1963.

19. United States v. U. S. Klans, Inc., 194 F. Supp. 897 (M.D. Ala. 1961); Lewis v. Greyhound Corp., 199 F. Supp. 210 (M.D. Ala. 1961).

20. Bailey v. Patterson, 199 F. Supp. 595 (S.D. Miss. 1961), vac. and rem., 369 U.S. 31 (1962); 206 F. Supp. 67 (S.D. Miss. 1962), rev'd in part, Civ. No. 20732, 5th Cir., September 24, 1963. The course of this litigation is examined in some detail in text accompanying notes 62–71 *infra*.

21. The Civil Rights Cases, 109 U.S. 3 (1883).

22. See Burton v. Wilmington Parking Authority, 365 U.S. 715, 725 (1961); Boman v. Birmingham Transit Co., 280 F.2d 531 (5th Cir. 1960); City of Greensboro v. Simkins, 246 F.2d 425 (4th Cir. 1957); Derrington v. Plummer, 240 F.2d 922 (5th Cir. 1956), cert. denied, 353 U.S. 924 (1957); Jones v. Marva Theaters, Inc., 180 F. Supp. 49 (D. Md. 1960); Lawrence v. Hancock, 76 F. Supp. 1004 (S.D. W. Va. 1948); Lewis, "Burton v. Wilmington Parking Authority—A Case Without Precedent," 61 *Colum. L. Rev.* 1458 (1961). See generally Henkin, Shelley v. Kraemer: "Notes for a Revised Opinion," 110 *U. Pa. L. Rev.* 473 (1962).

23. Addyston Pipe & Steel Co. v. United States, 175 U.S. 211, 228 (1899); *In re* Debs, 158 U.S. 564 (1895).

24. This reluctance very probably stems from the prohibition contained in 28 U.S.C. §2283 (1958) and its predecessors, but the checkered career of that rather vague statute suggests that judicial initiative has also played its part. See 1A Moore, *Federal Practice* ¶0.208, at 2301–11 (2d ed. 1961).

25. See notes 60–71 *infra* and accompanying text.

26. Lombard v. Louisiana, 373 U.S. 267 (1963).

27. See, *e.g.*, Taylor v. Board of Educ., 191 F. Supp. 181 (S.D.N.Y.), aff'd, 294 F.2d 36 (2d. Cir.), cert. denied, 368 U.S. 940 (1961).

28. Exclusion of Negroes from certain of the skilled construction crafts led to mass demonstrations against a public construction project. But although the fact of discrimination appeared to be

unquestioned, immediate relief was impracticable because few Negroes could be found who possessed the necessary training for the jobs. The upshot was an agreed procedure for facilitating Negro apprenticeship applications. See *The New York Times,* July 12, 1963, p. 1, col. 4.

29. Meredith v. Fair, 305 F.2d 341, 355–60 (5th Cir.), cert. denied, 371 U.S. 828 (1962).

30. In a number of localities children have appeared as demonstrators, sitters-in, and participants in other forms of protest. This probably reflects recognition of their relatively greater immunity from reprisal. Since they are usually not employed, they cannot be fired. Since they usually have no banking connections, their loans cannot be called. Since they usually are not primary tenants, they have no leases to cancel. If expelled from school, they have at least some legal remedies. There is more reluctance to inflict physical brutality upon them. And, if under eighteen, their arrest usually leads to an adjudication of delinquency rather than a criminal conviction.

It is difficult to say that a 20-year-old, or even a 17-year-old, necessarily lacks the capacity to make an intelligent decision to commit himself to such activity. But there is an age level below which the child must be regarded as unable to decide such a question for himself. Below this level (which cannot be precisely defined), the question arises whether the child is being exploited in a manner inconsistent with his own welfare so that the laws against contributing to the delinquency of minors can rightly be invoked.

31. The following are examples of such measures in various fields:

Voting: Grandfather clauses, see Guinn v. United States, 238 U.S. 347 (1915); *cf.* Lane v. Wilson, 307 U.S. 268 (1939); the white primary, see Smith v. Allwright, 321 U.S. 649 (1944); the poll tax, apparently about to be deprived of effect in Federal elections, by a constitutional amendment proposed by Congress in 1962, 76 Stat. 1259. The amendment has now been ratified by 36 states. Letter from D. C. Eberhart, Director, Office of the Federal Register to author, September 27, 1963.

Education: Segregation laws, see Brown v. Board of Educ., 349 U.S. 294 (1954); closing of public schools, see Griffin v. Board of Supervisors, 32 *U.S.L. Week* 2101 (4th Cir., August 27, 1963), stay granted pending cert. (Brennan, Circuit Justice, September 30, 1963); criminal prosecution of integrationist activity, see Bush v. Orleans Parish School Bd., 194 F. Supp. 182 (E.D. La.), aff'd per curiam, 367 U.S. 907 (1961).

Housing: Segregation laws, see Buchanan v. Warley, 245 U.S. 60 (1917).

Common carriers: Segregation laws, see Browder v. Gayle, 142 F. Supp. 707 (M.D. Ala), aff'd per curiam, 352 U.S. 906 (1956).

Privately owned places of public accommodation: Segregation laws, see Avent v. North Carolina, 373 U.S. 375 (1963).

32. *Voting:* Literary tests, see Alabama v. United States, 305 F.2d 583 (5th Cir.), aff'd per curiam, 371 U.S. 37 (1962).
   Education: "Deliberate" integration plans, see notes 34–38 *infra* and accompanying text; pupil placement laws, see Note, 62 *Colum. L. Rev.* 1448 (1962).
   Housing: Enforcement of restrictive covenants, see Shelley v. Kraemer, 334 U.S. 1 (1948).
   Common carriers: Prosecutions for breach of peace, etc., see Bailey v. Patterson, Civ. No. 20732, 5th Cir., September 24, 1963.
   Privately owned places of public accommodation: Prosecutions for breach of peace, see Garner v. Louisiana, 368 U.S. 157 (1961); prosecutions for trespass, see Lombard v. Louisiana, 373 U.S. 267 (1963).

33. *Voting:* Eviction of Negro tenant-farmer registrants, see United States v. Beaty, 288 F.2d 653 (6th Cir, 1961).
   Education: Mob violence, see Cooper v. Aaron, 358 U.S. 1 (1958).
   Housing: Boycotts by brokers, insurers, and institutional lenders, see *U. S. Comm'n on Civil Rights, Civil Rights U.S.A.—Housing in Washington,* D.C. 10–15 (1962).
   Common carriers: Mob violence, see United States v. U. S. Klans, Inc., 194 F. Supp. 897 (M.D. Ala. 1961).
   Privately owned places of public accommodation: Boycotts, see Institute of Human Relations, *The People Take the Lead,* 34–45 (1963); Peters, "Who Chooses the People You Know," *Redbook,* June, 1959, p. 40.

34. Brown v. Board of Educ., 349 U.S. 294, 301 (1955).

35. Morland, *Southern Schools: Token Desegration and Beyond,* 4–5 (1963).

36. Morland, *op. cit. supra* note 35, at 4, 6.

37. Abuse of the formula has become a national scandal. By placing the burden of judicial initiative on the district courts—the sector of the federal judiciary which is most exposed to community pressures and which, therefore, has most difficulty in challenging local mores—the Court has invited the invention of artificial reasons for delay. (The "grade-a-year" program has been used sometimes to start with the first grade and work up, and sometimes to start with the twelfth grade and work down. It is hard to see how they can both be right, except on the premise that delay is desirable for its own sake.) Whatever considerations of supposed practical expediency may have impelled adoption of the formula in 1955, they have now been demonstrated to be ill-advised. And, as noted above, *supra* note 6 and accompanying text, the Court has not hesitated in the past to re-examine its decisions in the light of their effect in actual practice. At the last term, for example, it overruled Betts v. Brady, 316 U.S. 455 (1942) (limiting to capital cases the constitutional right to counsel), when a strong showing on this score had been made. Gideon v. Wainwright, 372 U.S. 335 (1963); see especially the opinion of Harlan, J., con-

curring, at 372 U.S. 349, and the Brief for the American Civil Liberties Union as Amicus Curiae, p. 29. Indeed, the 1954 *Brown* decision was itself a result of the failure of Plessy v. Ferguson, 163 U.S. 537 (1896), to achieve equality in real life. See note 2 *supra.*

Conceptually, the "deliberate speed" formula is impossible to justify. It creates a new category of constitutional rights, which are declared to exist in the abstract but which cannot be enjoyed unless and until local administrators get around to implementing them. Since Marbury v. Madison, 5 U.S. (1 Cranch) 137 (1803), judicial review has been founded in the judicial duty to give a *litigant* his rights under the Constitution. But the apparently successful plaintiff in the *Brown* case got no more than a promise that, some time in the indefinite future, other people would be given the rights which the Court said he had. It may be noted that the Prince Edward County school district, which was involved in a companion case to the *Brown* decision, still has no integrated schools. See Griffin v. Board of Supervisors, 32 *U.S.L. Week* 2101 (4th Cir., August 27, 1963), stay granted pending cert. (Brennan, Circuit Justice, September 30, 1963).

38. On two recent occasions the Court has gone out of its way to express impatience with the deliberateness of the school boards and the lower courts. See Watson v. City of Memphis, 373 U.S. 526, 529–30, 533 (1963):

> [T]he applicability here [in a case involving segregation in municipal parks] of the factors and reasoning relied on in framing the 1955 decree in the second *Brown* decision . . . must be considered . . . in light of the significant fact that the governing constitutional principles no longer bear the imprint of newly enunciated doctrine. . . . Given the extended time which has elapsed, it is far from clear that the mandate of the second *Brown* decision requiring that desegregation proceed with "all deliberate speed" would today be fully satisfied by types of plans . . . which eight years ago might have been deemed sufficient. . . . The rights here asserted are, like all such rights, "present" rights; they are not merely hopes to some "future" enjoyment of some formalistic constitutional promise.

And see Goss v. Board of Educ., 373 U.S. 683, 689 (1963):

> Now, however, eight years after [the *Brown*] . . . decree was rendered and over nine years after the first *Brown* decision, the context in which we must interpret and apply this language to plans for desegregation has been significantly altered.

The whole Court joined in each of these expressions.

39. Unless, of course, by mistake. Such mistakes do occur and inevitably make their contribution to the general humiliation of the Negro. For example, in 1960 Dr. Jane Allen McAllister, a Columbia Ph.D. and veteran professor of education at Jackson State College for Negroes, was arrested for sitting on the third

seat from the back of the bus on which she commuted from Vicksburg to Jackson. The arresting officer, not knowing that she had occupied the same seat for years and that it was generally recognized as "her" seat, had demanded that she move to the back seat; being surprised, she did not immediately comprehend the order. The policeman evidently realized his error and released her, and the Trailways regional manager later came to the college to tender his apologies. Trial Transcript, pp. 483–93, Bailey v. Patterson, 197 F. Supp. 595 (S.D. Miss. 1961), vac. and rem., 369 U.S. 31 (1962). But apologies cannot erase the reminder that, as a Negro, she is exposed to special risks regardless of her compliance with the local ground rules.

40. See Eubanks v. Louisiana, 356 U.S. 584 (1958); Reece v. Georgia, 350 U.S. 85 (1955); Strauder v. West Virginia, 100 U.S. 303 (1879).

41. See Johnson v. Virginia, 373 U.S. 61 (1963).

42. See Bullock, "Significance of the Racial Factor in the Length of Prison Sentences," 52 *J. Crim. L., C. & P.S.* 411, 415–17 (1961).

43. See *ibid.*

44. See, *e.g.*, Edwards v. South Carolina, 372 U.S. 229 (1963); Chase v. McCain, 220 F. Supp. 407 (W.D. Va. 1963), argued on appeal, Civ. No. 9081, 4th Cir., September 23, 1963.

45. See Gibson v. Florida Legislative Investigation Comm., 372 U.S. 539 (1963); *cf.* Bates v. City of Little Rock, 361 U.S. 516 (1960). This technique is one aspect of the growing effort to equate Negro protest with Communism.

46. 360 U.S. 72 (1959). See also Uphaus v. Wyman, 364 U.S. 388 (1960).

47. Gibson v. Florida Legislative Investigation Comm., 372 U.S. 539 (1963).

48. *The New York Times,* June 13, 1963, p. 1, col. 8, p. 12, cols. 1–6.

49. Early in September 1963, public schools in four Alabama cities prepared to begin integration pursuant to court order. The order had terminated four years of litigation, and efforts had been made to prepare the four communities for compliance with it. The Tuskegee High School was scheduled to open Monday, September 2. Early that morning, Governor George C. Wallace issued an executive order declaring that violence was threatened because of the "unwarranted integration," and ordering the school to stay closed for a week. At 6:25 A.M., without prior notice to school authorities, 108 state police arrived and enforced the order by surrounding the school. The mayor and other local officials opposed the action, expressing the desire "to avoid any racial incident" in Tuskegee, where Negroes outnumber whites more than 4 to 1 and have a voting majority. The school board said the school was and would remain open. Thereupon the force of state police was doubled. *The New York Times,* September 3, 1963, p. 1, col. 1, p. 9, col. 7.

The Huntsville schools, at the Governor's request, had meanwhile postponed their scheduled September 3 opening for three days. *Ibid.*

Three Birmingham schools were due to open September 4 on an integrated basis. The preceding afternoon state police arrived in town. The city council thereupon adopted a resolution urging the Governor to keep the state police out because they were not needed for preservation of order. Also on September 3, while Tuskegee officials threatened legal action to compel the removal of state police. *Id.*, September 4, 1963, p. 1, col. 1, p. 26, col. 3. The next day two Negro children registered in a Birmingham elementary school and were to enter integrated classes the next day, as were three Negro high school students. But on the night of September 4 the home of a Negro integrationist lawyer was bombed, and three Negroes were shot (one fatally) in the ensuing rioting. The Governor termed the riot "very tragic" and expressed regret at the violence. *Id.*, September 5, 1963, p. 1, col. 8. The next day the Board of Education, at the Governor's request, closed the three schools because of the bombing and rioting. *Id.*, September 6, 1963, p. 1, col. 6. Said the Governor, "What this country needs is a few first-class funerals, and some political funerals, too." Although again expressing regret at the violence, he contended that whites who physically resist racial integration "are not thugs—they are good working people who get mad when they see something like this happen." *Id.*, p. 14, cols. 3–4.

On September 6 a new executive order was issued, pursuant to which the state police were sent to keep pupils out of four Huntsville schools that were scheduled to admit one Negro each. Some white pupils forced their way in, but the Negroes were kept out. The local police chief criticized the exclusion as "tyrannical" and "shameful," and the mayor and city council wired the Governor to remove the state police. State police were also dispatched to Mobile, but they permitted the high school to open upon assurances that Negroes would not attend. *Id.*, September 7, 1963, p. 1, col. 3, p. 9, col. 1.

Before dawn on Monday, September 9, the Governor issued three executive orders directing that Negroes be excluded from the Birmingham, Tuskegee, and Mobile schools. (The Huntsville schools, not covered by the orders, admitted Negroes that day without incident.) The orders made no reference to danger of violence but said that integration would deprive white students of equal protection and due process. State police enforced the orders. Later that day, all five of the federal district judges in Alabama enjoined the Governor and the state police from further interference with integration and from failure to maintain order at the schools. The Governor thereupon withdrew the police and called out the National Guard to take their place. The Guardsmen took up positions at the schools before dawn on September 10. But at 8:15 A.M. Washington time, President Kennedy federalized the guard and removed it from the schools forthwith.

Negroes then entered the schools. *Id.*, September 11, 1963, p. 1, cols. 1–2.

Boycotts of the schools by white students took place at Birmingham, Tuskegee, and Mobile, and segregationist demonstrations occurred at Birmingham and Mobile. *Id.*, September 13, 1963, p. 14, col. 1. On Sunday morning, September 15, the Sixteenth Street Baptist Church in that city was bombed and four Negro schoolgirls were killed. Angry crowds of Negroes flooded the streets. Cars containing white youths flying Confederate battle flags drove through the crowd and were stoned by Negro youths. Police appeared to quell the disorder. A policeman killed a sixteen-year-old Negro boy with a shotgun blast in the back. Later that day a thirteen-year-old Negro boy on a bicycle was shot and killed by two white boys on the outskirts of the city. *Id.*, September 16, 1963, p. 1, col. 8, p. 26, cols. 1–4. Two boys accused of slaying the bicyclist were charged with murder, *id.*, September 30, 1963, p. 1, col. 3, and were later indicted, but there has been no prosecution of the policeman who killed the other boy, a grand jury having "no-billed" the matter. On September 15, Governor Wallace caused a $5,000 reward to be offered for apprehension of the bombers, saying: "The church bombing in Birmingham today is a tragic event, which has saddened all Alabamians. The perpetrators of this vicious crime must be brought to justice." *Id.* September 16, 1963, p. 26, col. 1. On September 16, President Kennedy declared in a public statement: "It is regrettable *that public disparagement of law and order has encouraged violence* which has fallen on the innocent." *Id.* September 17, 1963, p. 1, col. 8. (Emphasis added.)

50. The distinction between encouraging with intent to cause crime and encouraging with knowledge that crime will result is rarely articulated. Juries are generally able to find that encouragement with knowledge that crime will result implies an intent, if there is no proof of other motivation. See Warfield v. Commonwealth, 334 S.W.2d 913 (Ky. 1960). Generally speaking, American law restricts accomplice liability to cases in which the accused acts with the purpose of participating in criminal activity. See, *e.g.*, United States v. Moses, 220 F.2d 166 (3d Cir. 1955); United States v. Falcone, 109 F.2d 579 (2d Cir.), aff'd on other grounds, 311 U.S. 205 (1940); Snell v. State, 139 Ga. App. 158, 79 S.E. 71 (1913); Dalzell v. Commonwealth, 312 S.W.2d 354 (Ky. 1958). *But see* Masses Publishing Co. v. Patten, 246 Fed. 24 (2d Cir. 1917).

The Chief Reporter of the *Model Penal Code* sought to impose accomplice liability on one who, knowing that another is contemplating an offense, substantially facilitates its commission. The Reporter believed that society's interest in crime prevention outweighs the individual's freedom to act in such circumstances. *Model Penal Code* § 2.04(3)(b), comment (Tent. Draft No. 1, 1953). The American Law Institute rejected this view and chose to require a showing of criminal purpose, fearing that the broader formulation might attach liability to socially inoffensive conduct.

51. On February 12, 1962, Ronnie Moore was indicted in Baton Rouge, Louisiana, for criminal anarchy (punishable by imprisonment for not more than ten years). *The New York Times,* May 26, 1962, p. 126, cols. 3–5. On August 8, 1963, five Negroes were arrested at Americus, Georgia, for attempted insurrection (punishable by death). *The New York Times,* October 10, 1963, p. 28, col. 1. The prototype for these prosecutions was Braden v. Commonwealth, 291 S.W.2d 843 (Ky. 1956), in which a white man who purchased a house for a Negro in a "white" neighborhood was prosecuted for advocating sedition, and upon conviction was sentenced to fifteen years imprisonment and a $5,000 fine. The conviction was reversed after the defendant had spent seven months in prison pending the making of a $40,000 appeal bond.

See also the Jackson Freedom Ride prosecutions, at text accompanying notes 60–77 *infra.*

52. See, *e.g.,* Screws v. United States, 325 U. S. 91 (1945) (sheriff convicted of killing Negro prisoner, reversed on legal grounds); Sellin, "The Death Penalty," in *Model Penal Code* (Tent. Draft No. 9 at 79, 1959).

53. See Lusky, "Minority Rights and the Public Interest," 52 *Yale L.J.* 1, 15–19 (1942).

54. The need to weld recently independent states into a single nation focused particular attention in the early days upon implementation of the privileges and immunities clause of Article IV, §2 of the Constitution. It provides: "The Citizens of each State shall be entitled to all Privileges and Immunities of Citizens in the several States." Such implementation was accomplished by the grant of diversity jurisdiction to the lower federal courts, which made available to the outlander a tribunal in which he would suffer least disadvantage because of his nonresidence in the forum state. More recently, as sectional prejudice has tended to wear away, *diversity* jurisdiction has been narrowed and *federal question* jurisdiction—made necessary by local disapproval of the requirements of federal law—has been expanded.

55. See 5 Elliot, *Debates on the Adoption of the Federal Constitution* 155–56, 158–59, 331 (1896).

56. *Id.* at 159.

57. *U.S. Const.* art I, § 8, cl. 9.

58. Judiciary Act of 1789, ch. 20, § 1, 1 Stat. 73.

59. See generally Peltason, *Fifty-eight Lonely Men* (1961).

60. See Bailey v. Patterson, 199 F. Supp. 595, 612–13 (S.D. Miss. 1961) (Rives, J., dissenting), vac. and rem., 369 U.S. 31 (1962).

61. See Edwards v. South Carolina, 372 U.S. 229 (1963); Garner v. Louisiana, 368 U.S. 157 (1961); Thompson v. City of Louisville, 362 U.S. 199 (1960).

62. Bailey v. Patterson, 199 F. Supp. 595 (S.D. Miss. 1961), vac. and rem., 369 U.S. 31 (1962); 206 F. Supp. 67 (S.D. Miss. 1962), rev'd in part, Civ. No. 20732, 5th Cir., September 24, 1963.

63. 28 U.S.C. §2281 (1958).

64. The preliminary injunction motion was first assigned to be heard on July 10, 1961, thirty-one days after it was filed. On that day the three-judge court, over the dissent of Circuit Judge Tuttle, granted a continuance until August 7 because of the indisposition of one of the assistant attorneys general of Mississippi. On August 7, the court gave priority to argument of a number of technical motions that defendants had made; and though all of them were either overruled or reserved for decision after full trial, it was then too late in the afternoon to hear the preliminary injunction motion. The case was continued to September 25, at which time the court said it would hear the evidence and rule on the prayer for permanent as well as preliminary injunction. At the close of the September trial, plaintiffs again pressed their motion for interim injunctive relief pending decision of the merits, but the motion was denied. The court's decision was rendered November 17. Thus, despite the congressional mandate for quick disposition of preliminary injunction motions, 28 U.S.C. §2284(4) (1958), and despite the fact that illegal arrests of Freedom Riders were meanwhile proceeding by the hundreds—they totaled 315 by the end of the summer—the plaintiffs were unable to secure an *adjudication* of their motion prior to disposition of the case on the merits. Such an adjudication would have been appealable under 28 U.S.C. §1253 (1958). See Bailey v. Patterson, 199 F. Supp. 595, 621–22 (S.D. Miss. 1961) (Rives, J., dissenting).

65. Bailey v. Patterson, 199 F. Supp. 595 (S.D. Miss. 1961).

66. Louisville, N. O. & T. Ry. v. State, 66 Miss. 662, 6 So. 203 (1889), aff'd, 133 U.S. 587 (1890).

67. Alabama & V. Ry. v. Morris, 103 Miss. 511, 60 So. 11 (1912).

68. 28 U.S.C. §1253 (1958). There are exceptions not pertinent here, see, *e.g.*, Act of May 18, 1933, 48 Stat. 70, 16 U.S.C. §831x (1958) (review of condemnation awards under Tennessee Valley Authority Act by three district judges with appeal to court of appeals).

69. Bailey v. Patterson, 369 U.S. 31, 34 (1962); see text accompanying notes 85–93 *infra*.

70. Bailey v. Patterson, 206 F. Supp. 67 (S.D. Miss. 1962).

71. Bailey v. Patterson, Civil No. 20372, 5th Cir., September 24, 1963. The court did not reverse the district court's denial of an injunction with respect to the Attorney General of Missis-

sippi, because he had indicated an intention to comply with the court's determination of the constitutional question. Other parties were enjoined.

72. For a history of the statute see 1A Moore, *Federal Practice* ¶0.208, at 2301–11 (2d ed. 1961); Warren, "Federal and State Court Interference," 43 *Harv. L. Rev.* 345, 372–77 (1930).

73. See Leiter Minerals, Inc. v. United States, 352 U.S. 220 (1957).

74. See *Ex parte* Young, 209 U.S. 123 (1908); *cf.* Browder v. City of Montgomery, 146 F. Supp. 127 (M.D. Ala. 1956).

75. In support of this view, see Morrison v. Davis, 252 F.2d 102 (5th Cir. 1958), cert. denied, 365 U.S. 968 (1958); Cooper v. Hutchinson, 184 F.2d 119 (3d Cir. 1950); *cf.* United States v. Wood, 295 F.2d 772 (5th Cir. 1961), cert. denied, 369 U.S. 850 (1962); memorandum for the United States as Amicus Curiae, pp. 3–27, Chase v. Aiken, Civ. No. 9084, 4th Cir., September 1963.

76. One argument would be that if after the federal action is commenced for the purpose of protecting a federal right such as the right to travel unsegregated in interstate commerce, the state can prosecute all claimants of that right and burden them with such expense that they will no longer seek to exercise it, the federal case will become moot and the federal court's jurisdiction thus defeated.

It has also been suggested, more broadly, that since the statute is not a jurisdictional one, see Smith v. Apple, 264 U.S. 274, 278 (1924), it leaves the federal court free to "mould its process to accord with the factual situation." Moore, *Commentary on the Judicial Code* §0.03(49), at 415 (1949).

77. See, *e.g.*, The New York Times, May 3, 1963, p. 1, col. 4 (Birmingham, Ala.); *id.* July 31, 1963, p. 13, col. 1 (Clarksdale, Miss.); *id.* July 17, 1963, p. 1, col. 3 (Charleston, S.C.).

78. Railroad Comm'n v. Pullman Co., 312 U.S. 496 (1941); see Young, "Discretion to Deny Federal Relief Against State Action," 28 *Texas L. Rev.* 410 (1950).

79. See Harrison v. NAACP, 360 U.S. 167 (1959); Darby v. Daniel, 168 F. Supp. 170, 195 (S.D. Miss. 1958); Lassiter v. Taylor, 152 F. Supp. 295 (E.D.N.C. 1957); Bryan v. Austin, 148 F. Supp. 563 (E.D.S.C. 1957), vacated as moot, 354 U.S. 933 (1957).

80. See Harrison v. NAACP, *supra* note 79, at 179 (Douglas, J., dissenting); Leiter Minerals, Inc. v. United States, 352 U.S. 220, 230 (1957) (Douglas, J., dissenting); AFL v. Watson, 327 U.S. 582, 606 (1946) (Murphy, J., dissenting). Chief Justice Marshall might also have been critical; in Cohens v. Virginia, 19 U.S. (6 Wheat.) 264, 404 (1821), he said: "With whatever doubts, with whatever difficulties, a case may be attended, we must decide it, if it be brought before us. We have no more right to decline the exercise of jurisdiction which is given, than to usurp that which is not given. The one or the other would be

treason to the constitution." And see Clark, "State Law in the Federal Courts: The Brooding Omnipresence of Erie v. Tompkins," 55 *Yale L.J.* 267, 293 (1946). *But see* Wright, "The Abstention Doctrine Reconsidered," 37 *Texas L. Rev.* 815 n. 9 (1959) (asserting reluctance in lower courts to apply doctrine as rigorously in civil rights cases).

81. See Young, *supra* note 78, at 418–19.

82. See Sheldon v. Sill, 49 U.S. (8 How.) 440 (1850); Martin v. Hunter's Lessee, 14 U.S. (1 Wheat.) 304 (1816) (Story, J.); Hart, "The Power of Congress To Limit the Jurisdiction of Federal Courts: An Exercise in Dialectic," 66 *Harv. L. Rev.* 1362 (1953).

83. The abstention doctrine is based on a value judgment that it is more just to delay adjudication pending authoritative state-court interpretation of state law than to render a final decision premised on a tentative interpretation which may be later repudiated by the highest state court. Desirable as it is to decide questions of state law correctly, it is sometimes more important to decide them quickly; and the yearning for certainty as to the meaning of state law cannot rightly be indulged at the expense of federal rights that can be preserved only by prompt and vigorous federal court action.

Inasmuch as some district courts have practiced informal abstention by simply delaying adjudication for abnormally long periods, it would also be desirable to provide a statutory priority for the hearing and decision of racial discrimination and racial protest cases, as is done for important antitrust cases, Expediting Act, 56 Stat. 198 (1942), as amended, 15 U.S.C. §§28–29 (1958), and cases in which interim injunctions are sought to prevent the enforcement of state statutes, 28 U.S.C. §2284. In order to be effective, however, it might be well for such a statute to provide that a district judge who failed to hear and decide the case within a specified time would be obligated to file an explanatory statement with the court of appeals, and that if the explanation were unsatisfactory, a new district judge might be assigned to the case upon motion of the party claiming relief against discrimination or protection of protest.

84. The knowledgeable comment by Young, *supra* note 78, suggests a negative answer to this question.

85. 28 U.S.C. §1253 (1958). It is not unprecedented for orders of three-judge district courts to be reviewable by courts of appeals. See note 68 *supra.* As an alternative, it would be possible to do away with the three-judge requirement in these cases. But doing so might lessen the likelihood of avoiding error at the trial level; the three-judge requirement makes possible a decision contrary to the views of the local district judge. Note that two circuit judges can be designated to sit.

86. Bailey v. Patterson, 369 U.S. 31 (1962). See note 69 *supra* and accompanying text.

87. *Id.* at 33.

88. *Ibid.*

89. See *Ex parte* Poresky, 290 U.S. 30 (1933); Bell v. Waterfront Comm'n, 279 F.2d 853 (2d Cir. 1960).

90. Memorandum for United States as Amicus Curiae, pp. 2–3, Bailey v. Patterson, 368 U.S. 346 (1961) (stay denied per curiam).

91. Bailey v. Patterson, 369 U.S. 31, 32 (1962).

92. Record, p. 20, Bailey v. Patterson, 369 U.S. 31 (1962). Since the plaintiffs alleged that the threat of prosecution constituted a direct threat to them, it seems legally immaterial—from the viewpoint of standing to complain—whether the threat was to prosecute *them* or *other* Negroes who violated the segregation statutes. In either case, the threat would hamper the plaintiffs in the enjoyment of federal rights.

93. If the Supreme Court's reluctance to bypass the courts of appeals in such cases is attributable to a belief that appellate decisions of Southern federal courts would command particular respect in the South, the conclusion would be the same.

94. See 2 Wharton, *Criminal Law,* §1550 (12th ed. 1932). See also authorities collected in People v. Clemente, 285 App. Div. 258, 136 N.Y.S.2d 202 (1st Dep't 1954) (Breitel, J., dissenting), aff'd, 309 N.Y. 890, 131 N.E. 2d 294 (1955).

95. Moreover, the federal judge has broader powers in jury trials than do most state court judges. See Note, 27 N.D.L. Rev. 199 (1951).

96. Stack v. Boyle, 342 U.S. 1 (1951).

97. See Martin v. Hunter's Lessee, 14 U.S. (1 Wheat.) 304 (1816).

98. 28 U.S.C. §§1442, 1442a (1958).

99. 28 U.S.C. §§1444, 2410 (1958).

100. That acquittals were ultimately directed by County Court for fifteen of them (white Protestant ministers) does not invalidate the inference. Since the facts of their cases were not materially different, the difference in their treatment only compounded the denial of due process and equal protection.

101. *Cf.* Thornhill v. Alabama, 310 U.S. 88, 96–98 (1940).

102. 100 U.S. 313 (1879).

103. See *id.* at 317, 320.

104. See *id.* at 321–22.

105. See Kentucky v. Powers, 201 U.S. 1 (1906); Gibson v. Mississippi, 162 U.S. 565 (1896). See generally 45 Am. Jur. *Removal of Causes* §109 (1943).

106. Baines v. City of Danville, 4th Cir., argued September 23, 1963. The Memorandum for the United States, as Amicus Curiae in the district court, summarizes the facts as follows:

The evidence adduced at the hearing in Danville on June 24–25, 1963, reveals, *inter alia,* that Judge Aiken, who will hear all of the pending contempt charges, was himself involved in attempting to disperse crowds of demonstrators at an earlier date. He also testified that he feared that trouble or violence of one kind or another might occur as a result of the demonstrations; indeed, at one point in his testimony he said that he considered that certain types of demonstrations which he had observed amounted to "violence," and were "sinister" and "menacing," although no actual physical violence occurred. In view of this evidence, it is difficult to believe that petitioners will be able to obtain a fair trial before Judge Aiken. And if they cannot do so, whatever defense they may wish to assert grounded upon their right to demonstrate for the purpose of obtaining the equal protection of the laws may well go for nought in Judge Aiken's court. If that is true, then, we submit, petitioners should be classified as persons who are "denied or cannot enforce in the courts of [the] State a right under any law providing for . . . equal civil rights . . ."

Indeed, there is much more involved here than the mere denial of a fair trial. The trial itself is being conducted in a most unjudicial atmosphere. The Judge conceded that he has been armed with a pistol which he removes only when reaching his office. One witness testified in fact that Judge Aiken was armed on the bench. However that may be, the fact remains that it is common knowledge that the trial Judge is armed, and this alone is bound to intimidate Negro citizens of Danville, to reduce their expectations of obtaining a fair trial in the Corporation Court, and thus to interfere with their campaign for equal civil rights. Moreover, the evidence reveals that Negro counsel, male and female, have been searched upon entering the courtroom; that the courtroom has been closed to the public (except to the press); that perhaps 40-odd armed police officers were stationed throughout the courtroom during the two contempt trials which have already taken place; that the Judge had prepared, in advance of trial, a written memorandum of his decision finding the first two defendants guilty of contempt; and that Judge Aiken refused to examine into the contention made upon motion of the defendants just prior to the first trial, that the Corporation Court had no jurisdiction to proceed because, as this Court subsequently held on June 25, 1963, filing of the removal petitions transferred the cases to this Court and ousted the Corporation Court of any power to act upon them. This conduct of Judge Aiken surely suggests that he will be somewhat unreceptive to arguments grounded upon controlling federal law. Furthermore, Judge Aiken refused to release on bail, pending appeal, the two defendants convicted of contempt. Since the sentences imposed are relatively short, this ruling—which Judge Aiken apparently intends to apply to all the pending contempt cases—effectively denies appellate review of his judgments of guilt. And, finally, the practice of imposing 45 and 60-day jail terms in contested cases, while imposing either no confinement as in one case, or only a two-day term, as in the second case, upon the two defendants who pleaded guilty, simply exacerbates the situation by suggesting that those who choose to assert their rights will suffer the consequences.

The combination of a trier of fact who has apparently prejudged the issues and was a participant in the events culminating in the very charges to be tried, considered together with the general atmosphere of the proceedings and its inevitable results, makes it quite clear, it seems to us, that a fair trial cannot be had in the Corporation Court. But that is not all. It is not simply that whatever rights defendants have to demonstrate for the equal protection of the laws will be disregarded in the contempt trials. The situation is further aggravated by the fact that racial antagonism lies at the root of this denial. The entire controversy now before this Court stems from the conflict over Negro equality, and the proceedings in the Corporation Court, which are here challenged, are a direct result of this conflict. We do not suggest that Judge Aiken is racially prejudiced against the defendants; but a Court would have to close its eyes to the realities not to notice that the peculiar proceedings in the corporation court are the direct consequence of this racial conflict. Judges, and especially federal judges, are not "forbidden to know as judges what [they] see as men." [Ho Ah Kow v. Nunan, 12 Fed. Cas. 252 (Civil No. 6546) (C.C.D. Cal. 1879)] . . . The denial of a fair trial in these circumstances, then, is in the most fundamental sense grounded upon race.

Under these circumstances, if the original intention of section 1443 (1) were to govern these cases, we think they would be properly removed.

Id., pp. 5–8.

107. See Peltason, *op. cit. supra* note 59, at 10 *passim* (1961).

108. See Baines v. City of Danville, 4th Cir., argued September 23, 1963. The argument runs thus: (1) The 1866 Civil Rights Act, creating federal remedies for racial discrimination in the state courts, included a removal provision which is the predecessor of 28 U.S.C. §1443 (1958), ch. 31, §3, 14 Stat. 27 (1866). A similar provision appeared in the 1875 Civil Rights Act. Ch. 114, §3, 18 Stat. 335 (1875). It was carried over into the Revised Statutes of 1878 as §641. (2) Until 1875, remand orders were not reviewable on appeal or writ of error because they were interlocutory orders. They were, however, reviewable by writ of mandamus to the federal trial court, directing it to hear and decide the case. Railroad Co. v. Wiswall, 90 U.S. (23 Wall.) 507 (1874). (3) In 1875 they became reviewable by appeal and writ of error also, along with interlocutory orders generally. Civil Rights Act of 1875, ch. 137, §5, 18 Stat. 472 (1875). (4) In 1887 the 1875 provision for review of interlocutory orders was repealed, but all rights under Rev. Stat. §641 (1878) and certain other statutes were expressly saved. The effect

was to leave untouched the reviewability of remand orders in §641 cases not only by way of appeal and by writ of error, but by way of mandamus (in accordance with the practice since 1866). (5) The same saving clause was carried forward into the 1888 statute which was enacted to correct the enrollment of the 1887 statute. Ch. 866, §5, 25 Stat. 436 (1888). (6) In Cole v. Garland, 107 Fed. 759 (7th Cir. 1901), an appeal case, the court held that no rights were saved by the saving clause in the 1887–1888 legislation because §641 conferred no power to review a remand order (the review provision being contained in another statute). This was an erroneously restrictive interpretation of the saving clause, and frustrated its plain intention. Moreover, by implying that the only avenue for review of remand orders was to preserve the question through the state courts for ultimate Supreme Court review, the court in Cole v. Garland overlooked the possibility of review by mandamus, which had been untouched by the judiciary statutes of 1875, 1887, and 1888. (7) Cole v. Garland was accepted as a correct statement of the law, though its teaching was never reviewed by the Supreme Court; and in the 1911 codification, which was intended to systematize but not to change the law on matters such as this, S. REP. No. 388, 61st Cong., 2d Sess., pt. 1, at 2, 28 (1910); H.R. Doc. No. 127, 61st Cong., 2 Sess. 23 (1910), the general prohibition upon review of remand orders by appeal or writ of error was carried forward without the supposedly nugatory savings clause. Even then, the right to mandamus was left untouched. (8) There has been no subsequent effort on the part of Congress to change the law. In the 1948 Judiciary Act, the prohibition upon appeal of remand orders was inadvertently repealed entirely, and for a brief period they became appealable. (The writ of error had meanwhile been abolished in 1928. Ch. 14, 45 Stat. 54 (1928).) This mistake was corrected by insertion, through a technical changes act, of the present 28 U.S.C. §1447(d) (1958). The stated purpose was "to remove any doubt that the former law as to the finality of an order of remand to a State court is continued." H.R. REP. No. 352, 81st Cong., 1st Sess., 15 (1949). Use of the language "on appeal *or otherwise*" resulted from the assumption that Cole v. Garland stated the then-existing law correctly, but if read literally it would cut off three modes of review that had been available in civil rights cases at least since 1875: (a) appeal, (b) mandamus, and (c) Supreme Court review of state court judgments.

To summarize: In 1887 Congress evinced a clear intention to leave civil rights cases untouched by the broad prohibition upon appeal of remand orders. In no legislation since 1875 has there been any indication that Congress desired to change the law in this respect. And Congress has *never* indicated an intention to abolish review on mandamus, which has existed since 1866.

In Baines v. City of Danville, review is sought by way of mandamus as well as appeal.

109. H.R. 7152, 88th Cong., 1st Sess. (1963).